SELDOM

SELDOM

A MEMOIR

DAWN RAE DOWNTON

Arcade Publishing • New York

FIRST U.S. EDITION

First published in 2002 by McClelland & Stewart Ltd., Canada

Library of Congress Cataloging-in-Publication Data
Downton, Dawn Rae, 1956–
    Seldom : a memoir / Dawn Rae Downton. —1st U.S. ed.
        p. cm.
    ISBN 1-55970-665-1
        1. Downton, Dawn Rae, 1956—Childhood and youth. 2. Seldom (Nfld.)—Biography. 3. Seldom (Nfld.)—Social life and customs. I. Title.
    F1124.5.S45 D69 2002
    972.8—dc21   2002074628

Published in the United States by Arcade Publishing, Inc., New York
Distributed by AOL Time Warner Book Group

Visit our Web site at www.arcadepub.com

10 9 8 7 6 5 4 3 2 1

EB

PRINTED IN THE UNITED STATES OF AMERICA

for Harry and Jack
for my mother
and her mother
angels sing thee

The first noble truth is suffering.
— *Siddhartha Gautama, the Buddha*

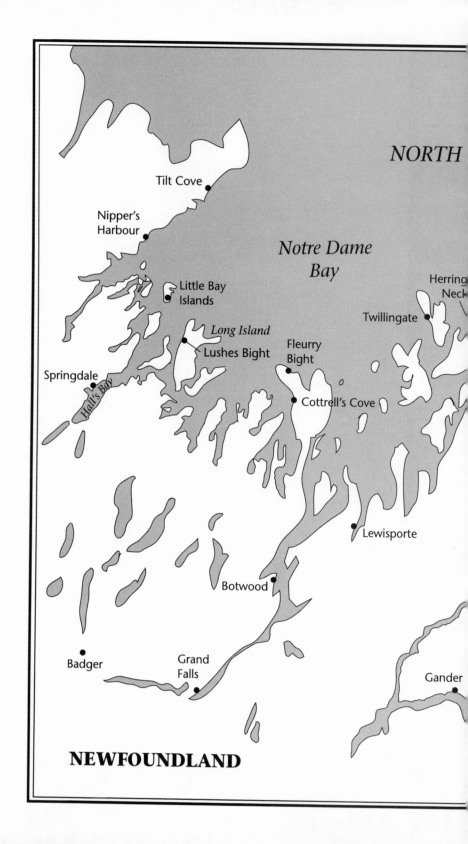

NORTH

Tilt Cove

Nipper's
Harbour

Notre Dame
Bay

Herring
Neck

Little Bay
Islands

Twillingate

Long Island

Fleurry
Bight

Lushes Bight

Springdale

Hall's Bay

Cottrell's Cove

Lewisporte

Botwood

Badger

Grand
Falls

Gander

NEWFOUNDLAND

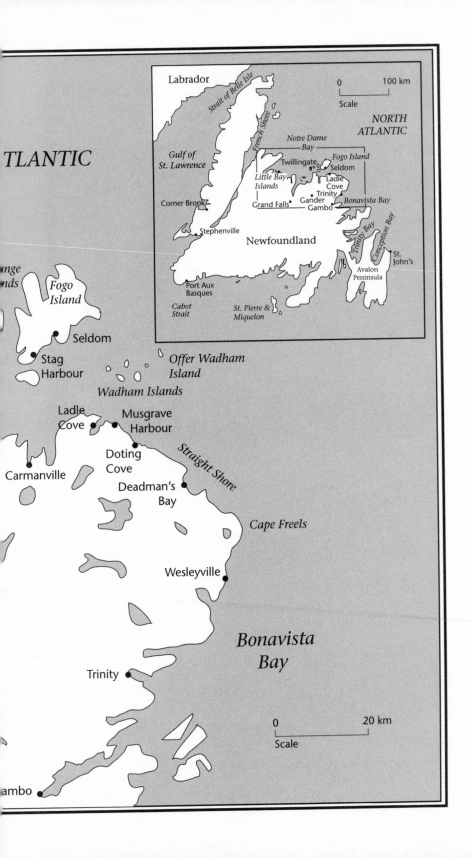

LITTLE BAY ISLANDS

NORTH
ATLANTIC

Northern Harbour

The Lockes
The Bottom
Pole Hill   The Joneses
School
Ensign Store
Government Wharf
Campbell's Point
Southern
Harbour

Delphi Wiseman's
Uncle Nelson's
Uncle Harold's
Tickle House

Back Beach
Big Tickle

Goat Island

Salt Rock
Bert Strong's
Tennis Courts   Strong's

Mack's
Island

Burnt Woods

Shoal Tickle

Sulian's Cove

0   1 km
Scale

The Wisemans and the Wellons of Notre Dame Bay

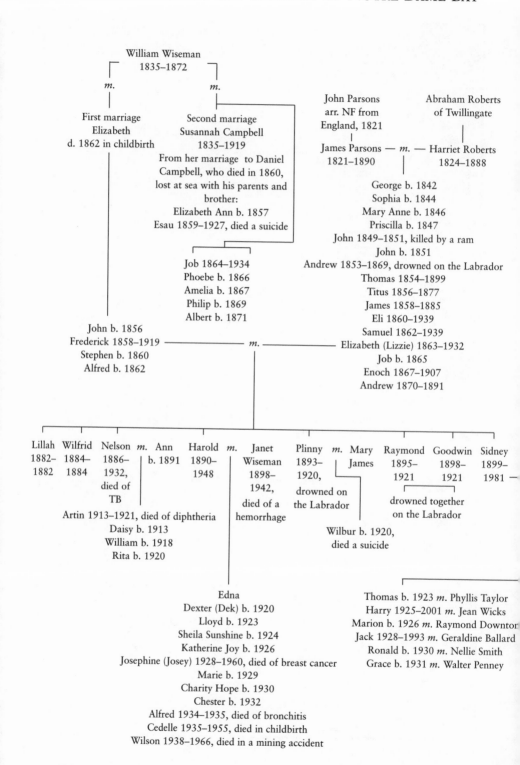

William Wiseman
1835–1872

m.

First marriage
Elizabeth
d. 1862 in childbirth

m.

Second marriage
Susannah Campbell
1835–1919
From her marriage to Daniel
Campbell, who died in 1860,
lost at sea with his parents and
brother:
Elizabeth Ann b. 1857
Esau 1859–1927, died a suicide

John Parsons
arr. NF from
England, 1821

James Parsons — m. — Harriet Roberts
1821–1890   1824–1888

Abraham Roberts
of Twillingate

George b. 1842
Sophia b. 1844
Mary Anne b. 1846
Priscilla b. 1847
John 1849–1851, killed by a ram
John b. 1851
Andrew 1853–1869, drowned on the Labrador
Thomas 1854–1899
Titus 1856–1877
James 1858–1885
Eli 1860–1939
Samuel 1862–1939
Elizabeth (Lizzie) 1863–1932
Job b. 1865
Enoch 1867–1907
Andrew 1870–1891

Job 1864–1934
Phoebe b. 1866
Amelia b. 1867
Philip b. 1869
Albert b. 1871

John b. 1856
Frederick 1858–1919 ———————— m. ————————
Stephen b. 1860
Alfred b. 1862

Lillah
1882–
1882

Wilfrid
1884–
1884

Nelson
1886–
1932,
died of
TB

m. Ann
b. 1891

Harold
1890–
1948

m. Janet
Wiseman
1898–
1942,
died of a
hemorrhage

Plinny
1893–
1920,
drowned on
the Labrador

m. Mary
James

Raymond
1895–
1921

Goodwin
1898–
1921

Sidney
1899–1981 —

Artin 1913–1921, died of diphtheria
Daisy b. 1913
William b. 1918
Rita b. 1920

drowned together
on the Labrador

Wilbur b. 1920,
died a suicide

Edna
Dexter (Dek) b. 1920
Lloyd b. 1923
Sheila Sunshine b. 1924
Katherine Joy b. 1926
Josephine (Josey) 1928–1960, died of breast cancer
Marie b. 1929
Charity Hope b. 1930
Chester b. 1932
Alfred 1934–1935, died of bronchitis
Cedelle 1935–1955, died in childbirth
Wilson 1938–1966, died in a mining accident

Thomas b. 1923 m. Phyllis Taylor
Harry 1925–2001 m. Jean Wicks
Marion b. 1926 m. Raymond Downton
Jack 1928–1993 m. Geraldine Ballard
Ronald b. 1930 m. Nellie Smith
Grace b. 1931 m. Walter Penney

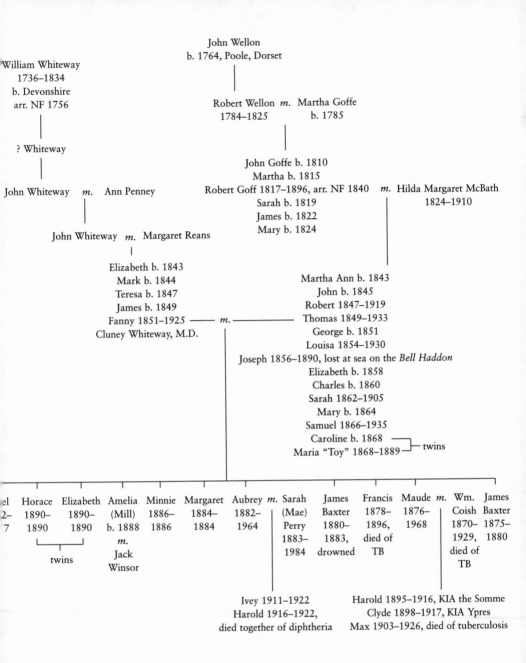

John Wellon
b. 1764, Poole, Dorset

William Whiteway
1736–1834
b. Devonshire
arr. NF 1756

Robert Wellon *m.* Martha Goffe
1784–1825   b. 1785

? Whiteway

John Goffe b. 1810
Martha b. 1815

John Whiteway *m.* Ann Penney   Robert Goff 1817–1896, arr. NF 1840 *m.* Hilda Margaret McBath
                                                                                    1824–1910
                                         Sarah b. 1819
                                         James b. 1822
John Whiteway *m.* Margaret Reans   Mary b. 1824

Elizabeth b. 1843
Mark b. 1844
Teresa b. 1847   Martha Ann b. 1843
James b. 1849   John b. 1845
Fanny 1851–1925 ——— *m.* ——— Robert 1847–1919
Cluney Whiteway, M.D.   Thomas 1849–1933
                                 George b. 1851
                                 Louisa 1854–1930
                         Joseph 1856–1890, lost at sea on the *Bell Haddon*
                                 Elizabeth b. 1858
                                 Charles b. 1860
                                 Sarah 1862–1905
                                 Mary b. 1864
                                 Samuel 1866–1935
                                 Caroline b. 1868 ———┐
                                 Maria "Toy" 1868–1889 ┘— twins

el   Horace   Elizabeth Amelia   Minnie   Margaret Aubrey *m.* Sarah   James   Francis Maude *m.* Wm.   James
2–   1890–   1890–   (Mill)   1886–   1884–   1882–   (Mae)   Baxter   1878–   1876–   Coish   Baxter
7   1890   1890   b. 1888 1886   1884   1964   Perry   1880–   1896,   1968   1870–   1875–
        └———┬———┘   *m.*   1883–   1883,   died of   1929,   1880,
          twins   Jack   1984   drowned   TB   died of died of
                                     Winsor   TB   TB

                                          Ivey 1911–1922   Harold 1895–1916, KIA the Somme
                                          Harold 1916–1922,   Clyde 1898–1917, KIA Ypres
                                          died together of diphtheria Max 1903–1926, died of tuberculosis

THE TICKLE

I

ETHEL

They were married at Seldom on December 10, 1922, a Sunday, in the home of George R. Wheaton *in accordance with the Law of Newfoundland and the Ceremonies of the Methodist Church*. Across the ocean in Stockholm that afternoon Professor Fridtjof Nansen of Oslo, the polar explorer, scientist, diplomat, and humanitarian, was presented with the Nobel Peace Prize for his work on behalf of war refugees in Europe and Russia, and promptly devoted his prize money toward ongoing relief. Far to the southwest in California, an ill and frail William Antrim, stepfather to Billy the Kid, had taken to his bed to breathe his last. There were significant differences between the bride and groom standing in the Wheaton parlour in Seldom, Fogo Island, that day. The bride, had she known, would have been interested in the professor; the groom in the moribund Uncle Billy.

The bride was educated, refined, with an unselfish, peaceful soul. Did the groom have a soul at all? Skipper Sid, he was called back then. Later, by his children, the Old Man. Himself.

On his way home to Little Bay Islands from business in St. John's, Sid had sailed to Ladle Cove and fetched his bride-to-be. They would be married in Seldom, where the minister was, but Seldom harbour was no place to park a schooner in December. Like so much of Newfoundland, Seldom gives and takes. Its poor bit of shelter from the North Atlantic is all there is for miles around, yet schooners seldom got in for the ice; its name, shaved down over the years from Seldom-Come-By, tells the tale.

The oldtimers say otherwise, like travel agents shilling their bit of turf at the expense of another: in this case, at the expense of Stag Harbour Run, the next harbour west and so forbidding that no one would venture to dock there except under the balmiest skies. No one went there, ever, the Seldom oldtimers say. Everyone came here. Seldom-Come-By means Seldom-Gone-By, seldom bypassed.

The oldtimers could be right. Seldom was a busy place in days past. It was a busier place in summer than winter, and it was an unseasonal time for Sidney Wiseman's schooner to be touring the outports of Notre Dame Bay on anything but the most urgent business. But Sidney couldn't wait. Yes, it was December and a terrible time to be ferrying a woman around for marrying, but Ethel Wellon had run from his advances, and he had to get her back. Ethel wouldn't have much to do with a man outside of marriage, so marry her he would. She'd run to her family home in Ladle Cove and was teaching there, and that was where he had found her in the fall and made his proposal.

Now Sidney tied up his schooner at the Wellons' wharf in Ladle Cove. He'd fetch Ethel and ferry her the hour across the channel to Seldom in a trap skiff covered with a canvas tent, the vessel he used on the Labrador to go the few miles between his schooner and his cod-traps. Ethel wasn't keen to carry on with the plan; she wanted to postpone things. Just the Sunday before, Harold and Ivey, her little nephew and niece, her brother's children, had died in a single day, of diphtheria. The family was in deep mourning; for the Wellons, living next door to a cemetery was turning out to be a terrible thing. But Sidney had his plans made. He had it all set up. That was the way in Newfoundland; you just got on with it, whatever happened. Surely Ethel couldn't disagree. He'd turned down the minister's invitation to meet in the church in the east end of town. He didn't need a church. He was only going to Seldom in the first place to check in with the Fisherman's Union Trading Company store where he owned shares. It was just luck that he was fetching Ethel at all and fitting the wedding in. It had worked out well; the company man Wheaton would supply his parlour for the ceremony, and the company would even put up the schooner's crew of six for the weekend. Sidney would stay over until Monday and see his partners at the store.

In Ladle Cove, Ethel's parents watched the wedding skiff depart. Fanny and Thomas Wellon didn't feel left out. Fanny was an old woman now, full of grief this week at the loss of her grandchildren. You never got used to something like that, no you didn't, not any more than you ever forgot your own childhood. All that stuff in the middle – sometimes, if you were lucky and had the Lord's blessing, you could forget all that. But your old age and your childhood – either end of you – somehow those stayed. She was nearly seventy-one and was peering out her window with all of her faculties but less of her sight than she'd been used to, watching Ethel leave. A trap skiff, indeed.

Ethel was the third of Fanny's daughters, after Maud and Mill, and the last to go. Until now she'd taught school for more than ten years up and down the Straight Shore and around Notre Dame Bay. *Yes Miss Wellon, no Miss Wellon* – Ethel heard it every day and loved it, but all the same, teaching was hard. Still, she had a head on her shoulders, a pretty one but full of wisdom too. Ethel always knew what to do, even if it only meant staying put, holding ground, doing nothing but steadying herself.

Ethel was her mother's treasure, and Fanny didn't like this Sid Wiseman one bit. He was as rough and coarse as his brother Good before him. Good had caught Ethel's eye first; and who but the Lord Himself could ever say why? With the heart of gold the girl had, Good's name alone would have been enough to win her notice. Ethel had had a lot of admirers – the Goodyear boys from right here in Ladle Cove when the kids had all been teenagers; Bert Strong, the wealthy one who proposed to her so many times and who would mourn her all his life; stylish George Hicks who went off to the war and sent her postcards of himself sitting on camels in front of the pyramids in Egypt. George was a Hicks from Carmanville who'd gone to Grand Falls, the newsprint town where things were said to be booming.

Fanny sniffed. She watched the skiff retreat through the snow. Did they get snow all the way to Grand Falls, or were those mill folks somehow excused? Fanny had grown up in a ragged, poor outport farther down the coast, and it had done her fine. But no one else, not any more. Grand Falls, or any place else inland, for that matter, or anything down to St. John's, it was all surely better than it was on the coast anyway, that's what everyone thought now, as if every hurt in the world blew in straight to the coast on an ill nor'easter, dropping its calamity on the bluffs and wharves and boat stores below, spending itself by about Botwood, never so much as sighting glorious Grand Falls. *When the wind is in the east, it's neither good for man or beast.*

Oh, you never know – that's what Ethel had told her mother she thought about George Hicks. When she'd thought of George at all, that is, between the chores and the schoolroom and all the demands on her. Ethel had been clear about one thing. She preferred her hapless outport sky to Grand Falls, so far from home.

Fanny sighed. George Hicks hadn't been the one for Ethel in any case. In the end, Good Wiseman was the one the girl had wanted. But Good had died young, gone the way of so many local boys; and now this Sidney Wiseman, the younger brother, had sprung up like a weed in his place. They might have means, these Wisemans from Little Bay Islands, but this one in particular, shined and buffed from the war, was no match for her daughter. Underneath his hero's sheen he was black and rough as coal.

Fanny watched only snow at the window now. The skiff was gone. She didn't feel left out. She just felt a bit sick at the thought of it, that was all.

~

The marriage was solemnized by W. S. Mercer, Methodist minister, whose ornate script filled out the marriage certificate, a small, unprepossessing and fragile document the size of an airline ticket. His signature was witnessed by Sid's crewman Joseph. Locke., who wrote downhill and with careful periods after each of his names. It was also witnessed by Mrs Isaac Collins, who didn't use periods at all, and who seemed to have practised for weeks.

The newlyweds signed their names, Sidney Hayward Wiseman writing in a cramped yet childish hand, the tails of his *y*s bent under in conspicuous afterthought. He ended his signature with a comma, as if he already knew the place his bride would take in his life: dragging along behind like something fallen from a cart. Behind him, beneath him, an addition, another afterthought.

Ethel watched him sign, distracted only by the harshest shrieks of the gale raging past the Wheaton parlour window. It seemed to carry the voices of her lost nephew and niece, the voices of everyone she had lost. But Good was gone and she was in love with his successor, for now and ever. Sidney had a charm like none other, he had prospects but he'd be marrying up all the same; he told her that. He was in love with her and he told her that too. And while it all mattered, she didn't think of herself as the prize he told her she was. She didn't think of how many men had loved her. She thought of the one who said he loved her now. She thought of herself as his wife; how lucky she'd be now, finally, after all her heartache.

She was not a girl to talk herself up. She was warm, tender, generous; and she looked for these gifts in others. Maybe she hadn't found them in him yet, but what counted most was just this: she was in love with him. She watched him sign – she didn't take her eyes off him – and then she signed below: *Ethel Winnifred Wellon*.

Hers was the articulate hand of a schoolmarm, more stylish even than the Reverend Mercer's, which entered their ages as twenty-two and thirty respectively; their "conditions" as bachelor and spinster; and Sidney's occupation as fisherman. Though the reverend entered no rank or profession for her, by 1922 when she stood in front of him that Sunday in George Wheaton's parlour, Ethel Wellon had been to university in St. John's and taught school for several years around Notre Dame Bay – just up the coast from Ladle Cove at first, at Carmanville and Frederickton, and then on to Greenspond, the tiny harbour where her grandfather had met her grandmother three-quarters of a century before. She came from a long line of Wellons, one of the Straight Shore's most stalwart, upright, accomplished families, and now she was joining a long line of Wisemans.

She paused a moment before she signed. What was stopping her, what was holding her back? Whose foot was treading so lightly on her hem?

Oh Ivey, oh little Harold. The faces of the dead were a pantomime, their voices, far off now and retreating, were an elegy in her ear. She was mixed up. Was this a wedding, or a wake? The children's voices murmured again on the gale outside the Wheatons' window. Three Wellons lost from the family in a week; one Wiseman gained. The Wisemans were a good family, too; everyone said so. It was a fair exchange; it was progress of a sort. Ethel was lost to the Wellons but found to the Wisemans. *Reverend*, she wanted to ask William Mercer, *isn't it progress of a sort?* Leaving George Wheaton's parlour that Sunday, she found herself standing in the hall, turning it over. The reverend was leaving too, in a hurry to make evening service in the church despite the gale. What did he know of progress in a place like this? One more winter and he'd be lost himself, in a snowstorm after Sunday service as he tried to make it home for supper.

Ethel was mindful of the time, but still she stopped him as he buttoned his coat.

"Reverend," she said, a gloved hand on his arm. "I lost a niece and nephew Sunday last. Might we have two prayers?" And so they returned to the parlour and prayed, while Sidney fretted in the hall, his crewman Locke standing beside him, turning his cap in his hands.

Jay-sus. Exasperated, Sidney Wiseman swayed on his heels in George Wheaton's hall. God and death and children and women. It was ever thus – one or the other of them was forever getting in his way.

~

Ethel was the youngest child of the prosperous Wellons from Ladle Cove, a sail of a few hours east from Little Bay Islands along the coast of Notre Dame Bay, and she knew many pleasures her friends did not. Her mother, Fanny, had a younger brother who was a doctor, a rare accomplishment for a local boy at a time when the province's medics were often American imports from Johns Hopkins, like Dr. Olds of Twillingate; where one local or another could declare himself *an intelligent man and a partial practitioner of the best of his knowledge among the destitute of that quarter*; or where with a few miles on you as a hospital orderly you could hang out your shingle as *Physician, Surgeon, Accoucher and Everything Else*. Fanny's husband, Thomas, had a thriving business as a Ladle Cove merchant. Thomas had inherited the enterprise from his own father, who had ensured its success by shipping Ladle Cove produce almost all the way west around Notre Dame Bay. When Thomas visited Ethel in her married life at Little Bay Islands, her brood would wake to find candies and a twenty-five-cent piece under each of their pillows. Grandpa Wellon was better than Santa, and Ethel loved him dearly.

Ethel's family had a farm and a hired hand and a maid who went to church with them on Sunday, and so much extra milk that the floors of the Wellon home were washed in it to make them shine. Because of its varied economy – lumber, commercial farming, fishing, and, until 1900, a copper boom – Ladle Cove itself was prosperous by Newfoundland standards. It had a road that went nowhere, but that made it self-contained and self-sufficient. You got up and down the coast by boat or, in winter, over the ice by foot or on a horse, or by komatik with a dog team. In later years you could even cross the ice by snowmobile, a skiied affair far larger than its modern derivative, large enough to transport goods. All Ladle Cove needed was its maze of paths, house to house, its collection of beaches and fish stages and its assortment of wharves, one for nearly every rough frame home, and the great sea and all its bounty at the Funk Islands and the Wadhams beyond. With the exception of Buchans in central Newfoundland, the site of one of the richest base-metal mines in the world, Ladle Cove collected the least dole of any Newfoundland community during the Depression. It had a reputation among St. John's bureaucrats as a model outport.

As it was for most outport Newfoundlanders, nonetheless, tragedy was Ethel's constant companion, and coming from a large family didn't necessarily mean what it said. Most of Fanny and Thomas's eleven children died young – of diphtheria, consumption, and the household accidents that seemed as common then as the days were long.

Fanny was forty-one when she had Ethel, her last. Starting late at age twenty-four, Fanny did well to produce her brood over the course of seventeen years, even if she couldn't keep it. Her firstborn, James Baxter, made it to five. A second James Baxter was born shortly after the first died but fared no better, drowning at three; the name was abandoned after that. Two girls died in infancy a few years before Ethel was born, leaving barely a trace, and newborn twins followed them shortly after. By the time Ethel arrived, Fanny had buried six children. Another son, Francis, made it all the way to eighteen before he died of consumption when Ethel was four, right on the heels of Ethel's beloved grandfather Robert Goff.

Ethel grew up with her sisters, Maud and Mill, her brother, Aubrey, the family's only surviving son – and a house full of ghosts.

Sudden and unprovided death stalked the living as well, into the next generation. Ethel's sister Maud had three children, all boys. In years to come, young Marion, Ethel's older daughter, would think her cousins exceedingly handsome. She would stand on a chair to talk to them in the large, gilt-framed photograph Ethel had of them hanging high in a bedroom, as was the style. Their picture was all that remained of the boys – the Great War had taken them all. Harold and Clyde died in combat. On hearing his older brothers had both been killed, Maud's youngest, Max, determined to go and "get them back," walking forty-five miles to Grand Falls and forty-five miles back in the sleet and snow of the Newfoundland winter to enlist. He caught a cold, came down with pneumonia, and suffered "weak lungs" until he died a few years later.

The Wellon family had a way of making the best of things, and on the day Harold died with so many young Newfoundland boys on a battlefield in France, a child was born to his Uncle Aubrey, Ethel's only surviving brother. Aubrey named the baby Harold, but the name proved no luckier than James Baxter had a generation earlier. On a single day just a week before his sister's wedding trip to Seldom, Aubrey lost both his Harold and his little daughter, Ivey, to diphtheria. Little Harold was six, Ivey just ten. The small bodies were wrapped and passed out a bedroom window for immediate burial in the cemetery next door. The circuit preacher was in Greenspond. Thomas Wellon, a lay reader, said a few prayers for his grandchildren in his stead, though he couldn't make his voice settle, and Aubrey and his wife stared at the graves.

Ethel wept and wept. She loved children, and these two she loved most. They were lost to her now, as she herself would be lost to the family in just another week.

~

Ethel had much of her father in her. She had even more in her of her grandfather, though she'd been only four when he died, just a sprite. Around 1840, as a young man in his early twenties, Robert Goff Wellon had come to Ladle Cove from England, from Poole in County Dorset, stopping a while at Doting Cove, Musgrave Harbour, and Herring Neck, even playing lighthouse keeper on the Wadhams Islands. Back in England Robert's own father had been a glazier, and

that, Robert said, was how he'd bluffed his way into keeping the Offer
Wadhams light. He'd be good with glass, he told them, and those
lights had a lot of glass. Prisms and lenses, at least.

Robert was one of the Wadhams' first lightkeepers. Truth be told,
there was nothing to getting the job. The Wadhams were an outpost
at the end of the world, east of Fogo, east of everywhere, and no one
else wanted it. The lighthouse at Offer Wadhams was built after the
1852 Spring of the Wadhams, when some forty sealing ships foundered
in the ice nearby, leaving their crews to swarm up the cliffs by the hundreds and camp out in summer fishing shacks abandoned for the
season. Eventually, they walked down across the ice to the mainland
for help. But there would still be incidents, this new light or not. It was
the North Atlantic; it was Newfoundland; there'd always be incidents.
A lighthouse keeper on the Wadhams would always have the devil to
pay and no pitch hot. But Robert liked his post well enough. Many of
his fellow countrymen had struck out for Newfoundland, especially
from Poole and Dorset. It was a tradition. A migratory fishery to
Newfoundland from the West Country of England had been running
for nearly three centuries. Devon mariners like Robert were thought
to be particularly up to the journey, particularly tough.

> If Poole were a fish Poole
> and the men of Poole fish
> there'd be a pack for the Devil
> and fish for his dish

went a 1766 British *Proposal for Encouraging the Fishery*. Some of
the West Countrymen wanted to quit their back-and-forthing year
after year after year and stay in Newfoundland, but Britain legislated
against it. The country's young men could go away only if they
returned with their income. It wouldn't do to set up a competing profit
centre elsewhere, or a merchant marine in training.

Robert Goff Wellon might have been leaving his country, but he
was going to be joining his countrymen. By the early eighteenth
century many of them had stopped commuting across the Atlantic
and had settled permanently in Newfoundland. Robert was well

inclined to make a lasting move. Arriving in the world in 1817 on
the bloodied heels of Napoleon's last hurrah, he had entered a Europe
that now swirled around him, chaotic, manic. His own large family
was no calmer. He'd been born into its dead centre, and he left behind
an older and a younger brother as well as two older sisters and two
younger ones. In a family like that, in a climate like that, a man could
get lost. It was a good time to get away.

Nothing stopped him – nothing, that is, but Hilda Margaret
McBath of Greenspond, whom he met almost the moment he arrived,
and took with him to Herring Neck. It was as if she'd been waiting
for him, Margaret with her Highlands lilt and her green, green eyes
like a cat's. Two generations on, her grandson Aubrey inherited those
eyes, but on him they had less charm.

~

After a spell in Herring Neck long enough to produce a brood, Robert
Goff was off to the Wadhams lighthouse with Margaret and their
eleven children, Thomas, Ethel's father, among them. With their move,
Robert Goff and the bonny Margaret populated the Wadhams single-
handedly. A last son, Samuel, was born on the Wadhams and toddled
around with the gulls.

The Wadhams were a dream after Herring Neck, where the bait
herring were plentiful but the cod were not and where nearly a
hundred families stuffed themselves into half as many shacks, all squat-
ting haphazardly on the cramped, craggy shores. It was hard land to
build on, so you shared, and for Robert the place had begun to feel like
the family he'd left in Dorset – brimming. At the Wadhams, they were
alone. Except in the summer, when the fishermen came in droves from
the mainland, only the eggers sought the islands out, killing the gulls
for the feathers they sold for bedding, and collecting their eggs for sale
in port. There was no repeat of the Wadhams Spring and its broken
ships. The lighthouse shone its swath down the ocean waves, and the
Wellon family was unbothered by calamities. They stank of the seal oil

that fuelled the light, and they gathered round every four hours as Robert rewound the gear that turned it, pulling on the long ropes that held the weights. In summer, they cleaned away the damp rot and repainted, and Robert sailed to Seldom to fetch his pay in light dues collected from passing vessels. He grew a long, long beard which he never cut, not even later in life. He watched his children play, and he read at night and in the long days too. He owned a leatherbound set of the *Encyclopaedia Britannica*. Later, his granddaughter Ethel would run her hands over the books.

Robert Goff Wellon was a man, as Robert Frost put it a century later, out far and in deep.

Eventually he and Margaret moved to Ladle Cove, where the last two girls were born, twins. Margaret Wellon had borne a lot in life, and her throng of children remembered their mother fondly when she died, just before Christmas, in her eighty-sixth year. *Our mother here lies underground/The dearest friend we ever found/But through the Lord's unbounded love/We hope to meet in realms above* her marker reads in the old Ladle Cove cemetery, ornate compared to the stone for her husband, whom she outlasted by fourteen years. Most of her children had equally untypical long lives. Margaret lost a couple of her girls, but only one of her sons predeceased her. He'd gone down on the *Bell Haddon* off Twillingate years before. *T'was but three days out from Newfoundland*, they used to say about him, *when overboard he fall'd. And as he was a-goin' down, upon the Lord he called.*

The Wellons called upon the Lord a lot. They were devout; they were sure in their faith and sure of themselves. Robert Goff had made himself over, time and again; within the bosom of his family he'd made the most of himself. He'd set his sights; he'd been around; he'd cut the family cloth; he'd spun it richly for ages to come. He'd relied on God but he'd known himself. He'd had in him what his granddaughter Ethel aspired to.

～

Two generations later, Ethel had gone off to teachers' Normal School at Methodist College in St. John's. In those days, many so-called teachers got by on their high school credits alone. Ethel was different; she pitched high. She'd taught school now for years. For the last three until her marriage to Sidney Wiseman she'd been schoolmarm in Little Bay Islands, a horseshoe of specks in Notre Dame Bay tied together by a hand-hewn, rust-coloured bridge. It was an isolated spot, poor by times and forgotten by the world, connected to it only by the coastal boats that came weekly in summer, less often in winter: the *Clyde* out of Lewisporte, the *Prospero*, the *Northern Ranger.*

It was where she was returning with her husband now, to set up house and family. She was one of the many young girls in those days who went into an outport to teach and didn't come back. She was like them – and she was altogether different. Something played at her. On that December morning, as she stood newly married on the wharf at Seldom, the gale that had blown out the previous day's snow, tamed now, teased her hair. At the side of the wharf, Sidney readied the trap skiff that would take them back to Ladle Cove, where they'd pick up his schooner and be on their way to Little Bay Islands and home. She watched him work. It was winter, it was Seldom. She was scrammed, blue with cold, and she was uneasy too. The wind chattered at her in the voices of the dead. *Ethel. Auntie Et.* Harold and Ivey. *Ethel, my lovely* – that was Good. *Ethel, my lovely, speak us some verse.* And then a new voice in her ear, her grandfather's voice. Robert Goff who'd stepped up onto this very wharf so many years ago, who'd sailed over each summer to collect his light dues. *Where are ye now, Thomas's little Et?* Ethel stopped short, lifted her face to the sky. Only a gull wheeled far overhead. There was no one there, no one at all. She could plunge her hands into the air around her and come up empty as a net in a bad season. For the first time in her life, Ethel felt a little lost.

Before her marriage, as the schoolteacher for Little Bay Islands, Ethel had lodged with one of Little Bay Islands' "best" families. Frederick and Elizabeth Wiseman showed off their new boarder. She added to the civility the Wiseman estate showed the community.

She even brought them more visits from the circuit preacher, Elizabeth was sure of it. The minister had come by more often these last couple of years than he ever had to the Strongs over at the other end of the harbour. The girl could be counted on for erudition, to carry a conversation with men of the cloth. Her father was virtually a man of the cloth himself. Frederick laid and lit the fire in the parlour, and there they sat with biscuits and tea.

With the Wisemans, things were seldom what they seemed – but from the outside looking in, Ethel didn't know that yet. She was a bright girl but school-learned, protected by her home-bound mother, Fanny. Ethel was good-hearted, and around men she was green as Frederick Wiseman's roofing paint. Installed down the hall from the Wiseman boys in their house at Big Tickle, the channel from the North Atlantic into the harbour, she got a bird's-eye view of the marriageable ones. In the long evenings she did the books for the Wiseman family business, fleshing out her income of about twenty dollars a month – most of which she turned over to Lizzie and Fred for room and board.

It was young Good Wiseman whom Ethel thought about as she worked the Wiseman ledger. Bert Strong, too, from just down the road, George Hicks, the Goodyear boys, how she was twenty-six now, nearing twenty-seven. How March came and went each year surrounded by ice and darkness and barely a day's sun, bringing another year upon her. No, she wasn't getting any younger.

Good, now, he had such a face. There he was, now, turning a potato over and over in its jacket in the ashes in the stove, the evening half finished and one of Lizzie's huge dinners down him not so long ago. He was such a one, that boy: he looked younger every day. He had a way with that face, even now smeared with potato and butter and pepper, angling it at her just as she caught his eye so that his auburn hair danced on his forehead.

For Ethel, in the early years in the house at Big Tickle, her heart's content was in sight – and life was, well, Good. She drew the oil lamp closer down the table to her ledger. It was hard to keep up with her work, to keep her mind on it; hard to see in the dark.

For their part, the Wiseman boys were only too glad to have Ethel Wellon on hand. She was pretty and smart, with a lovely sad face and a shapely waist, and they weren't used to her as they were to the local girls. Ethel had been to teacher training in St. John's. They'd been nowhere for nothing – just to the Labrador for fish. Ethel could talk Spanish and French to the skippers of the foreign ships in to pick up salt cod, and sometimes the call went out to have her come down to Strong's wharf to translate. With her learning, Ethel could talk rings around the Wiseman boys, but she didn't, and they liked that too. She was demure, with a winning small smile and rosy cheeks. They lined up.

~

But the line shrank, devastated by fate – and the pitiless Newfoundland fishery. Like Ethel, Sidney was himself a youngest child, of nine. An older brother, Plinny, drowned on the Labrador where he'd been working the season. One hot August afternoon he was in a small boat in Perry's Gulch, hauling a trap. Suddenly a sea – no one called it a wave – broke over the skiff, throwing him out. Spotted by the white soles of his boots, Plinny was retrieved the following morning from beneath the edge of a large boulder that had trapped him. Talk was, he still had his pipe in his mouth, but his eyes had been eaten straight out to sockets by the shrimp that were so plentiful along the Labrador rocks. *Full fathom five thy father lies*, the kids taunted each other back at home when the death ship came in. *Those are shrimp that were his eyes*. They'd been reading *The Tempest* in class.

Preserved in a rough box with salt spared from the catch, Plinny was sailed home for burial on the salt-bleached deck of his own schooner. From the Wiseman house at the narrows of the Little Bay Islands harbour, Lizzie spotted the vessel returning unaccountably early, and then she saw its flag at half mast. She didn't go down to the wharf.

Oh, it was too, too bad, all too bad.

Ray and Good Wiseman followed Plinny into the sea the next year, in October 1921. "We got a ticket straight to hell," said Ray to Good, as if he knew something was up. The boys were leaving Strong's wharf to go "down" to the French Shore at Fichot Island (up, actually, along the east coast of Newfoundland's long northern peninsula that sticks up like a defiant finger at the North Pole and God). They were to bring back a load of fish for Strong's, the wholesaler. Bad weather was brewing; shouldn't they wait it out?

Ray and Good weren't the type to wait for much. They loved a good time, and a sail in a gale promised as good a time as any. Alas, the storm that blew in around the *Helen C. Morse* once it departed Strong's wharf was a fierce, three-day frenzy that came to be known as the October Gale. She went down north of Cottrell's Cove with all hands, and only small pieces of her were ever recovered.

Sidney's brothers, Harold and Nelson, stuck at the trade and somehow survived, Harold producing fourteen children over the course of two marriages. But it was a hard life, he lost his beloved and beautiful first wife, and his nerves frayed in time. Harold was big-hearted, sentimental, readily moved; once, a struggle to get a canvas cover in place on his boat at the end of the season reduced him to tears.

Like their father before them, the Wiseman boys who lived and stayed hale had no trouble doing well. It was a skipper's market, and the Fisherman's Protective Union formed along the east coast by William Coaker in 1909 had suddenly made the vocation lucrative. No more buying your gear from the company store for some price disclosed later and guaranteed to blow your boots off, when the company also decided what your catch was worth. No more twisting in the wind on the company store's credit. *Let me know if you got a berth for me,* Robert LeDrew wired Fred Wiseman from Pilley's Island about the coming season. *Keep my berth,* Thomas Dillon of Millertown wired, to confirm his. Alfred Earle cabled too, all the way from St. John's. *Have you berth for me this summer. If not I will try somewhere else.*

But downs followed ups like the waves that roiled. *If it be marvellous in the eyes of the remnant of this people in these days, should it also be marvellous in mine eyes?* The Lord asked Zechariah, and the Lord said no. After the death of her husband, Fred, in 1919, Lizzie blackened faster than peeled potatoes in the sun.

~

Fred had lived long and prospered for a man of his time and place, lasting into his sixty-first year and becoming that rare outport success, both master and owner of a fishing schooner, and then another and another, all docked at one of Strong's three long wharves. On Frederick's death, Lizzie sold the schooners, except one, to Strong's, at whose dock they remained, and by 1921 the Little Bay Islands census of "330 Persons in 69 Households" noted her as a woman of private income and independent means. But better she hadn't stopped short of the final sale – Fred's last schooner was an ill-fated ship, determined to follow its master into the dusk. It went to Plinny and came back from Perry's Gulch without him, met by a bleak old woman staring out her window. Ray and Good took the ship over after that, and then it was gone forever, sunk with all hands. The older brothers, Harold and Nelson, didn't mourn its loss. Long contracted to Strong's, they were already mastering schooners and fathering families of their own. They were drifting from their mother, from the family holdings. Strong's, after all, had fifty schooners going each year to the French Shore and on up to the Labrador. Who needed another?

Lizzie walked from window to window after Fred's death, after Plinny's and Ray's and Good's, on clear nights watching the moonlight on the ice sheets that cracked and burst up, butting each other and jamming the harbour like a train wreck. How was she ever to get any sleep, the damn moon glaring like that? No doubt the schoolmarm was snoring away in the next room. Shallow people slept well; Lizzie had always thought that. Oh, what did she care how devastated the girl said she was over the loss of the boys? She, now, Lizzie: she had troubles, worries. Who would batten down Lizzie's hatches now, and take over Lizzie's family? Which one of her no-good sons would remember there was a name to keep, a living to make, and find a schooner to make it with?

And then – here he was, Sidney, the lad, the dear one and the youngest and the one she'd waited for all her life. Here he was, home from the navy, a little late, having tarried a few months to gallivant and explore the world. With Lizzie's stash he bought into Strong's as well as St. George's Coal Fields, White Bay Mining, Fisherman's Union Trading, you name it. Sidney Wiseman was a grand young man come home to a ready-made fortune and a fine old house. He had the schooner the *James Strong* built for him, 139 tons with materials from Strong's mill and constructed on Strong's dock and with a few strings attached to it that Strong's could yet pull, but it was *his*.

He'd rowed his mother over from Big Tickle in the punt to see its bones go up. All the way across the harbour, him rowing her like that! She'd put on her best hat. Lizzie didn't make that trip much any more, but there she was again, going places with her son. Wasn't he that rare outport success now, ship owner and master both? It'd taken his father all his life to accomplish what the youngest son had at the tender age of twenty. So what if it was Fred's sweat that gilded him now? Wasn't he the flanker, wasn't he the Wisemans' bright spark! His older brothers crewed for him. Skipper Sid Wiseman sang his little ditty everywhere, the one about the Wisemans, the Wellmans, the Richmonds, and the Campbells, all the Islands' great men: *A wise man, a well man, a rich man – and a camel to carry them all.* There he was, the wise man, right at the head of the list.

But a single line for Lizzie forever had two hooks. It was like her good hat that day on the harbour when she visited the *James Strong*. The scarf on it was stiff, and slapped her face all the way. It wasn't a hat for wind. Nothing worked for Lizzie, nothing really did. Maybe Sidney could make things work, if he had his chance. She'd make sure he did. *Y'let naught stand in your way, my son,* she told him all his life. *Y'walk right over it.* She'd seen him gaff his first lobster at the age of five, beating the thing to pieces on the wharf when it pinched him. What a rage he'd been in. Yes, he'd do fine; even at five he could cut a notch in the beam. With the return of her golden boy from the war, Lizzie had warmed to the idea of life without Fred.

Then Sidney married Ethel.

~

As fine as the house was that Fred had built and left Lizzie, like every other building in Little Bay Islands it had not a scrap of insulation, and in it you got cold very quickly. Lodged at the top of the Tickle, it was breezy and chill. No outport building had a basement, and ill winds blew in everywhere. At Big Tickle, the only sanctuary some winter days was the wood stove in the big kitchen, with its ever-present drying line of socks and mittens hung up at the rear, its ever-present line of boots warming in back.

The house itself was splendid, overlooking the Tickle like a uniformed sentry with a fob watch. With its ornate scrollwork, mantles, and mouldings, it was huge for its day, nearly a mansion. For Little Bay Islands it was the house of a lifetime, outdone only by Strong's estate with its tennis courts across the harbour. It had high front steps and a long front porch. It had decorative bargeboard trim and even sported a billiards table in the panelled room where Dr. Lidstone, the community sawbones, and other family friends congregated. Arthur Lidstone came up to the house most Sunday mornings, to sit in the rocking chair by the billiards table where he smoked his Gold Flakes and drank two bottles of homemade dogberry wine.

The good doctor was a boozer, practising in Little Bay Islands where the long arm of the law seldom reached, but he delivered Ethel's firstborn ably enough to be made a family namesake. Thomas Lidstone Wiseman was a Christmas baby that Dr. Lidstone made a gift to the newborn's parents. Ethel was just grateful she had someone other than her mother-in-law at her side for the delivery. The balance of her brood was helped into the world by Granny, the local midwife, a stout old

crone smelling of camphor who pulled at her stockings as she beat out
the time for Ethel's contractions, snapping them smartly against her
ankles in a finale each time Ethel completed a push and lay back,
exhausted. Granny was a mixed bag. She knew her stuff, but made her
patients feel they were labouring inside a marching band. There'd been
a time you could go to Dr. Abraham at Pilley's Island Hospital and wait
out your confinement. Dolphe Strong had sent his wife to Pilley's on
the *Clyde* to deliver her third son. What a commotion there'd been
around that; you'd think it had been their first. But they'd wanted the
best care. The first boy had had something go wrong at birth, and had
a wry neck. This time, a flurry of wires had gone back and forth, sometimes more than two a day. *All well home. Youngsters first rate. How is
everything at home. All fine at home. Have spare room ready and a nice
cup of tea.* Dolphe's cousin had even wired St. John's: *Ship by rail 1
gallon good rum.* But the Old Pill Box at Pilley's had closed in the early
1920s. It was Granny for a time after that, and then Arthur Lidstone.

Lidstone and Sid Wiseman were great cronies. Sid himself wasn't
much of a drinker in those years, but the billiards room at the house
at Big Tickle was one of the few places he seemed content. In years to
come he'd let his boys up to the table to play, standing them on biscuit
boxes. *Watch the felt, watch the felt, mind you don't tear the felt!* He
was always yelling at the little boys. But despite that, for a brief time
at the house at the Tickle, Sid was happy too.

For his mother, however, it was always winter. Lizzie had lost a boy
and a girl in infancy as well as a husband and three grown sons, and
now the Wellon girl had taken her youngest. Her Sidney hadn't been
the girl's second choice at all. Her Sidney had rescued Ethel, that
was the way it was. And now Ethel's presence just meant more socks
to hang behind the kitchen stove, and a litter of kids too. Two already.
Tom had been followed by Harry.

With her own beloved mother dying out of reach down the coast
at Ladle Cove, Ethel had spent her second pregnancy distracted. As
she welcomed her darling new boy she grieved her mother, who would
be gone in six weeks. *Oh for the touch of a vanished hand/And the*

sound of a voice that is still, reads Fanny's marker in the Ladle Cove cemetery. She died in late October, on her fifty-second wedding anniversary. She had ailed a long time before she went, but by the time the *Clyde* was running again through the slob ice, Ethel was too big with child to go to her to say goodbye. Harry, the new baby, was born sickly, with a chest condition for which his remaining grandmother prescribed daily swaddlings in a poultice of cod liver oil and cotton wool. Trusting no one to oil and swaddle as well as she, Lizzie rubbed the baby down herself and then wrapped him up in the wool. The schoolteacher was causing far too much disruption, loading the household with work. When Marion, the next child, was born only ten and half months after Harry, interrupting his treatment, it was hard to say whom Lizzie blamed more – Ethel or the new baby. Certainly Sidney had nothing to do with it.

Lizzie coddled the little boy, at least, and Ethel made herself grateful. Baby Harry considered himself his Aunt Liddy's pride and joy. One day he ran in from the yard, agog, to tell her that a lobster was crawling on the sea bottom near the wharf. The harbour teemed with lobsters year round; Little Bay Islands fished seals, herring, salmon, crab as well, in later years packing crab at a plant near the end of the horseshoe, but its waters ran with lobster too, and before the Islanders ever packed crab, they packed lobster. Lots of it – four thousand cases one summer alone. If you looked down from anyone's dock you'd see the bottom crawling with them. After a gale you had to pick up your feet so as not to trample them on the rocks, where they'd been tossed up by the wind and the waves. But a lobster on the loose was still a sight to a little boy.

Every Little Bay Islander kept a gaff on his wharf. Lizzie's had several – you never knew what you were going to have to haul in. She fetched one and speared Harry's lobster from the water for him, expertly, as if she'd been knifing things all her life.

～

Lizzie had no patience for the new child, Marion. Nor any for Ethel. On top of everything, the girl was a sentimental fool. One morning well into Ethel and Sidney's marriage, Lizzie had had enough. She came downstairs to find Ethel thawing baby chicks on a towel she'd spread out on the oven door, turning them over and moving them around until a tiny wing shuddered here, a scrawny leg twitched there. As usual, Ethel had gotten up ahead of everyone else to light the fire and start her day. Well, thought Lizzie, why shouldn't she get up? She had a lot to do. That morning, though, Ethel had asked the maid, Ede, that other wretched girl loitering in Lizzie's house, to light the stove while she went down from the kitchen through the long covered corridor to check the henhouse behind the house. It had been a frosty night, and one of the hens had been nesting: chicks had hatched and frozen overnight. Ethel had carried the stiff little lumps back to the kitchen in her apron, transferring chick after chick between the warmth of her bodice and the oven door until all but one was restored.

Ethel's children were fascinated, cheering the survivors as each came to, grieving the single casualty. It was unthinkable that their mother, splendour of their little lives who delivered them from every hurt, could not save everything. "Put him in your bosom, Mommy, put him back in your bosom!" they pleaded.

Lizzie had been standing on the back stairs. Striding into the kitchen now she spat at the children and their mother, disgusted. It was hard to know which she disliked more. As for the wretched birds, they should have entered Lizzie's kitchen plucked and cleaned and in a stew pot or not at all. They should have been pitched straight into the stove, every one.

Things between Lizzie and her daughter-in-law went from bad to worse. One day Lizzie threatened Ethel with a kitchen chair, holding it over her head to crash it down. Ethel and Ede wrested it away from her.

"Fine," said Lizzie, reaching into her great gaunt mouth and, with a bony thumb and forefinger, extracting the last of her loose teeth.

She held it up in front of Ethel. "You wait, my girl, until Sidney gets home," she leered. "You wait until Sidney hears how you knocked out my last tooth when you beat me over the head with this chair."

When Aunt Lizzie had her stroke, she fell and knocked over the high chair of baby Ron, Sidney and Ethel's youngest. It was the most she'd ever had to do with him.

~

Lizzie was carried out from her sickbed in a coffin. She had lingered for a week; now Ethel headed the procession down the stairs. She was crying, carrying the basin she'd used to wash the body. Ethel had attended the old crone's every whim for days, but still she wasn't crying in relief.

"She's gone, Marion. Grandmother has died," she told her daughter as she pitched the grey water down the kitchen sink.

At six, Marion was amazed. Was there any monster her mother couldn't love? Aunt Lizzie used to stop her in the upstairs hallway and pinch her spiny fingers into the child's shoulders. Aunt Lizzie had the fingers of a witch. "No luck comes of little girls," she'd hiss into the child's face, and Marion would run away crying. "You! Child!" she'd grab Marion at the shoulders again; the rest of them, too, but Marion most often. "Let me see into your mouth now." She'd try to reach her fingers in, searching for signs of the diphtheria that had taken her first grandchild, Nelson's boy.

Bite her! Bite her! the boys would say, and Marion cried harder at the prospect of being bitten back.

When Aunt Lizzie died Harry was six, just as Marion was. They'd been born so close together that for a few weeks every year he and his little sister were the same age. Harry ran around the kitchen now, his arms outstretched like a plane. "Aunt-y Lid-dy, Aunt-y Lid-dy," he cooed. "Where you gone?"

"Shut up, you. For Godsake." That was Sid, from his daybed along the far wall of the kitchen, where he stretched out day and night under the flowered wallpaper, waiting for his life to arrive now that his mother, his ally, had gone.

~

After his mother's death, Sidney came apart. Walking the road to the Tickle house one night with Ethel, he erupted in a froth and ran down the shore, swearing to drown himself in the harbour.

Ethel picked her way across the beach after him and coaxed him back. "It's low tide yet, my darling," she said to him reasonably. "You couldn't drown much there."

"I'll wait, then," he cried. "I'll wait for the tide and I'll toss myself in," he said. But he never did.

Ethel coaxed Sidney to leave the Salvation Army citadel, too, when he began picking at Jimmy White as he testified to the assembly about God's goodness.

"You know naught o' goodness, my lad," Sid heckled young Jim. "You pay me for that engine I sold you and then you can be good all you want." Sid still wore his naval uniform from time to time, and while it had thrilled her once, Ethel wished now he'd retire it. It hadn't taken her long to learn all about his darkness. It was getting so much worse now, with his mother gone, and long before that it had already been bad enough.

Ethel had already left Sidney once, only a few months into the marriage, waiting until May when he was gone to the Labrador for the season and then booking passage on the *Clyde*, to escape home to Ladle Cove. She met her parents on the wharf with her trunk. She was leaving the marriage, she told them, and she wasn't going back. She paused for a moment, clutching her middle. Seasickness. On the *Clyde* coming over, she'd been green to the gills. She hauled down a few breaths. Back in Ladle Cove the air seemed somehow better than it had in Little Bay Islands. Sidney was a madman, she went on, born of a madwoman, and life with him was not going to get better.

About that, she was right. About never going back, she was wrong.

Even restored to the bosom of her family and the ministrations of Fanny and Thomas, she continued sick. She tried her mother's Prescription A, a specific for stomach complaints from Stafford & Son which Thomas had brought in from St. John's. Spruce-bud tea was no help either; it only made her woozier. Granny Gudger, who had a nose for these things, went into the woods for a shrub which she stripped down and boiled up, but when she brought the brew over to the Wellons' she took one look at Ethel and poured it out on the step.

Granny Gudger had the calling. She knew.

When Granny left, Ethel sat on the steps and stared at the stain her tea had left. Ethel's parents had the means to support their daughter. But now they didn't have the inclination. A woman's place might once have been debated by the Wellons, for they were kind and intelligent folk and they loved their daughter fiercely. But Fanny herself was ailing by then, less than two years short of her own death. Thomas could see the writing on the wall. A woman's place was with her husband, that was all. And a woman with child – well, Ethel just had to go back, and they all knew it, even Ethel herself. Family was the most important thing to her; it must be kept together at any cost. It was her father, after all, who'd taught her that. But she'd hoped she could make her family anew; she'd hoped that by returning to her parents in the face of her dreadful blunder, she could step back into their family and make it her own once again.

> I do not ask, O Lord, that life may be
> A pleasant road;
> I do not ask that thou wouldst take from me
> Aught of its load.

It was her father's favourite hymn, and now she could see that he was right. She loved him fiercely too. For Ethel, Thomas was always right. A child should have its father. Death alone should take her from her husband – and death alone would.

II

FIRE AND WATER

In Notre Dame Bay, the water was cold year round, and Little Bay Islands' beaches were pebbly. In summer, kids took out the family punts and rowed around the harbour to errands along the shore. In winter they crossed the ice rather than walk the length of the horseshoe road to school and church. They weren't supposed to play on the ice on the margins of the winter, but they did – coppying on the pans, hurling themselves from one slab to the next. If you fell in, you simply grabbed onto a pan and waited to be hauled in.

It was cold, so what? This was Newfoundland; everything was cold. Rescue, now. Rescue was what mattered. There was salvation from without – or there wasn't. You couldn't save yourself.

People in the outports were resigned to water, bringing to it a learned helplessness that they brought to nothing else in their lives. Water was fate. When they grew up, those who went out on boats did so to work, not to worry about what would happen if the boat went down. If the boat did go down, not likely they could swim, even to flotsam where they might cling and be saved. *And the life of man nasty, brutish, and short* – the words of Thomas Hobbes rang in the coves for those with enough learning to recognize them.

The life of fishermen, they might have added. *Hauling, dawn to dusk.*

Sidney couldn't swim and there were times in the skiff or the punt with his father when Tom found himself having to resist the temptation to push the Old Man over. It would have been a solution of sorts to the family's misery. Sidney did take pains, however, to "teach" Marion – by dragging her into the punt in her underwear and rowing her far out into the harbour, where he knotted a rope around her waist and dropped her in. The other kids had all learned to swim on their own, perfecting their abilities by showing each other what they'd learned, and the summer he was twelve Marion's youngest brother, Ron, swam the entire length of the harbour just to show off. But Marion hung back, terrified. She had a horror of water and Sid knew it, especially the depths off Strong's, near big Salt Rock. Ships left loose salt in its red warehouse for the foreign boats that came in to buy the catch from the local fisherman. These were boats from all over the world – France, Spain, Greece, Egypt, India. These were the skippers her mother talked to, translated for. Later, when Ethel opened her shop, they went to her for provisions rather than to Strong's, where they weren't on the payroll and had neither credit nor obligation.

Southern Harbour, Little Bay Islands' main harbour, was one of the most beautiful in all of Newfoundland and, for its size, one of the finest. The main entrance through Big Tickle was narrow, at some points only a hundred yards from shore to shore, and the water was deep enough to accommodate steamers of four thousand tons. It gave safe anchorage to all it sheltered, and Strong's had set up a fish processing and salting centre and an international fish brokerage to rival any in Newfoundland. When they took on their loads of fish, the foreign ships dumped the sand they carried as ballast there. Little Bay Islands kids imagined they had some of the same sand there that had made the Pyramids, that Mahatma Gandhi had walked on in his dusty sandals. There, in the midst of it all, rose Salt Rock. A man was said to have fallen from the Rock and drowned there, a foreigner, perhaps, and Marion imagined his body floated there still, just below the waves, whispering of home in Mandarin or French, waiting and watching in some sort of lonely death trance to pull in others and hold them down.

Whenever she rowed past Salt Rock with Tom or Harry, Marion averted her eyes from the water, studying the skyline until the boat was well past. If she didn't watch for the dead man, surely he wouldn't watch for her.

Now, she had to worry not only about a bloated corpse in the water, but her own father as well. Would Sid take this opportunity to drown her? She cried and whimpered at the end of his grip, shivering to blue in her underwear even though it was summer. She wouldn't scream, not in front of the Old Man. "You have to go," Ethel said to her, hugging her daughter on the wharf. "We'll all be right here watching." In the water, the child kept herself afloat until Sid grew bored with his lark. She wouldn't scream either if they came anywhere near Salt Rock – she'd die keeping her own counsel from the likes of him.

She swallowed a lot of water and stroked alongside the punt.

~

It was common enough, the drowning of children, in wells or ponds or the harbour or the dire North Atlantic itself. Water would drown you as soon as wipe your bum, and many outport children were scalded to death in kitchen mishaps. The first person Marion ever knew to die was a drowning victim, a schoolmate who fell off his family's wharf at the age of six. The neighbourhood men curved the limp body over a barrel from the cooperage next door and worked on it for a long time before they gave up. Water dripped from the blond curls and ran down the barrel onto their boots.

Children were taught to climb onto boats and climb off them, to scramble up and down the ladders on the sides of wharves. Nothing more. Living around water, working on it – one way or another you had to take your chances. There was no quiet water on the coast, and no one was taught to swim. Most adults didn't know how. Who had time to learn, or to teach anyone else? Why would you encourage your children to go anywhere near the water anyway? There weren't beach parties. No one supervised children playing around water; there was no time for that either. Unless they were in a boat on business, children were told to stay away. They disobeyed at their peril.

Men working on wharves were nonetheless keenly tuned to children in the vicinity, chasing them away when they could, and it was Adolphe Strong who returned Marion to her mother the day the child nearly drowned. He'd been working Strong's wharf when he heard the splash far below.

"All she did t'whole way home was moan about her muff," Dolphe told Ethel as he docked his motorboat at the Tickle wharf and handed her the sodden child. The Wisemans' empty punt bobbed behind his boat on a tow line. It was baking day, and Marion, just turned seven, had been determined to row the punt across the harbour to Strong's shop for supplies. It would be Marion's first solo outing, and she could hardly contain herself. She had pleaded; finally, Mom had relented. A debutante at the oars, she'd put on her powder blue skirt and jacket and her white muff to match. The muff hung down from her sleeve most of the time; it got in the way of the oars. But when she arrived at Strong's wharf and tied the punt up, climbed the Everest of the wharf rungs and scrambled over the top, she slipped her hands in it again. Oh, that muff. It was grand, it was. She wore it while she waited in the shop. Black Bob Wiseman was going through the tobacco, searching as he always did for the blackest plug. Effie Howell waited behind the counter, her hands on her hips. Young Bob Wiseman was in the shop too, but no one could mistake the one Bob for the other. Black Bob turned a hard, shiny plug in his hand. "You got nothing blacker'n she?" he asked Effie.

"Some muff," Young Bob said to Marion.

Black Bob looked. "Some white," he said mournfully, and Marion stepped back.

Back past the men on the wharf, she balanced the tin of baking powder and the pound of butter on top of the muff. At the side of the wharf again she shucked it off and climbed back down the ladder. Untying the painter, she stepped out – into the deeps. The boat had moved. Down she went, muff and all, tossing the baking powder and the butter into the punt as she fell.

~

Sailor was Skipper Sid's dog, one of a neighbour's litter given him when the children were small. A big friendly woolly sook, the dog had white patches that gave him a hodgepodge look uncharacteristic of a Newfoundland. He was amiable, always in the way, not much help – that, too, uncharacteristic of a Newfoundland.

Sailor, Ethel named him, and she and the children adored him anyway.

Sid's love for his dog was more conditional. To Sidney, a dog was just a dog, and it had better not get in the way. There'd been dogs in the Wiseman household before, and they hadn't lasted. In the end, dogs were as useless as anything else. Like Dolly, Sailor's predecessor, who ate the hens whenever she could break into the henhouse and who lay around having pups and pups and pups that Sid had to find time to drown.

Sid wasn't lucky with dogs. He'd had a fine team of huskies that hauled his sled in the winter, since on land, dog team and sled was the only transport. Jim Strong had had a car brought in once on the *Clyde*, and the thing had been beaten to death in a week trying to make a road of the Islands' rocky path. While Sidney was away, alas, the children fed his huskies dried, split dogfish without realizing they should cut the spines out first. The fish bones perforated the dogs' intestines, killing every one.

A bad combination, children and dogs, Sidney thought as he surveyed the corpses and the cowering kids. He'd shot a weasel once, right by his root cellar door. Just got it in his sights and fired, it didn't matter how quick and crafty the thing was. Sid was a crack shot. Why shouldn't he just shoot the lot of them one day, just up and shoot them all?

Sailor lacked for most things a man like Sid would want in a dog, including the rescue instinct of his breed. When Tom fell off the wharf of the Tickle house Sailor was no help – the little boy had to haul himself in and up the pebble beach on his own. Young Harry ran for Aunt Lizzie, but no one caught it that day. Both Sid and his mother let the boys get away with things that Marion was thrashed for.

That was why Marion blamed Sailor the next time someone fell off the wharf.

~

Ten years before Ron swam the harbour at age twelve, he was knocked off the wharf at the Tickle house and nearly drowned. The accident was Marion's fault, and rather than accept the inevitable penalty at the hands of her father, she blamed it on Sailor. Dressed only in his napkin, when the baby toppled he fell far out from the wharf. Marion, five, stood and stared, riveted to the spot. Someone ran for Ethel. Eight months pregnant with Grace, the last child she was to have, she flew from the house weighted down by her maternity smock that flapped at her as she ran. She climbed down the wharf rungs. Tom scrambled down too, and Marion watched the top of his little bib hat bob below her as he descended. There was Ron, too, floating off to the side, his rear puffed up in the air of his ballooning white napkin while the rest of him was submerged. A bit of blond hair crowned the water.

He looked dead already, and back on the wharf Marion wished she were dead too.

Three times Ethel stretched out her hand from the wharf ladder, her face white from the strain *I do not ask, O Lord* and her arm quivering; three times Ron bobbed away, just beyond her reach.

Tom stretched his little arm out too. His mother's smock loosened from its tie and dragged in the wet.

There was no sound at all, not from any of them. Blood beat in Marion's ears. She felt an immense pressure in her head, as if she'd been holding her breath too long and would blow apart, as if the whole world in another moment would blow apart too.

Each time Ethel's hand stroked the water beside Ron, imploring, under he went. With her middle finger, the longest, she barely touched his head, inching it closer to her. Once, twice – when he went down the third time Marion, looking on, died a thousand deaths. Even at five, she'd heard the saying: you go down the third time you don't come up again.

For the little girl on the wharf, time crawled and stopped. For her mother on the wharf ladder below, time stopped too.

But Ron did come up again, and Ethel did finally reach him. She caught a corner of his napkin where the safety pin was, and the strain on it as she pulled snapped it open into her hand. Blood mixed with the seawater streaming out of the baby as they lifted him up and pulled him up the wharf ladder, Ethel on one side holding the corner of the napkin, little Tom on the other grasping his baby brother by the heel. Upside down, Ron drained back into life. It was Sailor's fault, Marion told her mother once everyone was reassembled on the wharf and Ethel had Ron held at arm's length to drip. Ethel had clasped the baby to her first and walked around with him, streaming water down onto the wharf. Her own blood still ran from the pin stick, and dripped on the wharf. "My child! My child!" she'd cried, and Ron cried too. When he was less afraid, he began to wail and shriek.

"It was Sailor's fault," Marion said solemnly. She knew the story would get back to her father sooner or later, and she'd be called to account. Sailor knocked Ron in, she told her mother, staring into the dark, knowing eyes, not daring to breathe.

It was the only time she ever lied to the one she loved best.

Sailor *had* been in the way, she rationalized, walking behind her mother, who still held the baby as they filed up the lawn to the house, a small, troubled troupe of well-wishers for Mom and Ron both. They had to see things through, to make sure Mom and Ron were all right. Sailor came too, at the end of the line. But Ron had only bounced over the dog when Marion pushed him, finding both of them in her path. Ron was a toddler; he wasn't supposed to be anywhere near the water to begin with, and now he was in the way of her fun. She'd just been turning him around to send him back to the house. Yes, that's all she'd been doing – and then look what happened! But her guilt stayed with her for years. It hurt far more than even her father could have hurt her, and it came back to haunt her when Sailor paid the price.

~

Sidney was pleased as punch. All day he'd worked in the store – the huge, two-storey shed below the house where he kept his boats and nets and all his gear – and he'd finally got them in, the huge windows he'd had shipped up from St. John's on the *Clyde*. They'd been plenty dear, even for a man of Sid's means, and they'd been hell to install. But Sidney's store was bound now to be the best on the Islands, better even than anything the Strongs had on the other side of the harbour. Let them come look at Sidney's store now, at Sidney's grand, gleaming windows wrapping all the way around both floors.

Today he'd finished the windows on the second floor, just under the natty, square-topped roof. Well, the men he'd hired had finished them. He'd supervised. Who else even *had* windows? Everyone else made do with the double doors on each end of a store. You opened the wharf end to haul in your fish from your boats, and you made do with the light the doorway threw in as you worked.

Sid's store was a mansion by comparison, a palace.

Come one, come all, have a look at Wiseman's. He'd put the word out tomorrow; it was too late now. He was hungry and tired and he didn't even stop to take a last look around before he went down the stairs and out, locking the door behind him.

Sailor woke in the evening, climbing to his feet and shaking himself out. Where was everyone? The place had been busy before he'd gone to sleep in the sun where it shone warm and buttery on the plank floor through that new glass that had just gone in.

Sailor went downstairs. What was this? The door was shut, there was no one here, and he wanted his supper. He went round the first floor, sniffing and whining in the corners, and then up the stairs and around the top. He stopped at each of the gleaming new windows, pressing his nose against the glass to look out on the dark.

Nothing.

He went downstairs again, barking in earnest now. Still, no one came. He was going to have to pee soon, too, and he knew he should never do that inside. Up and down he went, back and forth, barking himself into a frenzy. But the house was too far away from the store, and no one could hear him. No supper, no children, no warm bed by the big kitchen stove overnight.

He was all alone.

If Sailor could have put words to his plight, he might have called it the saddest night of his life. He could not have known it would also be the last.

Sidney went out in the morning early, without stopping for his tea. To Ethel, working in the kitchen, it seemed strange that he came back so soon. Surely he'd want to stay for a moment in the store, admiring the new windows in first light. And now, stranger still, there he was going for his shotgun.

He turned to her, and she caught her breath. His face was sheeted with rage, nearly unrecognizable. "He smashed every single window trying to get out," Sidney spat at her from between his teeth. "He didn't miss a single one." Then he was gone.

She gathered the children to her and pulled the blinds. "Cover your ears, my children," she said, trying to fit her own hands over the ears of the youngest. "My poor children. Poor, poor Sailor." Harry couldn't be comforted; he ran upstairs to his room, crying. Tom ran out to the wharf in time to see his father tying the dog to a post on the wharf.

Two shots rang in Tom's ears, in the kitchen over the children, in Harry's bedroom, in Ethel's heart.

Marion looked all over Back Beach for the dog's body, but never found it. Her father had thrown it in the punt and rowed it into the harbour, weighting it with a slab and dumping it into the deeps by Salt Rock.

~

Water gave life and snatched it back and closed over the dead forever, but fire was worse. People depended on fire and dreaded it, and every house had a ladder to the roof. The chimney caught fire, you ran up the ladder with a bucket and doused it – it was as simple as that. Or so you hoped; so you prayed. In Little Bay Islands they still talked about the fire on the coast, west across Hall's Bay, that had nearly destroyed the entire town of Springdale thirty years before. The men put their women and children out on schooners anchored in the bay while they stayed behind to fight the fire, concentrating on saving the mill and the lumberyard so that they'd at least have timber left to rebuild the homes that incinerated in front of their eyes. Only one house survived – Skipper John Delaney's woodframe on the shore.

"He had the divil behind that," someone said.

"Nah. He had the wife. Pulled her back from the women boarding the schooner and made her stay to water down the house all night."

In Little Bay Islands house fires were extinguished at night, and the smoky house each dawn that came with the lighting of the kitchen stove was as common a wake-up within as the clattering Strong's sawmill, starting up, was without. When the Grimes place burned down during the day it was as much a lesson as a spectacle, and the children were let out from school to watch. Marion's brother Jack sought her out in the little crowd that ringed the yard, standing back from the smoke and heat. As it caught fire the Grimes's ammunition went off in a cascade, exploding a cartridge at a time. An iron bedstead glowed and twisted and fell with a crash through a bedroom floor onto the gutted parlour below, showering the air with ash and embers and a whoosh of heat. Jack held his big sister's hand and squeezed it hard.

Even with their old iron stoves the outport schools were cold in winter, but nothing was colder than an outport church. No one made fires there at all. Too many of them had burned down, and even churches that could afford them were no longer equipped with stoves. All boasted the hot passion of God. "The last night the Bay was frozen over in the course of an hour," wrote a circuit preacher, "not less than six leagues over. How astonishing! But nothing is impossible with God." For pulpit duty he piled on two pairs of worsted gloves and two pairs of socks inside thick leather buskins that reached to his knees. After prayers he performed three baptisms and a love feast, the water for all of it boiled in a teakettle and rushed to the church from a house nearby, and all of it frozen on arrival. Winter winds rushed through the floors of buildings as if they weren't there, but the love feast generated its own heat. God poured forth like a steam bath. The preacher stamped his buskins on the brittle floor and led in a hymn, but no one wanted to go home, to hell with the cold and all their troubles. No one but Sidney Wiseman, and soon he never went at all.

Season of gales and drownings and lost schooners, summer on Newfoundland's east coast racked up a fearful body count. But winter gained its edge from the ocean gales at the end of the fall that swallowed ships like fodder, and from sealing casualties on the ice that wrapped the land in spring. Winter was a cruel season that took no prisoners. Like children everywhere, Ethel's brood loved it, and for at least one reason they looked forward to the bitter cold: the walk to school shrank when the harbour froze. For five long months, from November right through to March, it froze solid enough to cross. All the way around by road in summer it was more than a half hour, running. Many a time they'd all arrived panting, clutching their sides to ease out the stitches. Only Harry revelled in the race: it was all training for the records he'd be breaking as a middle-distance runner when he grew up. At least the school wasn't where it used to be, farther away still. The first school had been built halfway between the Southern and Northern Harbours, so that children from Mursell's Cove, Western Cove, and Northern Harbour could attend. These tiny hamlets were all but deserted now, and another school was built closer to Southern Harbour, where the population had consolidated. In 1913 the United Church opened the newest school right in the centre of town next to the Orange Lodge. There was a small Salvation Army school at Sulian's Cove, where the United Church had also once run classes, but the new Southern Harbour school was the place to go. The ground floor held two classrooms; the upstairs was big enough for a community hall. The whole thing, costing thousands, was built entirely from donations. It was progress. The last year Miss Wellon taught there, before she became Mrs. Sidney Wiseman, the school became a Superior and went all the way to grade eleven.

For the Wisemans the trip to school shortened once again. In winter, it was a mere saunter, a leisurely twenty minutes straight across the ice. Climbing up from the ice to the shore each morning, they had plenty of time to stop and gather an armload from the cordwood piled outside that each was expected to contribute daily to the school's old pot-bellied stove. Even so, the teacher, Mr. Winsor, didn't like to race the fire, and once in their seats the kids made a great production of seeing their breath. They cleaned their wood-framed slates with water, icing them over with each wipe. When Mr. Winsor wasn't looking, Marion put her slate pencil aside and pressed her fingertips into the film of ice on her slate, melting it into funny faces. She flashed them at Jack to make him smile.

The trip across in the morning was never as good as going home. Crossing the ice was a whole lot shorter than slogging all the way around on the track of road, but the wind straight to your face made things a whole lot colder. Mr. Winsor had the children circle their mitts on the floor around the stove and hang their wet clothes to dry, but the heat was half-hearted and they sat and shivered all the day long. Coming home was a dream, though, and Marion could forget her father's orders to return directly, stopping for nothing on the way.

Her father had so many orders; what was one more or less? They only ever seemed to apply to her, anyway. Tom and Harry got away with murder. After school they'd stop with their cousins, Uncle Harold's boys Dexter and Lloyd, and play hockeysticking and pucking, shooting a stone the size of a pancake across the harbour ice with a couple of sticks shared among the group. Marion sat down on the ice one day to watch after school, and by the time she scrambled up and across for home she'd lost her mittens. They'd been warm from the school stove, too warm. Once she'd taken them off and laid them down beside her on the ice, she couldn't find them anywhere. Coming home she was very late, and without her mitts her fingers were frozen. Nothing had pockets in those days; the best she could do on the crossing was to shrug her hands up into her sleeves as far as she could. They were red, painful, stiff as sticks.

But that was hardly to be the worst of it. He was waiting for her, there, on the shore below the house. Her cousins, her brothers, her salvation: everything lay far back on the ice below the schoolhouse, squealing and diving and jumping loop-the-loops on make-believe skates. Ede, the maid, was up at the house, invisible from the shore. Mom was at the Ensign shop, way back across the ice, farther back even than the schoolhouse. Marion and her father were alone.

She was only six, and she was in for it.

He jumped out at her from behind the corner of the boat store, slamming her frozen hands with a split of firewood from the winter woodpile. He held her by the throat with one hand to stop her getting away, and with the other, holding the split, he beat her hands raw. She'd never felt so much pain. Her head rang with it, flashing white behind her eyes with the kind of shriek and burst that made you jump and cringe all at once, like the guns that the boys shot at tins cans for rifle practice, *twelve-gauge and three oh three with the telescopic sight to pick off seals feel the whack against your shoulder how your head rings with the burst how your head goes white inside.* She vomited over and over again, onto her boots, onto the beach. Still he hung onto her and down the split came, again and again.

She lost count. She lost track of everything. The world fell away. Only the shriek of shots now, her head hanging, vomiting through her arms as he held onto her and hit. She lost track of everything but this – that she was only six years old.

And then the time changes to the eternal present as it does when he beats her, and she is always being hit and he will never stop. She prays for death; hers, his, both

She doesn't know how she gets to the house. She doesn't remember anything. Ede has her hands in a basin of warm water and she shrieks and shrieks and shrieks, for the pain of the water is worse than the pain of the wood. Ede asks her twice if she'll have some supper, she can sneak it up when he isn't looking – Ede tells her that the next day, I asked you twice, Muffin, you were white as a sheet except for your hands, the blood in the basin, on the floor, on your coat, I thought you'd die – and twice Marion says yes, supper, he said no supper, straight to bed, Ede tells her that too the next day, and then she vomits again, faints to the floor

Mom is leaning over her now, she is in her bed and Mom leans in and her smell is good and her hair is good and Mom will save her and they will die and leave this place together, they'll gather the boys and leave and Ede too, and they'll all be no more and they'll all be safe

Marion, Marion, Mom says, her voice a distant lullaby, did Daddy hit you on the head? Did he hit you on the head too? And Mom's good hands in her hair, checking can she still talk will she walk again is she all right in the head or has he smashed that too, split, cracked, shattered, burst, collapsed

And Mom's good hands then on her dead ones, bloated, swollen dead fish hands in ribbons, bleeding on the bedclothes even now and Mom's good hands touch hers and she screams again, the pain

So will I save you, and ye shall be a blessing: fear not, but let your hands be strong Mom is saying it, it's some Bible verse, and Mom's crying, saying it and crying like it can't be true

~

It was hard to believe that her father had been watching them on the ice at all. That was what Marion thought in the days that followed, when she allowed herself to think about it at all. She had time to think, since there was little point in going to school. Her hands were too swollen to hold a slate pencil. Tom and Harry told Mr. Winsor that Marion was sick and couldn't attend, nothing more. They knew they had to stick together, and keep the family together too. Nothing was more important than keeping quiet, protecting Mom, holding the family together. It was better that way – everyone thought it was. Best to keep it within the family. Anything else would be a monstrous betrayal.

Who could you complain to, anyway? They didn't bring the magistrate in from Springdale very often. They never brought a magistrate in just for families anyway, did they? Marion, six, asked her brothers.

Just for people, Harry said, his eyes welling up.

They brought the magistrate in that time Gwen Hillier's family was going to sue Cliff Stone's family, because Gwen said that Cliff had pushed her off the porch and hurt her back. Gwen had pushed him first, Cliff said in his defence. Everyone was on Cliff's side. The Stones were poor as church mice, after all, Uncle Will Stone a tinsmith and all, so you had to look out for them. Besides, Gwen's family was known to be picky.

Particular, Mom had said. Now, children.

All the magistrate had wanted Cliff to say was that he wouldn't do it again. Six times he asked the boy. *Now Cliff, my son. Will ye be doin' that again at all ever?* The magistrate was something of a disappointment – no robes, no wig like the pictures in the books from across the pond. But he had a way with words. *Now Cliff, my son.* Sidelined in the gallery, the kids and half the town held their breath. School had been let out for the day so that everyone could see firsthand how the judicial process worked. They'd discuss it in class the next day, write essays about it.

Say it Cliff, say it! Six times the kids held their breath, silently shot their instructions at young Cliff. *Say you'll never do it again!* What would happen if he didn't? Would he be arrested and his family ruined? Would he be strung up, pilloried?

Guillotined, Harry said under his breath, white-faced.

But Cliff was resolute. "I won't do it so long as she don't do it to me first," he said. Six times.

In the gallery, Jim Strong and Uncle Dolphe Strong were disgusted – with the Hilliers. "Saints preserve us and good morrow to you," said Uncle Dolphe, rising and snatching his hat. "Let the boy go. We all got stuff to get on with; let's not be here the whole day and tomorrow too." Uncle Dolphe put up Cliff's bond, paid his fine, and had the boy released to his custody.

Lying in bed, Marion picked at her bandages. She and Tom and Harry loved Uncle Dolphe, but not even Uncle Dolphe could help the Wisemans. If their own mother couldn't help them, how could anyone else? Ede had told Marion that the Old Man had promised to give it double, to Mom and the children both, if Mom told. And so Mom didn't tell. And anyway, their father was a business partner of the Strongs, a colleague. Maybe what was happening to them wasn't against the law or against decency anyway. Seldom had they heard of it happening anywhere else, not like it did to them. Their mother was hit far more than they were, and far more often, and she had her understanding of it. "Personal success," she told them, "is measured by the degree of grace and dignity with which you handle the atrocities of life." Their father was an atrocity; they should handle him carefully. Whatever that meant. All they knew was that making a move to change things, speaking about it even in a whisper, would be a monstrous betrayal. And if they lost, if he got off, they might all be killed – Mom first of all.

A betrayal of a monster is a monstrous betrayal – Marion turned it over in her head. How strange that the Old Man was watching them on the ice that day at all. Him, with his nose out of his *New York Times* for once; him, taking an interest in his children? It wasn't likely. Sometimes it was best not to think about these things. There was a book about spies and secret agents in the breakfast room bookcase with the glass doors, and in it lived a Mrs. Verloc, "confirmed in her instinctive conviction that things don't bear looking into very much." Marion liked Mrs. Verloc. Her husband was a spy or something; maybe better not to know exactly what. Things probably didn't bear much looking into. Marion would never understand her father, why bother to try? Maybe Mrs. Verloc had had a father like Skipper Sid. The book didn't say, but it did say that her Christian name was Winnie, like Mom's middle name, Winnifred, like the bear who went around with Christopher Robin in the sumptuous new five-volume set that was also in the bookcase now that Mom got books in by mail order. The bear set had come in on the *Ranger* on its last trip the year before. Mrs. Verloc was a young woman who kept a shop, just like Mom, and had "a full bust, in a tight bodice, and with broad hips. Her hair was very tidy." Marion had memorized Mrs. Verloc, she liked her so much.

Next to Mrs. Verloc there were books on the Boer War, books of poetry, even a book called *How to Write a Formal Letter*. Because of that one, Marion wrote the best letters of anyone in school. When she grew up, she'd take over the job of writing letters on behalf of Aunt Maud. How they loved Aunt Maud, she and Mom! The boys, too – everyone loved Aunt Maud.

Marion stopped picking at the bandages. They were fine; she needn't fuss. Mom had put ointment underneath the gauze for the swelling and had made a poultice of flour and molasses like the ones the men put on their gurry sores where their oilskins rubbed their wrists. Aunt Maud was what Marion should be thinking about; never mind her hands. *As you go though life make this your goal: watch the doughnut, not the hole.* Mom was always writing letters for Aunt Maud, because Aunt Maud had been the Wellons' eldest daughter and didn't get an education like Mom did, Mom being the youngest and having nothing more pressing to do. Aunt Maud mightn't have been to college like Mom, but still she was beautifully well-spoken. Marion thought her voice *mellifluous* – it was a word she'd learned in school – and quite unlike Aunt Mill's voice, which was scratchy and just like Aunt Mill herself. Aunt Maud was soft and rich, like a really good pillow. Aunt Mill was stiff and stretched, like the braids she wore wrapped around her head. How different they were, for sisters. Mom and Aunt Maud weren't very different at all. They were both like the plushest of pillows. You could sink down in them and never have to come out to face the world again. Marion thought the whole of Aunt Maud was like a sweet bit of yellow down from a duck, or a bit of Paris silk from the mail-order books.

Aunt Maud didn't think so. She didn't think she wrote as good a letter as did Mom, especially not a letter to the pension officials. Aunt Maud was supposed to get a pension because she'd lost her boys in the war, but after her husband died and Aunt Maud had remarried, she'd found her pension cut off. "Isn't that the way now," Mom had said, and she got out her fountain pen and her writing tablet and she wrote off her letters to the pension officials on behalf of Aunt Maud.

Soon, Marion fancied she'd be able to take over for both of them. Maybe soon enough she could also do Aunt Maud's hair for her when she visited from Ladle Cove, just like Mom did.

When her hands got better, maybe. And there she was again, picking at her bandages regardless of Winnie Verloc, thinking about things that probably didn't bear much looking into.

∼

Mom had been in to check her again. The house was quiet, cooling off, and Marion could see her breath. She lay flat on her back, staring at the ceiling, her hands under her quilts on the warm part of her abdomen in just the way she supposed you'd hold a baby or some other hurt, injured, fragile thing. The ointment still smelled. Tom said it was goo and it smelled like the Burnt Woods to Sulian's where the good berry picking was, and not so bad then, what? But Marion had her mother's allergies and the smell made her eyes water and her nose stuff up. She couldn't cry on top of that or soon she'd be so stuffed up she wouldn't be able to breathe.

So she didn't cry. She'd done her crying. At six, she stuck her chest out like a soldier in a picture book and repeated it to herself: *I've done my crying.* Instead of crying, she'd think about how she and her brothers came in from the cold in winter and warmed their hands in Mom's hair. Mom had such a toasty scalp. It radiated. She'd think about that, about Mr. Winsor's smile, Uncle Dolphe's laugh, Uncle Harold's hug, his warm and woolly touch as he lifted them one by one from the punt and deposited them on the shore below their house, where anyone would suppose they'd be safe. Jolly Uncle Harold, his touch warm like the water Mom made in the enamel basin on the stove, mixing hot with cold so it would be wonderful when you plunged your hands in. *Oh for the touch of a vanished hand,* that was what Mom and Aunt Maud had told the stonecutter in St. John's to chisel on Grandmother Fanny's headstone at Ladle Cove. Marion had never known Grandmother Fanny. It was too bad. Everything was all too bad. She pushed her covers away. Marion wished her own hands would vanish, take their pulsing and shrieking with them. She wished for the touch of her mother, for the touch of Uncle Harold. Uncle Harold lifting them one by one from the boats, to the safety of solid ground, the safety of home.

But all she got was the Old Man, who made the ground shake and the world fall apart.

Marion's hands rang in the night.

~

Sidney Hayward Wiseman was corrupt fruit of a rotting tree, and that tree had tangled roots. His background was complicated even by outport standards, where large families were bred to fill the spaces left by little ones who didn't make it through infancy or even much past birth. So many grown-ups died young – of drowning, dismemberment, sepsis from a hook in the hand, coughing up blood, what have you – that second and third and fourth marriages were as commonplace as the winter icefields six months of every year stretching eastward to the long grey horizon. The Parsons family in Lushes Bight was one of the lucky ones, remaining nearly as large as it set out to be. Sidney's mother, Elizabeth, had been among the last of sixteen children, most of whom lived and prospered.

Still, Lizzie was the only girl surviving among twelve brothers – her sisters had all died in infancy. Parsons girls brought no luck, but the boys fared well, only two needing namesakes to replace them. *George, John, John, Andrew, Thomas, Titus, James, Eli, Samuel, Job, Enoch, Andrew* – the boys in the family swirled around Lizzie and made her head ache.

She hadn't signed on for this. She was a Parsons, one of the grand Parsonses of Lushes Bight on Long Island, just below Little Bay Islands. Better'n Little Bay Islands any day of the week and Sunday too, for *we gives 'em our fish* – that's what the Long Islanders said. *We sells it to 'em, and without us they'd starve.* Lizzie didn't care what the Islanders were thinking back: *Lushes Bight, Lushes Blight. Nothin' there but a bit o' shell an 'erring gull dropped on 'is way to somewheres else.*

If Lushes Bight was grand, Lizzie's people were grander. They'd come not from Twillingate or anywhere around the Bay at all, but direct from the West Country of England. They were the first to settle the Bight, never mind the name that had drifted on it by way of William Lush of Burlington, who came down from the north and fished Long Island seasonally. The Parsons home was a long, two-storey affair painted splendidly white, a pearl on the strand with multitudes of large mullioned windows on all sides and a double row, my darling, all along the back wall overlooking the sea. It had luxuries unheard of and celebrated around Notre Dame Bay: eleven rooms, dormers, a long, enclosed porch.

Within its walls, young Elizabeth Parsons had been relentlessly miserable, waiting for any bit of love or notice her parents might throw her, the runt pup in the midst of her roiling brothers. At eighteen she whisked herself away to marry handsome Frederick Wiseman, a Little Bay Islands fisherman of means. And then, one after another, she tried to load her own children with the love she'd missed. And one after another, her love failed to stick to each.

Lillah, her only girl, died in infancy and wasn't ever replaced by a namesake. Parsons girls brought no luck, that was clear, but Lizzie mourned her lost girl all her life. Lizzie had never known baby girls. She was enchanted with them – unless they belonged to other women, like her daughter-in-law Ethel. Little Lillah was followed into her early grave by a baby boy, who stuck to life no better than his sister. Nelson and Harold lived, and side by each their houses were, just there on the Tickle, right next to Lizzie and Fred's. Their broods ran around Lizzie's lawn. But if Nelson and Harold still loved their mother at all they didn't love her fiercely, like she loved them. They loved their new families more. And so she transferred her doomed love from Nelson and Harold to their younger brother Plinny, and then to Ray, and then to Good.

Down it went beneath the black waves of the unforgiving Atlantic; down with her sons went Lizzie's love. And soon enough, all she had left was Sidney.

He would be all she ever wanted, as things turned out. He would be enough. Smothered in Lizzie's love and its sickness, he would be just like her.

~

If Sidney's mother's side of the family was overripe and crammed to bursting, crowding her out, his father Frederick's side was a camp of ghosts so changeable, so deserted, that a cold breeze ran through it. Frederick thought of it that way, as a decaying house where things kept leaking out. Someone should seal the windows, re-putty the glass.

Frederick's father, William Wiseman, lost his wife in childbirth. He remarried quickly; it was the way in the outports. Survivors had to get on with their lives; if they had young children, the quicker the better. It was too hard a life to go it alone. William had four young children, Frederick among them.

William's second wife was the widow Susannah Campbell, come to him trailing a ghost. William had seldom heard a story bad as Susannah's. Her husband, Daniel, had gone down on his father's schooner with most of his family in tow. The schooner was known for its frequent trips back and forth to St. John's. It had been on only a short sail this time, from Little Bay Islands to Twillingate. But a short sail was all it took; sometimes men were lost to a misstep even before they unhitched their schooners from their docks. Daniel's mother moved to Little Bay Islands from St. John's not so long ago that she'd forgotten what it was like to be apart from kin and friends and all you knew. She thought she'd be neighbourly; she thought she'd just take the trip to Twillingate along with the boys, Daniel and his brother, to greet Susannah's mother and bring her over for a visit. She packed two of her Spode cups and saucers, her special ones. They'd have tea on the deck if the sun shone. Women shouldn't be travelling alone on these damn boats.

Schooners, Daniel said, correcting her.

She'd set her hands on her ample hips. *Boats*, she said. *Damn boats*.

In Twillingate, Susannah's mother waited and watched, her eyes on the horizon, but the schooner never came. Susannah and the children might have gone down too, had the little ones not been too young for boats. Her boy Esau struggled under the loss of his father and his kin and the grievous disappointments of a kind of life he'd never antici-pated, and eventually he hanged himself from a tree at Sulian's Cove.

The Newfoundlanders hung loaded names on their children – Job, Esau, Susannah – as if suffering and tragedy would be a given in their lives, and grace, godliness, and just plain doggedness would too. Sometimes William caught her misty-eyed. She'd take little Esau by the hand and go down to the end of the wharf. She'd sit there at night-fall, ripe to bulging with his boy now, while Daniel's boy played along the shore. She'd sit and look out, as if there was something to look at. And there was; William knew it. Daniel, dead and gone, was a man with whom he couldn't compete. Dead men had no faults; they grew younger and handsomer in the memory, sweeter and uncomplicated.

The worst thing they would ever do they had already done. They held no more hope, promised no more disappointments; they wanted little and demanded less.

William and Susannah had five children together before William himself died young, at thirty-seven, leaving her with a young, hybridized, and troubled family.

For little Frederick Wiseman in the midst of it, home was a disconsolate place, populated by disappearing parents who themselves changed partners, leaving strange waifs behind for Frederick to make into brothers and sisters. The child had lost his own mother when he was just a scrap, four years old, and then he'd barely turned five when he had to bunk in with this pinch-faced and choked-up Esau, who came along with the sad new woman and the little girl, both of them, too, all thin and white and bony. Stuffed full of the past as she was, Susannah hardly seemed to notice Fred, let alone mother him – and worse, it seemed that no one could, or wanted to. Folks came and went so fast, there one minute and gone the next to a wave, a cough, a fever. Perhaps it was best to leave them where they lay. He'd seen a verse on a marker on the coast, at a gravesite in Little Bay:

> *Children weep not for me*
> *But pray while time to you is given*
> *Your tears may only wet my clay*
> *Your prayers may gain me heaven.*

No one was weeping for young Fred's mother, fine. But shouldn't someone be praying? He imagined her in a pretty dress, some sweet summer frock they would have picked out to bury her in, hammering away at the iron doors of heaven, her thin hands gone blue in the icy wind.

~

He needed his father more than ever then, and had him even less. Part of his bride Lizzie's appeal to Fred was that she knew who she was. She came from people, not ghosts – too many of them, really. Lizzie's family had too many people; Fred's had too many ghosts. Lizzie was a Parsons through and through, from that big white shell of a place at Lushes Bight, with all those brothers thronging her like moths around a lamp. He tried to lock on, to get himself a little of her certainty. But transience and change was for Fred a way of life; the permanence of bonds was not. And who could get close to a woman like Lizzie? He never got closer to his sons, either, than to haul nets with them like any of the hired men. Harold and Nelson, then Plinny and Good and Ray, then Sidney. Just like the hired men, any and all of them.

Sidney and Lizzie moved closer in the space Frederick left. When Lizzie died, a blackness filled the corner of Sid's heart where his mother had lived.

III

DEPRESSION

A child should have its father. How often Ethel thought of what her own father Thomas had said when he sent her back from Ladle Cove with a new Tom swimming in her, learning to keep himself afloat in the mire to come. A good thing her father hadn't lived long enough to rue the day. Sidney never even knew she'd been away. That a good thing too. Ethel didn't mind being rebuked herself. But what if he'd blamed the boy? Sidney could be like that; deeply irrational, blaming a child who wasn't even born for ruining his life.

Beside his mother now, young Tom leafed through a book, his head buried in its pages. Sidney's firstborn, Tom, alone with his thoughts. Fatherless – except when he found himself at the end of a fist. The child Ethel had returned to his father because that's what you did. Tom, the deep one, swinging his bony legs now against the desk in the breakfast room that formed the bottom of the bookcase with the glass doors. It was Marion's favourite spot, a nest where she could plant her feet on a chair in front of the bookcase and lean back into all the books about the world outside, yet just there at reach. Marion could never get enough to read, but Tom was on her roost today. Scrawny

Tom, first out but still the runt, as though he hadn't committed to life, as if he wasn't sure whether he'd stay or whether he'd go. And just what was there about his father that would make him want to stay? Tom was forever bullied, if not by his own father then by the likes of Gordo Gillard or by other boys at school who weren't as smart as he was. Usually the children came home to report to Ethel who had been after Bertie at school that day, the mongoloid child from the family up the hill. Ethel's children would get the lecture then: *Make the best of all things, the best of people too; give the world the best you have so the best comes back to you.* Did Gordo Gillard ever get the lecture from his parents? Ethel wondered. One lunchtime the children had come home to Big Tickle running, breathless. Marion and Jack, at least. Harry and Tom were nowhere in sight. Marion clutched at a stitch in her side. They'd got as far as Taylors' shed on the way home for lunch, she reported, gasping, crying still. It was a terrible thing. They'd been running with Tom from the outset, straight from the schoolyard, keeping up with him once Gordo started after him. If Tom ran, they ran with him. Ethel's children stuck together, presented a common front. She'd taught them that, and they had plenty of practice, running from their father.

They'd been running for hours and hours and hours, Jack piped up, panting and crying himself. Hours! Tom had dived under Taylors' shed, and Gordo had got bored and hungry and went off home for his lunch. But then Tom wouldn't come out. You could hardly even see him now. He was thin enough to have wedged himself high up where the shed lodged into the top of the grade it was on. He was never coming out, not ever again as long as he lived. So he'd informed them, gravely, from beneath Taylors' shed. Better get Mom, they'd decided. Harry should stay with Tom; Marion and Jack would go get her.

Ethel had reached back and untied her apron. Marion and Jack were made to stay and eat their lunch. Before they'd finished, she'd appeared with Tom in hand and Harry in tow. Ethel kept Tom home that afternoon, and afterwards had had something to say to Mr. Winsor, the teacher.

Tom sat on Marion's bookcase today, an all-around good day with school out for the summer, Gordo Gillard gone until fall, and Sidney nowhere in sight. It was fishing season, and he was off to the Labrador. They all breathed easy on summer days, though they knew hell's hobnail boot was just around the corner, sneaking its way back on the chill winds that yellowed the alders. Mom would start in on the season's double-balled mitts; knitting two strands together made them just that much warmer for winter. It would be time to run down to the *Ranger* to collect the scribblers she'd ordered in from St. John's for school, time to lime the outhouse and the well, time to try on their hand-me-downs. Harry would see how well Tom's pants fit him and old logans with the leather tops. As he pulled them on he'd feel a creeping up his back. The Old Man would be home soon; time to shore up and batten down.

It wasn't an overreaction. Sidney skulked. He spied on Ethel and the children alike, hiding in the pantry off the hallway that ran along the kitchen and the breakfast room. The Wisemans alone had a breakfast room, an English tradition of Robert Goff's that Ethel brought with her from the Wellon home in Ladle Cove. And while most everyone had a pantry, lined with big jars of pickled eggs and smaller jars of jam, no one had the kind of pantry the Wisemans had in their Tickle house. The Wisemans' pantry was so well designed that it had space below the cupboards for pull-down bins full of flour and sugar; extra shelves for home-canned rabbit, turr, salmon, and moose, and bottles of pickles, marmalade, and bakeapples; and barrels for fruit and vegetables from the root cellar when a storm threatened to snow it in. The Wisemans' pantry had space, too, for Sidney to pull the children in and hit them out of sight and out of range of censure. In the beginning, that was. Later, he didn't always care who saw. More than anything, the pantry had room for Sidney to wait and watch. It was a fact: no one had the Wisemans' pantry – and no one had the Wisemans' pantry spook.

The pantry afforded Sidney not only a view of the kitchen and the door of the breakfast room, and of who came and went within the house, but from there he could also see the front door and every-one's comings and goings to the outside. The pantry even had a window, so he could see anyone coming up the side of the house. Winter was no challenge to him, when doors to every room were shut tight to spare the heat. He bent to the keyhole in the breakfast room door from the hall, or the keyhole in the pantry door. The maid, Ede, had exposed him once, by accident, but they never spoke of it now. There was an understanding between Sidney and Ethel, sealed with a blow that had laid her out all the next day: it had never happened. Ede had been chatting, going to the pantry to get a bowl for Ethel, when mid-sentence she'd screeched like a wild thing, startling Ethel so that the partridge berries she'd been cleaning on the table sprayed around the room. Ede would not make another mistake. It took them no time to get used to Sidney's perches, his listening posts and his movements.

What had she been on about to Aunt Et that Himself found so interesting, now? Ede often wondered that. For the life of her, she couldn't remember. *Sidney Wiseman! You think yourself of rather more interest than you are.* She'd wanted to say that. *You come out of there, now. Aren't you ashamed of yourself?* Neither Ede nor Ethel ever looked through to the pantry now, never looked that way at all. There was nothing behind that door, Ethel told herself, and there never would be. It was in the past. Perhaps, as he said, it had never even happened. The pantry, the pantry door, it was all in another uni-verse, not a part of her life or her children's. And, when she could believe it, sometimes when he was far away on the Labrador, her husband was too.

Why can't I have a father like Uncle Jimmy? Marion had asked her that. Hadn't she asked herself the same thing? But to the children, she never let on. The children weren't perfect either. They had to learn. *As you go through life, make this your goal: watch the doughnut, not the hole.* There Tom had been, cowering under Jimmy Taylor's shed. Uncle Jimmy was short and stout, mismatched with Aunt Rose Taylor, his wife, who was long and thin as the stove poker. He worked as an accountant for Strong's; Little Bay Islands relied upon him, and the kids loved him. He hadn't been home that day for lunch, though, and Rose nowhere in sight either. There Ethel had been, crawling down under the shed, coaxing her boy out. *Tom, my son, Mommy's here now; come on out.* She left it at that – she could hardly promise him *it's okay now, it's safe* – and he came. He always came to her.

Today, Sidney was off somewhere for once, though if he were assembling his cronies around the harbour she'd be up all hours, cooking for the late night feed in the dining room. A dozen seal flippers, usually, and not served until nearly midnight, when they'd finally lay down their billiards cues and pull up chairs to eat. About eleven, Ethel would heat the skillets on the stove. It exhausted her. It was hot in the room, summer or winter, morning or night or midnight, but she never even pushed her sleeves up off her wrists to cool down a bit. She had polycythemia, too many red blood cells. She wasn't so young any more; its symptoms were coming on her now. She was beset by fatigue, but who wasn't? That wasn't the worst. The worst was the way her skin flamed bright red, blistering with swelling and welts. Ethel was a proud woman who hated the look of trouble, fixed it where she could, and otherwise didn't complain about it. It wasn't because she'd been so pretty not so long ago; it was just that it wasn't for anyone else to know that things were wrong now. You kept such things between yourself and God. *I do not ask, O Lord, that life may be a pleasant road.* She couldn't do much about the way her lips swelled with fluid, the way her face and eyelids puffed out, the itch and burning in her limbs. Sometimes between Sidney and the disease she couldn't tell of her wounds what was what, and the confusion between the two made it easier for her to bear both.

God knew, the Lord Himself had wounds. Blessed wounds. *What are these wounds in thine hands? Then he shall answer, Those with which I was wounded in the house of my friends.* When her symptoms flared she wore long sleeves that covered her arms. The sun made it worse anyway, and the heat from the stove.

The children worried about their mother's health, her welts and bruises. Without her, they'd be lost. In the bookcase with the glass doors there was a volume on herbs and ancient remedies; Marion consulted it habitually. Devil's Bit, now, that was a wildflower that grew on the coasts of Ireland. Wouldn't the coasts of Ireland be like the coasts of home? Everyone talked like they were from Ireland, that's what Cyril Tuffin's mother, Auntie Blanche, said; drank like it too. Maybe Marion could find Devil's Bit here, up in the Burnt Woods or over to Sulian's on the cliffs. Maybe it was like bakeapples that grew in the swamps of Labrador but only flowered inland, never fruited. To get the berries you had to look on the coast. Devil's Bit had a stumpy, abrupt end. *The greater part of the root seemeth to be bitten away –* that's how the book said you could spot it. *Old fantastick charmers report that the Divel did bite it for envie, because it is an herbe that hath so many good vertues and it is so beneficial to mankinde.*

Marion mouthed it aloud in the English she knew. *Envy. Virtues.*

She saw it all then. Suddenly she saw everything: not just why her father hit her mother and hit his children, why he could go fine for days and weeks on end but then detonate, but why he resented Mom's friends and their friends as well, and why he never had a good word for anyone except to his face. He was jealous of everyone; he was envy incarnate. Virtue, the kind of virtue that everyone loved except him – that was Mom. Everyone loved Mom, and for that the Old Man punished her. Marion kept turning the pages of the book. Tears blurred in her eyes; she kept her head down. She'd find something sooner or later to help Mom's welts. She was going to be a nurse some day. Minnie Strong was a graduate nurse, all the way to Boston. Christina and Gert Wiseman, and Pearl Parsons and Avice Anstey too. Marion would follow along soon enough. She'd find something for Mom then. It wouldn't be too late.

~

Tom had never been robust. He'd inherited Ethel's black hair, and it washed him out. All the other children – the whiteheads, Ethel thought of them – had Sidney's fair hair and blooming cheeks. But Tom forever looked ill. One winter he ate nearly half a batch of taffy she'd left to cool. They'd worked on it all evening, heating the molasses in the dipper over the stove, buttering their hands while it cooled and then stretching it back and forth, pulling it out and folding it between them like bedsheets off the washing line. Finally, they pinched it off into pieces and laid it out to harden. And then he wolfed it down. Ethel didn't mind; it was good for him to get that much molasses. It might pink him up. She hadn't seen anyone down with consumption, not close up, except for her brother, too long ago to recall. Was this how it started, this pallor of the skin, this sculpting of bones?

Her brood was luckier than most, with plenty to eat, wood for the stoves, clothes warm enough for winter. Warm at night, too, though fire was a force forever to be reckoned with. Though they banked the stoves with ashes at night, the water would freeze in the kettles by dawn. After Sidney, Tom was first to get a hot brick in his bed. She tucked him into his storm clothes tighter than the rest, buttoning his long coat in a stranglehold to the throat, knotting his wool scarf twice around his collar so that he couldn't tilt his head and walked chin up with a perpetually lofty air, as if he were searching for something above the horizon. Wool scarves were a luxury, and Ethel wanted to ensure the boy had his for a long time. She'd pull down the ear lugs on his cap and snug his mittens high up his wrists, inside his cuffs. She tied him up so tight that Tom kept his logans unlaced when he was older. He liked them that way, slopping against his shins.

Ethel's girls wore knitted wool stockings along with the rest of their gear. For waterproof leggings they had buskins, rubber sheaths that buckled high up their shins. Ethel had her connections with her St. John's suppliers and knew where to find them by mail order. She knew where to find lots of things, and she knew how to make things last too. She fastened the flaps of the children's boots with diaper pins when the buckles tore off and couldn't be sewn back on. Whatever she could spare or salvage of their belongings, anything her brood could do without, she gave away to the needy – and that was everyone. Edith Grimes, the maid, had come to them that way. Ede had been going without a winter coat as the cold crept in, and Ethel gave the girl hers. She gave her a job too.

Ede was a cheerful sort, and for all the toil the Grimes house had held she thought that Aunt Et worked harder – far too hard here at the Wisemans, hauling water all day, cooking and cleaning and sewing and running a shop too, and most of all putting up with the likes of . . . Ede was only too glad to help out. Her sister Nina missed her. Nine, they called her. She was a tender sort, spooked with life and everything in it, and she visited Ede daily for moral support. For the most part she'd sit, keeping quietly to herself, but during summer thunderstorms she'd come apart, screaming and spitting at the Wisemans' kitchen table when lightning cracked overhead and thunder rolled.

"She can't help herself," Mom said.

But Nine was way older than Ede, and Ede didn't go on like that. Harry couldn't understand it. Ede was young looking, his mother reminded him. Maybe Nine wasn't all that old either. But she was older, by seven years. She was nutty. "It's like the chickens," Harry said. "They run around too, all nutty, before thunder."

"Harry, it's nothing like the chickens. Nina," Ethel soothed the girl, on the crests of her shrieks. She never called the girl Nine. *What a beautiful name, Nina. Have some tea now, Nina, won't you, while the storm passes.*

Ede helped Ethel with the sewing. Like everyone else, the Wisemans went to school in rebuilt clothes. Really old clothes Ede tore into strips and hooked into rugs. She was expert at it. Most of Ethel's Sundays were spent sewing and mending – and tallying figures in the shop ledger. She was fast: she had to be. She had to be judicious too. "My children," she told her brood, "a patch is no disgrace." Every other child in town was worse off, more patched than they, but Marion dreaded the days she had to wear her pinned, "gaitered" boots to school. Feet and legs were the worst of it in the Depression, for girls. Inevitably, Marion and Grace's lisle stockings would go at the heels and knees. Some days, Marion just hated to look down.

She'd rather have gone hungry, like she heard some kids were, but when she told Mom, suddenly they weren't any more. Behind the Old Man's back, Mom was forever sneaking things out of her shop for the families hardest hit, and even in the worst of the Depression most of the town was snug and fed – by Ethel Wiseman. Why let her neighbours become government-registered paupers when it was just a matter of extending their credit a while longer? She didn't let Sidney know. Anything left over at the Wisemans' found its way immediately to someone else. The government distributed brown flour, but Ethel always managed to get her family the best of the white. Sidney wasn't prepared to eat anything else.

"It's white, I like it," he said. "It's not, I don't." What did the Commission of Government know, for God's sake, trumpeting its daft campaign about vitamin B in black flour in order to force it down the throats of the poor? Sidney Wiseman wasn't about to submit to any Dole diet, he wasn't poor and no one was going to treat him as though he were. The Commission of Government in particular. This beriberi business you heard, the weakness that was supposed to come from eating white bread and drinking tea. It was just made up, a fantasy, more St. John's propaganda. Sidney read; he knew. Only Chinamen got beriberi, from eating rice off sticks or something. And from drinking that terrible yellow tea of theirs, no doubt; it was little better than dishwater. They had rickets here, that was what they had in Newfoundland, and proper thing too. What did the government know? The government said that beriberi made you weak in the legs by stripping the packing off the nerves there. Stripping the resolve off the muscles, more than likely, Sidney thought. People who got weak legs were slackers, pure and simple. No old dog for the hard road, them. His own weak lungs, that was something else, and nobody's business but his own.

Sidney knew these things. He was a man of the century. He'd been born in the dying moments of the last, not two years before Joey Smallwood himself was born a Christmas baby, on December 24, 1900. Joey harkened from farther down the coast, Gambo way, down along Bonavista Bay from the Straight Shore. It was typical of Joey, to have been a Christmas baby. Just the thing he might have planned. *I have come to you from the clouds,* Joey would say to the people assembled for his puddle-jumping tours when his plane landed in the outports. Had Sidney believed in spitting, he could have climbed to Pole Hill in Little Bay Islands and spit a straight line right down on Joey in Gambo – or Bonavista, more properly, where Joey had lately returned from St. John's, to live there a few years again and organize a new fishermen's union. And Joey could have spat straight back at Sidney Wiseman – over the heads of everyone between them, all those they were better than.

"Sidney," Ethel said, "the flour is brown, actually. It makes wonderful hearty brown bread. It's the whole of the wheat. Eat white, and you eat less."

"It's white, I like it," he said again. "It's not, I don't." Whatever did the woman know either? Half these women around were in the employ of the Commission of Government just to make the men behave, he was sure of it. He'd read it somewhere.

Sidney's white flour shone like talc and came in hundred-pound bags of cotton twill. Ethel got it at her shop, the Ensign, which she ran atop the government wharf with Fanny Anstey, making bulk orders from the Royal Stores and Ayres & Sons in St. John's. And a good thing too; otherwise they'd have to be wiring down the coast for every little thing, and then waiting. They did enough waiting as it was. *Send baby's rocking cot by Prospero without fail, not expensive,* that's how the telegrams had gone in the past, even before the Depression. That one had been from the Reverend Pitcher to Ayres & Sons in St. John's. Sidney remembered the reverend. He'd been posted to Little Bay Islands for the exact duration of the war, poor bugger. All the condolence visits he'd had to make around Green Bay the whole time, it was a wonder he'd had time at all to father a child and order a cot. *Could you procure 3 gallons black currants send by Prospero.* Even Auntie Bea had to wire her niece in St. John's for her canning and preserves. *Am depending on you for tomatoes and plums.*

Once Tom had taken the motorboat to the *Clyde* where she was docked at the government wharf, to collect a shipment of the talc flour for the shop. Ron was to run up by road to meet him and help unload the huge bags, all one hundred of them. Tom brought Mom's bill of lading, and the purser ticked off the order on his manifest as it left the wharf. But Ron didn't show up, and Tom had had to do all the loading and all the ferrying himself, the motorboat submerged to the gunwales with the weight of each load. Ron had said he'd come, but then he'd turned over in bed and gone back to sleep. "Tom, you didn't say when," he defended himself. After that Tom had learned to specify.

Marion made tablecloths out of the flour bags, bleaching the lettering off and then embroidering the corners and crocheting the hems with coloured floss. Children had once had to wear clothes made out of these flour bags, she reminded herself. Depression or not, things could be worse. She didn't know much about it. They knew they were in it because their father's *Saturday Evening Post*s and his *New York Times* told them so. And how it went on and on! Marion went to school with knee patches stitched carefully over her lisle stockings, feeling less horror over that than to be in Mom's overshoes when Mom had none herself. Ethel had put her coat on Ede and her boots on Marion, binding them in with pins to fit. Dressed for winter and blinking back tears, Marion had stood in Mom's boots, looking down at the crown of her head.

They were all poor, but some were poorer than others. Poor Peter Grimes got his name for being hardest up of anyone, and witless too. He admired Bill Mursell's pocket knife, and Bill agreed to give it to him if Peter'd agree to have his nose broken. The Mursells had much; they married Strongs. Poor Peter didn't have a cent, and he hounded Adolphe Strong for a job. The sight of the mashed-nosed kid on

Strong's wharf was too much for Uncle Dolphe; like everyone, he knew the story. "Oh, start now then, my lad," he sighed. "You've wore me right down."

But Peter couldn't start now.

"Why not?"

"Hain't had me breakfast. You got breakfast here?"

~

Tom was dressed tighter than the rest of them put together, but when he coughed and sniffled Ethel worried. Was that how the weak lungs started, with a winter cold, progressing finally to blood on the hanky as bright as jam? No one knew. Back in Ladle Cove, Ethel had been a child of only four when her brother Francis left them forever. That had been right after Grandpa Wellon, the lightkeeper, had died of old age, his whiskers bleached like last year's stubble in the spring hayfields, as long as a hammock you could swing in. How Grandma Wellon had sobbed over him. He's gone to his gulls, Grandma said. Gone to his Wadhams gulls.

Grandma Wellon had lived years longer, well into her eighties, and died when Ethel was nearly twenty. But Ethel had been small when Grandpa died, and then Francis, right on his heels. For a little girl it was difficult to fathom, how a young man like Francis could die like an old man, but there it was. Had Francis, too, gone to his gulls?

Now Ethel knew Francis had died of consumption. Now she knew that was only the half of it – you could die of everything, at a moment's notice. Old age was the good thing, the lucky thing to die of. This morning, Tom had lifted his face out of the volume of the *World Book* he'd pulled from Marion's bookshelves. "Mommy," he said, "where do elephants go when they die?"

She didn't find these questions difficult. *I do not ask, O Lord.* "To heaven, my darling."

Oh. The boy couldn't grasp it. An elephant seemed a lot of weight to get up into the sky, all the way up to heaven. Heaven was such a faraway place, after all, far to the east beyond Big Tickle and the ocean. It was no place straight above them, that was certain – nothing could look down so pitilessly on him and Harry and Marion, and Mommy too and especially Jack; nothing could look down and refuse to help them out of it, year after year just leaving them alone. To get to heaven you'd have to row out or sail out a long way east into the sunrise where God lived and things were better, maybe all the way to St. John's, and then you could lift up. Like an aeroplane, Tom expected. The preacher said that with some work anyone could get to heaven, but if his father could, Tom didn't see the point of anyone else going.

He thought a while. "I mean, where do elephants go *to* die?" A lot of people died right here in Little Bay Islands, and animals too, their pets. Uncle Dolphe's cow they'd brought over on the motorboat – well, she wasn't dead, but it wasn't likely she could hold out either. Tom had seen that eagle skeleton in the Burnt Woods on the way to Sulian's Cove. It had been small, just an eagle baby. Perhaps this was where everything came to die.

"Well, darling, the jungle, I expect. They probably have a swim, the big ones, the really old ones, to cool down, and then they might die, right there in the swimming hole. It's hot in Africa."

"And India." He had his finger in the book. "They have elephants in India. Transport for the rajahs."

"And India. They probably have a swim, and they'd need longer and longer drinks, and sometimes they might just stay in the water where it's cool, and wait for God."

The elephant could come to Little Bay Islands to cool off. Tom thought of it, an elephant from India with his tassels still on from his service to the rajah, swimming round and round the harbour by Salt Rock, waiting for God. Perhaps Tom could row out and feed him peanuts, and wait alongside in the punt.

He lifted his head again. "Mommy. Can you order peanuts from the Royal Stores?"

~

Sometimes Ethel wished she and the children could all die together in a flash, rising like a fairy circle into some golden peace at the top of the sky. Tom had dreams where something gripped his ankles and hung on when he stepped out of the punt, toppling him over the side, letting his head thrash under the water. When she went to him in the night he'd thrash still, pushing her away as if in his dreams, too, only he could help himself. Tom was like that – when he'd fallen off the wharf that time, he said that Sailor had been no help at all; he'd had to drag himself up the beach alone. Where had she been, his mother? It was true, she couldn't help any of them. O ye wretched of the earth, that was how the old Wesleyan circuit preachers back in her father's parish had styled the Ladle Cove congregation, a poor flock of straggling sheep, forever off compass out of dull-wittedness or malice or worse; stupid, hapless, spiteful sheep ranging daily between precipice and famine. And wretched she'd been since then, truly, time and time again, when one after another each of her children discovered that she would fail them. She would size it up, their father's hands at their throats, and then she would take a breath and let it happen. She would decide to fail them, and then she'd do it. It tore her apart. It was the worst thing. It was far worse than her own suffering, a thousand times worse than any death she could imagine. She'd always fail them. She couldn't help any of them. When she tried to, Sidney only beat them harder.

Ethel imagined her children rising with her in their fairy circle, imagined Sidney grasping at their ankles, taking hold, bringing them down to reckoning.

She never punished them. A mistake was an opportunity to learn. Tom had apologized to her the night he'd eaten half the taffy. "My darling," Ethel had said, "eat all the taffy you want, but share it with the others too."

She was like that. What had Tom feared? His mother never even wagged a finger at him like Cyril Tuffin's mother Auntie Blanche did at Cyril. Even when old Aunt Jane, Uncle Job's wife, had laid her head back and snored in the rocker and Harry and Tom put marmalade in her mouth, giggling to pee themselves, Mom hadn't wagged a finger.

She'd tell the boys not to complain when she sent them to fetch Aunt Jane in the punt for her visits, Uncle Job dead, poor thing, and she without means and transport of her own.

"*Mom*. Why does she have to visit at all? She's a fat bat." Harry and Tom would have rowed the seven seas for Mom, anything to help her out. But Aunt Jane was a handful and a half.

"Fat bat! Fat bat!" Little Ron would chime, waddling around the kitchen in his napkin, flapping his arms.

"Now boys," Ethel would say. "Do unto others. She's Aunt Jane and she loves you, and you'll be old yourselves some day."

"Do you love me best?" Tom had asked her suddenly that night, over the taffy. *Say yes, say yes!* She had to, she *had* to; he loved her best; he loved her more than anything in the world. But they'd had that discussion before, the bunch of them pestering her, and it had gone badly. *Who do you love? Who do you love? Do you love me best? Do you love Grace best, because she's small? Jack, because he's sick? Who do you love?*

Mom had risen and gone into her room, distraught, shaking her head. I love you all the same, she'd said.

He could hope, though, since his father loved him not at all. Surely he was owed.

"I love you all the same," she said again, turning what was left of the taffy on the stone countertop. "But you, my darling, you are the one who can have all the taffy he wants."

~

Summer saw the Old Man off to the Labrador for months on blessed months. Most days in winter he'd be lodged in the house or down at Mom's shop like some mould that wouldn't scrub off. He was the original homebody; his home was his castle and in it the children were his servants. He relished the job of overseeing it all. When he was home, it was a rare fine day that he'd be out of the house, but then he'd be in all night at billiards with the neighbours, socializing while Ethel cooked for half the Bay. Summer or winter, Ethel's one bit of quiet time was Sunday, though Sidney had no interest in church. Had Ethel not wanted them to go, he would have sent the children to Sunday School anyway, to be rid of them for the afternoon. Sundays, Ethel caught up with both the mending and the shop books at the kitchen table, spreading them out as the kids spread out their primers for their home-work on school nights. Ron's primer spelled out rudimentary words, and the boy would chirp them out: *cat, dog, fly, tub, hen.*

Buzz, Sidney would add, passing by. *Off.* It was his idea of a joke. He didn't swear. He didn't even drink much. The kids wished he did – that way, there wouldn't be so much explaining to do. If your father drank then he could get plenty ugly proper thing; that would explain it. Look at Cyril Tuffin's father, after all. A few pints and he was on Cyril like a miner with a pick from the copper mine at Coffee Cove; on Auntie Blanche too. But Skipper Sid was mean and ugly all on his own. No one could understand it. They never knew just what it was they'd done to bring it on.

Later on Sundays, after Sunday School, they'd retire to the parlour, where Ethel played the organ. It was a splendid instrument, its small, ornamental galleries backed with mirrors. *Jesus loves me, this I know,* she played. *Softly and tenderly, Jesus is calling.* She sang, and the chil-dren sang too. Jesus, Him now, they thought. He'll come for us. Tom had a straight voice that wouldn't bend, and the other children were too young to help out much, threading their way high and thin over the chords. Their father had a good voice, but he seldom used it for singing. Certainly not for singing hymns. Now and then for show he sang along to Scottish songs or Harry Lauder on the gramophone.

"Sid, come in, darling, we need your voice," Ethel called from the parlour on Sundays, but he never came.

Finally, she closed up the organ and thanked them all for coming.

"You're welcome, Mommy," the children said, wide-eyed. Imagine being thanked for coming to the parlour. It was a treat to be in here, in this cold crypt that came alive in their mother's presence. It was the room the dead disappeared into, the room the minister disappeared

into and to which they were called as he left, to kneel down by the
chairs and receive his blessing. The minister called, the minister came,
but Jesus never did.

~

Sidney Wiseman ignored his family. He seemed not to care whether
his children lived or died, certainly not whether the wind blew up
unexpectedly on their way home, or the ice they stood on was strong
or might shake in the next minute, split open and swallow them up.
When a storm came up on a school day they'd hang on the ends of
one another's coat belts and plow their way home, and if there weren't
coat belts to hang onto they'd make the best of it somehow. Their
father never came for them. Around the harbour you'd see young children carried home in storms on their father's backs, but not the
Wisemans. Their father didn't ask after them when they came panting
in the door, didn't ask how the walk had been, if the storm was high,
if the wind had stung. Their father never even looked up from his
newspaper, unless it was to get up and tap the barometer. But what
did it matter to him if a storm was coming? The one time they did get
lost on the ice on the way home from school it was Uncle Harold who
came for them, not the Old Man at all. Skipper Sid said later how he'd
watched it all out the window, Harold going down on the ice and disappearing into the gale, but they knew it wasn't true. What a liar the
Old Man was, on top of everything else. He couldn't have glimpsed
them through the white-out if he'd wanted to, but the truth was that
he hadn't wanted to. He just wanted to seem a part of things
later.

There was a deviousness to him. His children couldn't really put
the words to it, but it didn't seem right, the way the Old Man sat back
and planned how he'd get them when they made him angry. Other
people just blew up. Uncle Nelson had stuck a hook into his hand on
Strong's wharf once and he screamed and screamed – at Dek, when it
wasn't Dek's fault at all, but Uncle Nelson had needed someone to

hear him scream, and there was Dek, nearby. The Wiseman children understood that. Their father did something more. He thought about things in a cold, dead way, and he didn't really scream at all. Instead, he thought and thought, and then he lay in wait.

Marion had been only five then, when but for Uncle Harold they'd nearly been lost on the ice.

Five. All the same she'd felt very old, old like Mom could look those times when she got very tired and had a tear in her eye. *Hope springs eternal,* that's what Mom said when she cried, and Marion thought it was a stream somewhere bubbling up, the River Hope, an underground spring with wonderful cool water that never flagged and never stopped.

Marion had just begun school that fall. It was her first after-school blizzard, and with growing unease she'd watched it blow up through the schoolhouse windows.

"Tom." She appealed to him, her older brother at the other end of the schoolroom, in a whisper that might escape Mr. Winsor's notice. The schoolhouse windows rattled so hard she had to hiss. "Tom! We going home in that?"

"In what?" Tom shrugged with all the bravado of an eight-year-old in charge of the family. When the time came, however, he found not only that he was in charge of his family but of Uncle Harold's too. Harris Winsor opened the schoolhouse door only to have it whipped back in his face. He was concerned; he wanted them to stay until the gale blew itself out. Harris kept an eye out for the Wiseman kids. They were Ethel Wellon's, after all, and it wasn't so many years ago now that she'd been the teacher in this very room. Ethel Wellon, now Mrs. Wiseman. She had a special something, everyone felt it, and for Harris Winsor she meant something more. He had her legacy to protect.

"We'll be fine, Mr. Winsor," young Tom said all the same, and off they went. He wasn't one to shy away from a little walk. It was said that old Levi Joe, the Micmac chief from Springdale, woke up one morning and set his kettle on the fire only to find he was out of tea. He tied on his skates and skated ten miles out to Little Bay Islands, where he bought his tea, and then skated ten miles back – and was settled back in his house with his skates off before the kettle boiled. *Levi Joe, here we go* – they said that whenever they had to cross the ice in snow and wind. Marion and Jack always wondered about Levi Joe. "Did Levi Joe buy his tea from you?" they asked Mom in her shop.

Levi Joe, here I go, Tom said to himself. It was a lot of kids to tie together and keep together on a day like this, he found; too many Wisemans and too many more of Uncle Harold's, more than you could count on both hands. Tom also found he'd underestimated the wind. The temperature had been dropping all day, and the gale picking up. The snow was disorienting, and in no time they lost their way.

There were drifts everywhere. The ice surface looked like an ocean whipped with waves and whitecaps and breakers, there were so many drifts. It was impossible to see. Hold a mitt up in front of your face to block the wind and breathe, and you couldn't see it till you pressed it right down on your nose and smelled whatever wet wool hadn't frozen. The others became shapes around you – that had been Marion but where was she now, and a minute ago that had been Harry. Even screaming didn't bring them closer because the wind was screaming too, and everything blended into a roar of whipping white. The snow was blowing hard now; you had to turn backwards to the wind and cup your mitts to your face in order to get a breath at all. The cold was stunning.

Marion wasn't worried. Tom and Harry were there, somewhere right there, and wherever her older brothers were, things would turn out fine. Lord, the wind was fierce. Was that someone calling now, over the gale? Imagine what you could imagine you were hearing, in a wind like that. *Imagine what you can imagine. Imagine what you can imagine.* She said it over and over to herself, spilling it steamily like a mantra into her scarf and down into her collar to keep herself warm, to keep her mind off the cold. It'd be fun to be lost in a storm with her brothers and her cousins. Surely. Wouldn't it?

"We're sealers!" someone yelled. Dek, probably. She couldn't make anyone out in the blizzard and the roar of wind, not a voice, not a shape, and especially not a face. They all had their ear lugs down and their scarves and collars up, and their free hands – the hand that wasn't holding on to the belt ahead – in front of their faces to cut the blast.

"Fall in, number up, get to it!" The same voice again; ghostly peals of laughter from the other boys over the force of the wind.

Marion stared at the white in front of her nose. She barely heard her own panting over the roar of the wind. Was this a good thing, to be a sealer? So many of them didn't come back. There'd been that terrible thing with the SS *Newfoundland* and the Kean brothers and the Kean brothers' father, the sealer captains, just before the war. All those men left on the ice to perish, and seventy-seven of them dead. Mr. Tippett and his boys frozen together on their feet, huddled into each other. Mr. Crewe frozen kneeling, his son in his arms; his son, not much older than Tom. They couldn't pry them apart. People didn't talk about it so much now – it was years and years and years ago and the war made so much more to talk about – but they hated their boys to go to the ice. The seals weren't so good around Little Bay Islands, and Marion was glad. At Little Bay Islands the fishing was good, and Strong's was busy enough with fish alone. She wouldn't want her brothers to go to the ice for seals when they grew up. She needn't worry about Tom and Jack; it was already clear they were going to be lawyers or something. That left Harry. Harry would be an airman, so that was okay too. Ron was a baby, not a person. Would he be a person some day? She couldn't imagine it.

Snow spat in her face. It stung. *Levi Joe, here we go.* She thought of Levi Joe's tea boiling over his fire. Had he had a can of milk for his tea, and sugar? Had he got that from Mom at the Ensign shop too? She could smell the fire; she could taste the tea. She fell into drift after drift after drift, regardless of how high she picked up her feet. It was as impossible to walk, to keep on, as it was not to.

The line of children kept staggering into the wind, step after step, in what must be the direction of home. It was pitch dark, it was sheer white in the blizzard, all at the same time. If they stopped moving, if they stopped struggling for a moment, it would be only another short moment before they were snowed under and frozen in their tracks. Whenever Marion fell in a drift she picked herself up again, screaming *I'm here here here!* into the white nothingness, in case anyone wondered. She'd check in her hand for the end of the belt ahead, and pull herself up by tugging on it hard. It was important not to let go of that belt ahead. Once she tugged so hard that they both went down, Marion and whoever was in front of her, and they both struggled up again without letting go. The whole line was falling and righting itself, forever going down into the snow now, forever climbing up, gasping.

Still they walked. The schoolhouse and the pot-bellied stove and Mr. Winsor's furrowed, worried face – it all seemed ages ago. Marion was a bit worried now. They'd been at this a long time. She was awfully tired; her lungs ached with effort. It was hard to know at any point whether she was standing and struggling or down on her knees in a drift. Everything was snow, up and down. Where was up any more, where was down? The snow in her mittens no longer felt cold. The storm had sucked all sensation out of her, had sucked all thought from her head. The wind whipped so hard it threatened to spin her head on her neck. She didn't want to lose her head; she didn't want her neck to snap; she kept her forehead down. She worried enough about bones snapping and bits of her coming loose with the Old Man; she didn't need to care about it out here. One foot, the next foot. *Imagine what you can imagine. Imagine what you can imagine.* Heavens, they'd been walking a long time! Her feet were like lead. She had never known such cold. *Imagine. Oh oh oh oh . . .* And suddenly she was imagining a great dark figure looming out of the blizzard. It was Uncle Harold, and there was nothing imaginary about him at all. Uncle Harold was as real as a mountain. He'd come with a rope.

"Big boys on the back!" Uncle Harold called through the high winds, looping one to another, pulling the rope down, over, and through itself with his huge, expert hands as if they were some immense net he was knitting up in his twine store. Uncle Harold's voice was flung away, miles down the ice like so much snow, but somehow everyone heard and knew, and found a place in the line. Marion was first, even in front of Josey and Joy, and right behind Uncle Harold, for which she was very glad, and roped to him now as she was, still she hung on to his big belt for dear life. Off the line went in single file, fording the vast drifts of snow, Uncle Harold kicking them away with his great boots, clearing the path. Every now and then he'd come to a screeching halt, and with her head down and nothing to see in front of her but snow, Marion would thud right into his back. He'd turn, count them, carry on again. *Joy,* he'd holler back to the tiny one, *Joy m'darling, is ya there?* Uncle Harold didn't talk like that. It was just his way of cheering them up. The line stopped whenever someone fell down; hands reached out and picked him up again. They progressed. Somehow Uncle Harold knew which way to go, and finally they were scrambling up the shore.

Uncle Harold had come. Uncle Harold had saved them. They would live another day, and another and another – and all their days they owed to Uncle Harold. Uncle Harold, lifting them up to the shore of home.

~

They couldn't stop talking about him, but knew they must.

"Uncle Harold," Mom said to them later in a whisper as they went up the stairs to bed, "is a wonderful uncle."

"He'd make a sight better father'n what we got," Jack whispered back. "Can he marry you and Aunt Janet both? Can I be brothers with Dek?" *Imagine what you can imagine.* Her mother had said it so often, something like it, at least: *If you can think it, my children, you can do it.*

"He can't, Jack my darling, and you can't," Mom said. "And your father is a good father. Don't you forget how he provides for you. Don't you ever forget that about your father."

There was little chance of forgetting anything about their father. They didn't much know what it meant to be provided for; it meant nothing in the face of all those other things about him that made

Skipper Sid so memorable. Jack went to bed every night with his door
open so that he could listen for Marion. Marion kept her door open
too. She'd alert Jack, if she could, or save him, if she could. If she
couldn't, that was okay as well. They all understood that. They would
do their best and sometimes that wouldn't be enough. Jack did his best
with what he had, and it would be okay either way. He just liked to
know that she was there, his big sister just down the hall, her door
open. It felt like a lifeline in a storm between them, and that night that
Uncle Harold had saved them, as the blizzard raged outside and rattled
the Tickle house windows, Jack said a prayer for Mom and one for
Tom at the head of the first line and one for Uncle Harold at the head
of his, the second line that had saved them. He said a prayer for Uncle
Harold's Dek, and for Harry and tiny Ron and the new baby, Grace,
and for Sailor whom he missed and never forgot to God, and especially
for Marion down the hall.

And for his father he said a little prayer too, because his father
provided.

∼

Once or twice Marion's father had been as kind to her as Uncle
Harold. Once or twice; that was it. His temper had fouled with the
years. When he wasn't angry he left them alone. How wonderful it
was to be ignored! But when he was angry, he was a madman, merci-
less. Most days it was impossible to keep him on an even keel. Worse,
you'd never know what was bound to set him off. The tiniest things;
nothing at all. But once or twice –

She'd seen her first dead person with her father, and he'd been kind
then. She'd worn her white fur muff and her blue outfit, and the white
fur hat that Mom had bought her that went with the muff. You always
wore a hat at a funeral. Marion had never been to one, hardly anywhere at all, but some things you just knew. Her father went to wakes
out of respect for his elders. He had seemed respectful that day, nearly
awed. He'd even taken her hand. Maybe it was because people were

around in the parlour where the body had been laid out, watching
them, but she didn't think so. He'd seemed genuinely shaken in the
face of something that outwitted him, defied any of his moods, stared
down his wrath and transcended them both. All the way across the
harbour, beyond Shoal Tickle Bridge on Mack's Island, ancient old
Uncle Tucker had died, and Mom thought Marion should go with her
father to the wake, see something of death for the first time. Sidney
had been quiet. He had even taken Marion's hand to help her into the
motorboat, and out of it again when they reached Uncle Tucker's
wharf. Her father had been a different man that day, someone she
wouldn't know now.

They'd gone up the broken stone steps from the wharf. They'd
climbed a gravel path, stepped into the house. *Oooh, little Marion.
Ethel's darlin'*. One of the women pressed a cup of tea on her, but she
dangled her muff at her side and gripped her father's hand. She was
too transfixed for tea. In the parlour, the casket sat on chairs, kitchen
chairs that would have been at Uncle Tucker's table until yesterday,
kitchen chairs that until yesterday Uncle Tucker might have sat on to
take his own tea. Kitchen chairs that Uncle Tucker would have painted
way back when, that he would have pushed in and out from his kitchen
table for his three meals a day. Marion stood there for an eternity, for
as long as Uncle Tucker had now. She gripped her father's hand.

What became of people in caskets? What had become of Uncle
Tucker? Marion tilted her chin up on her pillow now, remembering.
Most of all, where had her father gone, the one whose hand she held?

She opened her eyes wide to keep the tears back, and she remembered what she always remembered when she thought of how the
world had fallen apart.

*Baa. The baby is baaing at the sheep in the window. Baa baa.
Marion is two, she has an older brother who is very big and stringy
and strong and serious and she has a second older brother who is just
a little bigger than she is and thinks he is an aeroplane, he is funny
and round and pokes her, and there is a new baby and he is sickly and
he is called Jack, and Mommy kisses him and Daddy too, and though*

she's heard of sheep and been sung to of sheep these are not her sheep. They are not the sheep of her mommy and her daddy. They are a neighbour's sheep and they have come to the window and they are eating the grass under the window and Marion and Mommy and Daddy are all watching and laughing and the sheep are baaing and Marion is standing on the couch below the window, standing between her mommy and daddy where they are lying on the couch watching the summer out the window. The summer is a song. She is rocking, really, because she is little and has only just learned to stand on squashy things like the cushions on the couch. She watches those sheep. She'd like to be out there, eating that grass with those sheep, because the grass is the colour of Mommy, it's beautiful, it's the colour of Mommy's Sunday dress. Today is Sunday and Mommy has on the green print dress with the white collar and Daddy has on his Sunday dress shirt. She'd like to be out there but in here with Mommy and Daddy is pretty good too. Daddy takes his pipe out of his mouth and touches the stem to the back of Marion's knees, bending first one and then the other so that they buckle and she falls down on his lap. They all laugh, she goes up in giggles, she loved him then and he loved her and he loved Mommy too and they had their good times, and the moment goes on and on forever

To where? Where did it go?

Why hadn't their father come? It was a voice in Marion's head, whirling like the snow off the ice that she still saw in front of her eyes, but so small now that it was almost a whisper. So small she turned it off, and it never came again.

CAMPBELL'S POINT

IV

_____

_W A R_

"And that's all they gave you, after all we've done for them?"
Sidney threw the knife down on the counter in front of his wife.

She picked it up and replaced it in its box, looking sidelong at the
door. The middle of the day now, and someone was likely to come in.
She prayed for it. Sidney would turn into the Cheshire Cat at the drop
of a footfall – someone's foot other than hers and the children's. She
was tired, asthmatic, finding it hard to get her breath. She'd just come
up off the *Clyde*, walking up to the shop from the government wharf
with her parcels and her two carpet bags on the last leg of her trip
back from St. John's. She hadn't even been home to the house yet to
drop her things. She'd been on her yearly visit to all her suppliers:
Bowrings, Ayres, the Royal Stores. This time she'd stopped at Ladle
Cove to see Maud and to visit her mother's grave. She saw Aubrey,
too, and his wife, Mae, who still looked at her askance when she
poured tea into Fanny's cups, as if Ethel might take the cups back or,
worse, rise up and smack her sister-in-law right there in her Ladle
Cove parlour for ruining her romance with George Hicks of Grand
Falls all those years ago. Except for Sidney standing in front of her

79

now, waving her knife, a gift to her from the Royal Stores, Ethel might have smiled at the thought of it, summoning such energy for Mae. Aubrey's wife just made Ethel more tired. Some days – this one, for instance – she could barely remember what stories Mae had told about her to try to ruin her. For that matter, she could barely remember George Hicks. When he got to Grand Falls he would have caught up with the Goodyear boys, her cousins, and she did miss them all. But she'd never been to Grand Falls and cared not a whit. *Make geography your destiny* – she remembered that from somewhere, a reading she'd taught from one of the primers at Carmanville, wasn't it now? She remembered that: *geography, destiny*, a sea of shining scrubbed faces. *Good morning, Miss Wellon*. Well, Miss Wellon had had a destiny other than geography anyway. Hers had been the destiny of children. *In sorrow thou shalt bring forth children*, God had chided Eve in the Garden. *My punishment is greater than I can bear*. Hadn't Eve said that back? Or was that Cain? Someone early on, in any case. Imagine, saying anything at all back to God. But Ethel's children seemed one of God's few blessings to her; the rest of her life was His reproach. How she loved her little ones.

Her children, now, they'd have the destiny of geography, if they wanted. They'd go places. Young Tom, only twelve, already wanted to fly aeroplanes.

In front of her, Sidney wheedled; Tom in his aeroplane vanished. "What Bowrings give us now, my darling?" He picked up the knife again where Ethel had set it down and tested the edge against his thumb.

"Not much. Let me get unpacked now." She held her breath. Gently, she took the knife from him and set it back once more in its box. Sidney had an elevated view of all the wholesalers his wife did business with, for the whole of St. John's, in fact, as if money grew on trees there better than anywhere else. It was a common enough view, one that Aubrey had held himself since the death of his two little ones, to diphtheria, in a single day. It was all years ago, but Aubrey still dreamed about St. John's as he worked the business he'd taken over from his father, Thomas, in Ladle Cove. St. John's wasn't the kind of place to have diphtheria. St. John's had no germs at all. It had clean streets, spotless. No one coughed up blood on the streets of St. John's. No one there had the white plague of consumption or anything else. The only thing you had in St. John's was prospects.

Sometimes Aubrey confused the streets of St. John's with the streets of heaven, paved in gold, and sometimes he realized clearly enough they were just rock and tar like any other, anywhere. He'd had enough of the outports, that was all.

"Bowrings give us nothing, then? My, my," Sidney said, with menace.

Still, Ethel held her breath. If the silver cake knife from the Royal Stores wasn't enough for Sidney, what would be? She eyed it, lying there on the counter between them where she'd set it back in its blue velvet bed, moulded into that lovely white cardboard box. Pearly white, the box, and a soft, buttery wooden handle on the knife itself. The long serrated silver blade had been inscribed just for her, for in St. John's they loved Ethel Wiseman. They always looked forward to her visit. MAY YOU NEVER WANT FOR BREAD OR CAKE, they'd had it inscribed, with the Royal Stores insignia.

She'd taken it out of her bag on the long train ride up the island, and again on the long steam from Ladle Cove.

Well, I never have, she'd thought, turning the blade back and forth on her lap. How it caught the light. *I've never wanted for bread or cake. Never wanted for anything.* Not even in March, the hungry month, when food ran low while the outports waited for the ice to melt and the boats to get in, while so many of the men, too, were off on the ice, sealing. Sometimes the women would say it was good timing, that – the men off on the ice when the food ran out at home. Fewer mouths to feed. But Ethel and her family had never gone hungry. She was a Wellon; she had a way of making the best of things.

"We can't know God's purpose," she'd said to her sister Mill when she'd seen her in St. John's, same as she did every year. "Shall not the Judge of all the Earth do right? That's what it says in the Bible."

Mill couldn't say. She worried about Ethel. Not that Ethel said anything – not to Mill, at least, and not even much to Maud. The things
Ethel kept in her heart you didn't turn over to the public, not even to
family. They'd only worry and wring their hands like Mill did, without
even knowing the half of it. This trip Ethel had gone first to Aubrey
and Mae's in Ladle Cove, then to Mill's in St. John's. She preferred to
close things off with the visit to Mill, because left to the end Aubrey
and Mae sent her home with a bad taste in her mouth. It was a bitter
taste, and Ethel tracked it to Mae's tea in her mother-in-law's china.
The two didn't mix – Mae and the Wellons, Mae's fancy Ceylon tea
and Fanny Wellon's English Aynsley cups. But Mae made Aubrey
happy, and Ethel loved her for that. Her sister Mill she loved well
enough, but not like she loved Maud. It was funny, wasn't it, so many
years between herself and Maud and only four years between herself
and Mill, and still it was Maud she loved best. It was as if Mill had
moved away from her, a little farther each year, once Mill had married
Jack Winsor from Wesleyville and moved with him to St. John's. They
had a house on LeMarchant Road by the butter factory, and that was
where Ethel visited, sitting in the parlour, the room that people in
town used, unlike the parlours in the outports that sat dark and drear
unless a body was laid out there, or the minister visited. Mill had her
yard laid out like the grounds of the butter factory. Her gardens were
smaller than the butter factory's but not by much. People went up
LeMarchant Road just to see the place – a low-slung building fronted
by patterned gardens and luscious green lawns, the building itself
painted creamy, sunny yellow, as if all God's goodness had drenched
its roof and spilled down the sides. Perhaps they'd stop at Mill's too.

At LeMarchant Road Ethel saw Jack Winsor again too. She always
saw Jack twice each visit, once with Mill at the house and once at the
Royal Stores, where he was chief salesman now. He always had things
laid out for her to choose among on the upper floor, and they talked
while he walked alongside her, holding the book in which he noted
her order. What a bounty there was. Ethel chose a little thing for

Marion each trip, and for the boys. Grace was still too small this time to have a gift from Mom.

"You're kind," said Jack Winsor. It had been he who'd presented her with the knife.

"Oh, my," said Ethel. It wasn't in her to be coy. "Well then, I hope I never disappoint you."

"Ayres, now, Ayres give us nothing either?" Sidney's voice was like wind with a curl of frost, and it snatched Ethel back to the Ensign shop and the present. Sidney loosed the knife from its velvet bed and raised it slowly, watching it catch the light. It was what she'd done on the *Clyde*, moving it up and down and around to get the shimmer, discreetly, so no one would wonder.

"Lovely, the way it plays the light, isn't it, my darling?" She chose her words as if they were filled chocolates and she were holding them out, trying to talk a child out of a tantrum. Bert Strong had been stared down by a moose once, years ago in the woods outside Witless Bay where he'd been picking berries on a day trip out from his boarding school in St. John's. He'd backed away carefully, talking to it. "Nice moose," he'd said. "Nice moosey." He'd been in his last year of school, nearly a grown man, and it was a story they'd all laughed at.

Sidney lunged. The tip of the knife pressed her windpipe. "You think twice now next time, my girl, before you go that far away and leave me with all this." With his free hand he waved at the Ensign shop, then far off in the direction of the house and the boat store and the wharf beyond that, and then the whole of the Islands beyond that, everything he believed was his or should have been. "You go away and leave me with this and all you have to show for my trouble when you come back is a damned penny knife. A damned tin penny knife."

He threw it down, clattering, on the floor and stormed from the shop. She sank down and retrieved it, her chest heaving. She sat there a bit. It felt good to be sitting down. There was a peace to it. She picked up the knife and pressed it between her hands. It was cool, and there was a peace to that too.

She couldn't go on like this. It was too hard. It was hard enough competing with Strong's. Strong's had all its men on account, and that was most of the families in town. Ethel had to rely on the come-from-aways: those in on the coastal boats; anyone from Long Island or down Hall's Bay way who'd come in on a passenger boat or a motor boat; the international ships whose skippers sought her out, *Señora, chère Madame*; and just anyone at all who happened to have a bit of cash outside his account at Strong's. She couldn't be away from the shop a minute, for fear she might miss a customer. Oh, it was all so hard, and she had to get home yet, all the way out to Big Tickle. They'd talked about moving to the middle of town, right here next to the store. They'd get on with it now. Sid could rest on his bonds and holdings for a year and stay back from the Labrador a season to build the new house and move them. He could keep Harold and Nelson back from their own season a few weeks to help him, and they could start dismantling the Tickle house and sail its fine mouldings and hearths across to Campbell's Point.

Ethel's breathing relaxed at the thought of it. It was a good plan. It was just too hard to walk all that way between home and the shop any more.

~

Sidney left the dismantling of the billiards room until last. It was his favourite corner of the Tickle house. The mouldings and cornices, the entire room, were still intact. It would be the first room reconstructed on the other side of the harbour, where the frame of the house was already standing into the sky. In fact, he might have even bigger plans than that for a new billiards room. Maybe he'd put it right in the new shop, for all the world to see.

Ethel leaned against the yellow wainscot. From Big Tickle she could look across the water nights and see the ghostly studs and braces of the new house, in lonely silhouette like some gallows abandoned or waiting, partitioning the moonlit sky over Campbell's Point. Was it any kind of place to go, after all? John Campbell had owned the land first, put his name to it long ago after coming up all the way from St. John's, and all it had got him in the end was the death of his wife and his two sons. Young Susannah, his son Daniel's widow, had had to start again with nothing.

"Rubbish," Sidney had said. "Campbell's Point is the best lot in town. Right in the centre. Right in the limelight."

Ethel didn't like limelight. "Mr. Campbell lost his wife and his boys, Sidney."

"Well." Sidney snapped his *Life* magazine and raised it under his nose. This discussion was ended.

"And his schooner." John Campbell had such ill fortune. Or had he brought it on himself? *You make your luck* – Ethel believed that. John Campbell had been the islands' first postmaster, built its first schooner; but he'd also shot the last of the Islands' Beothuk, out on Harbour Rock.

"Well, I expect he built another. You always can, those of us who got gumption."

The man, Campbell, had been one of Sidney's own forebears, but that wasn't why Sidney wanted Campbell's Point. He'd bought it for its limelight, Ethel knew. He didn't feel things the way she did, about where you came from and how you got here and who you were with now and who you were to become. Ethel felt things strongly. She felt the rightness and the wrongness of things. God had given her that: *Ye shall be as gods,* He had said to Adam and Eve, *knowing good and evil.* She wasn't sure it had helped Adam and Eve much. Maybe better not to know, but she did know things, and she did sense things. Something here, for instance, right now in the billiards room. She looked around the walls again to be sure. Above the yellow wainscot the walls were papered in tiny blue bellflowers, and Sidney's picture wasn't there. She could see it had been there, until recently. The paper had faded a little around it, marking its spot. Had he taken it down already to keep it safe for the move? That must be it. It would be bundled up and tucked away. She loved it. It was his portrait in his navy uniform, a middy blouse with white trim and a white lanyard. Years ago, the week before he'd shipped out for England, he'd gone into St. John's to have it taken by the war photographer there. He told her about it, how when he'd gone in the door to the photographer's shop the other boys all stood aside. They were all army, common as the day was long, but Sidney had been in full midshipman regalia, in his navy blues. Everyone wore full regalia for the studio appointments; most wore their hats. Who knew whether this would be the last look their families would have at them, ever? Who knew whether they'd be coming back?

Sidney was navy, glamorous and chosen; most of them there in the studio were infantry, brown as dirt. How wrapped up the infantry looked, as if things were over and done with before they ever set foot on a transport or a battlefield. Everything snugged in around them straight up to their ears. And lots of pockets. Useful, those. Sidney found everyone capricious, from deckhands to soldiers, undisciplined and snotty-nosed and bound to lose whatever you handed out. Their jackets buttoned tight to the throat with collars cut so straight their ends nearly overlapped. To keep them warm in winter, Ethel said, imagining it, the sons of Newfoundland caught in the snows of France.

His portrait had made him look so dashing. They agreed on that. But secretly he disliked it. He'd wished for an officer's tunic of dress blues, a four-in-hand tie and the coat with an open, notched collar, a collar like a gentleman's that called for a proper shirt and tie. In its pockets he would have carried nothing. What would a man like Sidney need? He had his pipe and his papers and the love of God and his mother, waiting at home.

The photograph was for her, Lizzie. He stood tall in front of the camera, middy and all, stretching up and holding his breath as he had when he was a lad, measuring up to the others. He'd longed for a white uniform cap with a visor. That would have sat on his head like the judgement of God. What he had instead was a witless white cotton sailor's gob, and he'd rumpled it in his hand, below the range of the camera.

To hell with uniforms anyway.

How handsome he looked in that photograph! Ethel thought. She wished he'd worn his hat.

"Sid, my darling," Ethel called, hearing him come in now. "I don't see your naval portrait that's been hanging here. Where can it have gone?"

He sauntered into the room. Champion, war hero, handsome darling – her notion of him vanished. Now, he wore that look. What had she done? She worked so hard to defuse things. Often she didn't even know what she had to defuse. She thought they'd made up from the other day. But with Sidney you never knew – days, months, years might go by and suddenly something was hurled back at you, driven into your heart with all the sharpness it had at the start. Now, advancing on her from across the room, he was the picture of menace, and he spread his hands apart on the cushion of the billiards table to lean toward her, the table between them. She imagined him jumping over it, springboarding. Could he do that?

"Well, my darling, my portrait went down with the ship," he said. He was sneering.

"Sidney. Darling."

"Ah. You liked it, did you, Ethel?"

"I loved it. You know I loved it."

"Well, then." He turned on his heel and left the room.

They'd had a fight. A disagreement, she preferred to think of it, and she told him so at the time.

"Do you now?" He'd smiled and looked his look.

Three women, young enough and all sisters of Minnie Grimes, had needed transport to Long Island and he'd offered to motor them over in his launch. It would have cost him nigh on twenty dollars for gas

for the motorboat, and then there was an overnight's lodging at Long
Island to arrange, but he *wouldn't think of it, girls.* He wanted to take
them for nothing, have his jaunt.

"We can't afford it," Ethel had objected. And they couldn't.

He'd pulled a twenty from his billfold. "I'll show you what it will
cost, my darling," he said, and lit a match to the bill. Holding it in
front of her face, he let it burn all the way down in his fingers, not
dropping it, not flinching, and then he'd gone anyway.

She found out the rest later from Audrey Grimes: how in the
middle of the sound he'd produced the portrait from under his coat
and peeled it from the frame, then tore it in four neat squares. These
he dropped ceremoniously in the water, chanting each down with a
splish and a *splash*, and following it with the ornate carved frame,
splosh. Is everything all right at home? Audrey wanted to ask Ethel.

"It was a fine likeness," she said instead, "but a finer frame. I could
have put my parents' wedding portrait in it."

Ethel wouldn't have put a picture of Sidney in anything less, but
she mourned the portrait more, languishing now at the bottom of the
sea. There was no getting it back; no getting anything back. The sun
never shone. *Ask ye of the Lord rain in the time of the latter rain; so
the Lord shall make bright clouds,* so Reverend Mr. Wood had said
once, in the Tickle house parlour. Soon, he'd be saying it in the
Campbell's Point parlour.

Bright clouds? Ethel hadn't known what she'd thought of that.
The Lord had his ways, that was sure. So many of them involved so
little sun.

~

Aunt Maud carried the clipping with her all the time. By now it was
nearly twenty years old, yellowed and fly-away like parchment. She
didn't need to open it, risk it falling apart like so much confetti.
She could recite it by heart and did so now, standing beneath the boys'
picture fastened to a stud, part of the framing of Et's new house. Ethel

had known she was coming. She'd pulled the picture out of its packing and hung it for her sister, out in the open air. A breeze blew in on Campbell's Point from the harbour, riffling Maud's hair. Her clipping was from the St. John's newspaper, what Field Marshal Douglas Haig had cabled to Newfoundland governor Walter Davidson after the July Drive. "Newfoundland may well feel proud of her sons," Haig had written. "The heroism and duty they displayed on 1st July has never been surpassed. Please convey my deep sympathy and that of the whole of our Armies in France in the loss of the brave officers and men who have fallen for the Empire, and our admiration for their heroic conduct. Their efforts contributed to our success, and their example will live."

As commander-in-chief of the Allied Forces in Europe, did Sir Douglas have time to do more than write sympathy notes? Sadly, the loss of the Newfoundland Regiment at Beaumont Hamel on the Somme in July of 1916 did not, in fact, contribute much to Allied success. Over the course of the war, Newfoundlanders suffered a higher casualty rate than any other overseas contingent – fully two-thirds of the 5,482 who went lay dead or wounded. Casualties were especially devastating in the ill-fated Somme campaign along a twenty-five-mile stretch of the Western Front. The July 1 sunset brought down its curtain on 19,240 British dead and twice as many wounded in a single day.

There, too, the Newfoundland Regiment fared worst of all, with every one of its officers wounded or killed. To escape being targetted by sharpshooters, officers had gone out dressed like their men. But they carried only their walking-sticks and pistols, no rifles. At nightfall on July 1, only 68 of the 778 Newfoundlanders who went over the top that morning answered roll call and returned to their St. John's Road trench. The official count, which took several days to make in the awful carnage, would close at 243 dead, 386 wounded, 91 missing.

Maud's boy, Harold Coish, twenty-one, was among the dead. His younger brother Clyde was luckier, for a time. He'd been one of the ten per cent of the battalion held back at Beaumont Hamel, as a few men were always held back from any battle to rebuild their regiment in the event it suffered heavy losses. Clyde's holdback was unusual: typically brothers were sent out side-by-side to fight, for morale and advantage. But Clyde had been sick. Infectious diseases – mumps, measles, scarlet fever, pneumonia, meningitis, all bugs that liked nothing so well as men crowded into barracks – had swept through home fronts and battlegrounds alike that year, so virulent that troops arriving in Britain were segregated from those already trained and leaving for the front. Measles alone delayed two new units of the Newfoundland Regiment from even proceeding overseas.

As the July 1 darkness pressed down upon him with the threat of gas in the air, Clyde felt sicker still. He heard how Harold had gone down, carrying pieces of the bangalore torpedoes distributed among the infantrymen with the rest of the gear and munitions load: flares, shovels, pickaxes, sledgehammers, trench bridges, and anything else that might help them secure the German line two hundred and fifty yards and four barbed-wire belts away across No Man's Land. One of the boys even carried a can of grey paint for claiming and identifying captured guns. Their loads were heavy in every way. Harold, too, had been sick, but not so sick as Clyde. His sections of the bangalores were just manageable, some forty pounds of metal tubes filled with explosives for blasting through his own barbed wire before he sprang out into No Man's Land and charged for the German lines.

Haig Ale and Haig Stout, named after Douglas Haig, had gone into production in St. John's early in the war years, but the Coish brothers were never to taste either. Such two per cent "near beers" got the rest of Newfoundland through to the end of Prohibition in 1924, and what Newfoundlanders back home didn't know about Haig Ale and Haig Stout's namesake didn't hurt them. Haig made a better beer brand than a leader and military tactician. His plan for France had been futile, his choice of front a grave mistake. It was impossible to win in the single stunning blow he imagined, pointless to win in any case, and devastating to languish in. Despite his mistakes at the Somme, Haig was made field marshal the following year by George V as the king's "New Year's gift from himself and the country." Despite the cost of his mistakes to the sons of Newfoundland in particular, Haig toured the Island after the war, unveiling the National War Memorial on the eighth anniversary of the July Drive in a week of events that came to be known as Haig Week. He was Earl Haig by that time, and he unveiled Newfoundland's memorial in France as well.

At Beaumont Hamel, the Newfoundlanders joined the second wave of the attack; trouble was not expected. But it should have been. The Battle of the Somme was one of those bloodbaths compounded by error after irony. Early after sunrise a mine exploded under one of the German trenches, and a bridge went up. It was the way Haig did things: a show of fireworks and bravado that did little to intimidate and everything to forewarn. The Germans yawned and stretched and trained their machine guns on the holes in the barbed wire covering the enemy line – on the Newfoundlanders, their dog tags, and the additional identifiers, meant to protect them from friendly air fire, but which only helped do them in. A large triangle of tin, seven inches to a side, was sewn on the back of every uniform – and in the brilliant Somme sun of July 1, these became shining markers by which the German snipers lined the boys up. Harold fell at about nine-fifteen in the morning, going over the top with the rest of his battalion on orders from the Divisional Headquarters. HQ had mistaken the white German flares for their own, and believed they'd been signalled a first wave of success. In reality, in just a few minutes, hundreds had been killed in the Newfoundlanders' advance party, the South Wales, King's Own Scottish, and Borders regiments. In half an hour, the Newfoundlanders – 710 of the 801 men sent out that day – went down, just eighty yards from the German guns.

At eight forty-five A.M., his troops still shuffling in the St. John's Road trench in front of him, Lieutenant Colonel A.L. Hadow, commander of the regiment, had checked with headquarters on his field telephone: "asked Brigade if enemy's first trench had been taken and received reply to effect that the situation was not cleared up." Neither could the advance of the Essex Regiment, on the far flank, be confirmed. The Newfoundlanders' advance, Hadow wrote, was ordered regardless,

> over the open from the rear trenches known as St. John's Road and Clonmel Avenue. As soon as the signal for advance was given, the Regiment left the trenches and moved steadily forward. Machine gun fire from the right front was at once on us and then artillery fire also. The distance from our objective varied from 650 yards to 900 yards. The enemy's fire was effective from the outset but the heaviest casualties occurred in passing through the gaps in our front wire. The men were mown down in heaps.

Harold never got a chance to use his bangalores. Many more holes were needed in the wires than had been cut and the soldiers bottle-necked, making easy targets. Corpses hung on the wire, one on top of another, flung there by enemy fire. The survivors staggered on. Only a handful got near the German wire. Hadow thought a few bombs might have been launched into the enemy trench. The Essex Regiment was stalled by the bodies they had to climb over in the forward trenches, and the Newfoundlanders who had made it out of those trenches went on without backup. Without the Newfoundlanders, a few minutes later the Essex, too, were mowed down.

For the rest of the morning the Allied trenches suffered heavy shelling. Survivors and wounded crawled back as they could; many waited for darkness. During the afternoon, the ten per cent reinforcements, Clyde among them, were brought in to the St. James Street support trench, and then on to the Fethard Street trench at their left. There, under cover of dark, they received some equipment as well as some of the dead and wounded that were clogging other trenches, and were told to prepare for counterattack and gas.

~

In Ladle Cove, July 1, 1916, dawned a beautiful summer day, marking nothing yet. Ethel's father was in the house preparing for tomorrow's service, and in that spirit, she supposed, Ethel found herself humming an old Wesleyan hymn through the clothespins in her teeth. Damp linens swayed on the washing line strung between the maples in the yard. *One army of the living God,* she sang as she pinned,

To His command we bow
Part of His host have crossed the flood
And part are crossing now.

Rain threatened for the night ahead but Ethel liked to leave the sheets on the washing line all evening, to air. The days were so long now it would be easy enough to pull them in at dusk. With the warm weather she didn't have to deal with her father's and her brother Aubrey's long johns anymore. Mae tended to Aubrey now anyway, but just today Ethel had been over to help Mae in her childbed and had brought a load of laundry home. The child had been born at the end of a long struggle that had started days before, and Mae, flushed and sullen and exhausted, lying back on her sodden pillow with her hair in her mouth, hadn't been ready with a boy's name. She was thirty-three; she was getting too old for the production of children and after today she would hate everything about it.

Her sister-in-law Maud, nearly forty, hadn't much patience with her. Ethel could see that, even though Maud had said not a word – not to Mae, not to Ethel, not to anyone. Maud couldn't imagine a greater blessing than children. Hers were grown and it made no difference; she worried about them constantly, even young Max right here by her side.

Maud had taken an early shift at Mae and Aubrey's with the granny. Then Ethel took over, sponging Mae's face. Mae hadn't wanted a boy. She'd wanted another girl to go with her Ivey. She was sick of boys who only turned into men, when men were so much work. If she'd had another girl to go with Ivey, she would have given the baby one of her own names, Sarah. Ivey and Sarah. It sounded like soaps in a ribboned box, or a china set from England.

Ethel had brought a silver coin with her in case the child finally came today, and he had. She bent in. The tiny thing hadn't the green eyes of his father and his great-grandmother Margaret, from Scotland; he'd need more luck. Tucking her coin in the newborn's hand to start it running, she went down to Thomas Wellon and Co. to fetch her brother. Aubrey closed up the shop, distracted. He was worried, he told Et.

"About the baby? The baby's fine. A boy." Aubrey hadn't seemed interested. "Mae's fine too. Worn out."

"I'm worried about Harold."

"Ah. And Clyde."

"Well, just Harold, I think."

"Well, Clyde's over there too." Ethel could hardly say it. She hated to think about it. Ethel wanted to comfort her brother, but couldn't think of what to say, any more than she ever could to her sister Maud. Something from Scripture; that would serve. "The Lord is a man of war, Maud," she'd say. "So says the Book of Exodus."

"The Lord is a man? God help us!" Their father was a lay reader in the church, and Maud and Ethel knew the Bible well enough to have a little fun with it, even in times like these.

Both Maud's boys were over there, all she had but for Max, the youngest and too small yet to go. It had been impossible for the other two to resist. Impossible for anyone's boys after they'd seen the Proclamation that ran in the St. John's paper and got circulated all around, offering a dollar a day, free rations and free passage to training in St. John's. And the finishing touch: a portion of the pay went to your family back home, where it would be so badly needed. *YOUR KING AND COUNTRY NEED YOU! Will You Answer Your Country's Call? We want to send our best, and we believe that Britain's Oldest Colony will gain greater honour and glory for Her Name.* Well, t'was not every day that Morris killed a cow. Especially not in the outports. Who could say no? A lad going off to war would be as fine a man, now, as ever broke a cake of the world's bread. If he got refused, for flat feet or bad teeth or a rheumy cough, whatever it was, he'd even get free passage back. But few said no, and few were refused.

Walking by his sister's side now, Aubrey seemed inconsolable. "Et," he said, turning to her on the doorstep, "let's call the baby Harold. Harold Francis."

"Harold's a good name," Et said. She saw him in the door, rolled Mae's linens under her arm and went home.

"The baby's a boy," she called as she came in the door. "Named Harold."

"Harold." Fanny came out from the kitchen, drying her hands on her apron.

"Harold?" Her father came out from the breakfast room, where he'd been working at his desk.

"Mmm. Harold Francis." Ethel pitched the laundry in the tub.

"Harold *Francis?*" Her father raised an eyebrow. His son Francis had died years and years ago. Thomas could barely remember it, though you never really forgot a thing like that. "Well," he said. "Harold's not dead yet. Harold's very much alive." He cleared his throat, went back to his work in the breakfast room. He was glad his daughter Maud wasn't there. That wasn't what he'd wanted to say. He wasn't sure just what it was he *had* wanted to say. Aubrey could name his boy whatever he liked.

After supper Ethel sat on the porch with the Sunday potatoes and watched the wide lengths of the sheets shift in the breeze, billowing and slackening like sails on the winds blowing in from the east. She had to get everything done tonight, Saturday evening, and she'd lost a lot of time attending Mae. Like any Methodist, her father allowed no work on the Sabbath. He didn't even shave. Meals were eaten cold – the potatoes in Ethel's lap now, rolled in her apron, would have to be boiled up tonight and served cold tomorrow. Even the Sunday bread was sliced the day before, the Sunday dishes left to Monday. They weren't even cleared from the table, and breakfast and lunch dishes were pushed to the side to make way for supper. Clearing the dishes would be an affront to God, Thomas said, but a mess would offend Him too, so Fanny threw a cloth over the whole thing once the family was done in the evening and had pushed their chairs back. She wouldn't throw out any water they dirtied, not on the Lord's day. She set plates over the buckets and basins to cover up the sight of it all.

Getting ready for Sunday was a chore; it kept you on your feet. But still Ethel sat and stared. What shapes drying sheets could take on, like the clouds. You could see the saints in the clouds sometimes, their faces, their blessed hands reaching out in intercession, even their martyrdoms. Below them, summer waxwings gambolled in the trees. It was a languid evening for a Saturday. Too languid, really; she should be getting on with things, gathering them together for tomorrow, and then gathering her own effects in her trunk in preparation for leaving. As soon as the summer ended she'd be off, leaving Fanny and Thomas to teach around the bay again for the winter. How she'd miss them, and Maud and Mill too, and Aubrey. She'd miss seeing the new baby Harold waddling about; he'd be doing that soon enough, running after big sister Ivey.

She felt a strain about it, an ache. Strange, how the day had dawned so fine, bringing a new baby, only to shroud itself in melancholy. She brushed away a bee that flew past her cheek. What a late hour for a honeybee to be out. It buzzed again but she couldn't see it. Her unease grew. Doubled over the potatoes the way she was, her chest grew tight as if there were too little room in her for breath. She felt closed in, suffocated. All afternoon she'd been smelling something strange in the air, as if some doom were creeping up on her. She'd set the potatoes down in a moment and go in and sit on the edge of her bed, bend over to try and get some relief from her asthma. Sometimes that helped. There wasn't much else to be done. Her mother had bought a little lamp from a pedlar of cure-alls on the circuit out of St. John's, but its smoke only made things worse for Fanny and Ethel both. Ethel was done with Stafford's Liniment, and poultices, too; they stank and kept you from your work and amounted to nothing else, and her mother's Phoratone, a mixture for cough, made her sleep. Ethel wasn't sleepy now though; she was on the edge of dread. She watched the sheets. Things seemed misplaced, like the bee. It was an unseasonal time to be bothered with asthma, with the pollens not blowing until October, but who could see into these things? Not she. That was what a God was for, a higher mind than hers. Leave it to Him.

And as she left it to Him and rose from her step, Ethel smelled something worse than she'd smelled all day, worse than Mae's blood and sweat or Aubrey's fear: pungent, acrid, like some great haymow lying fully rotted in the next garden. It smelled as if something were full to overflowing, about to burst its seams all over her father's yard. The sheet farthest from her on the washing line stiffened then, snapping, and Harold stepped out of it and onto the lawn just short of a stretch of wild columbine and lady's mantle. Smart, he looked, in his khaki, holding a rifle and in full uniform with his buttons shined. The rifle was in one hand; in the other was some sort of long metal cylinder. He was tall, lean, not much older than she, and not tanned at all for the season, but white, pasty white.

Not as white as she, though; she blanched, and felt her heart stop.

Harold saluted her with the bangalore, his child aunt, his childhood friend, and stepped back into the sheet, winding it around him like a little cyclone as he went, until he disappeared. The whole thing had taken a second, no more, and Ethel coughed and coughed, running to the camphor lamp. The lamp did her no good, and she climbed the stairs and for a while lay on her bed. Her heart heaved in her chest. Maud came over from her house later with eggs in her apron for Fanny's Sunday breakfast in the morning, and Ethel heard her and went down, composing herself. But she never said. She stared at her sister and never, never, never said.

Not even when the telegram came and William and Maud brought it over to Fanny and Thomas. Maud's knees were buckling. Sunday came and Sunday went; it was a rare event when the Wellons did not go to church. It was the thirteenth of the month that the telegram came, nearly two weeks after the battle. Ethel sat her sister in a chair and watched her shake.

All her life there were going to be things she never, never said –
and here was the start to all that. Granny Gudger said later that Maud's
boys had come to her in the pasture and given her long messages for
their mother: *be good, be brave, till we meet again.*

Did he have that cylinder? She imagined asking Granny.

*He did not. He had a bandage round 'is head, blood seepin.' He'd
been hit right bad.*

Let Granny Gudger tell it, then. Granny Gudger was always telling
things like that. Ethel wondered how the old woman ever got anything
done and got Horace Gudger fed at all, so busy was she receiving the
ghosts of all the outport boys who died, scores and scores of them from
all the way over to the Straight Shore of Bonavista Bay and Deadman's,
then west all the way up through Botwood and Bishop's Falls to
Leading Tickles. So many from Ward's Harbour on Long Island alone
that after the war they renamed the place Beaumont.

Let Granny Gudger tell it, then. She, Ethel, never would.

~

"It was a magnificent display of trained and disciplined valour,"
Major-General Sir Beauvoir de Lisle wrote after the battle to Sir
Edward Morris, prime minister of Newfoundland, "and its assault
only failed of success because dead men can advance no farther."

Maud knew about that note too, though she didn't carry it around
except in her heart. It troubled her too much. What was the man saying?

Sir Good Sight, Sir Beautiful Sight. Maud's French wasn't good
like her sister's – Ethel and her kids *parlez-vous*'d in the schoolhouse,
after all – but she knew enough to have the man's name, translated,
ring in her head. Was he saying that with more soldiers, more
Newfoundlanders, lots more to go down and some to advance, they
could have won the day? How many more did this wretched Beauvoir
want? She'd sent off two, Harold and Clyde. And poor Max had
meant to send himself off, as well, as it turned out – Max who'd sickened going and "getting his brothers back," walking forty-five miles

to Grand Falls and forty-five miles back in the sleet and snow of the following year to enlist. Max had never been the same again after that. Had any of them ever been the same again? But Max had caught that terrible cold, and then pneumonia, and ever after he'd had the weak lungs that finally carried him off. And three years after that, her beloved husband as well, lungs again.

Maud turned things over in her heart. What about Henry V, she asked Et, the king of England in the play, praying on the eve of his impossible battle? *The day, my friends, and all things stay for me.* They did stay, so the story went. It was the enemy who went. It was an unlikely story, impossible. Ten thousand casualties for the French, a handful for the English. And yet it seemed to Maud that the king hadn't more than that handful to begin with, and certainly no good weapons. A few sticks, really; swords and spears but certainly no horses like the French. Probably no bows and arrows either – the French had them all as well. The British might have had a slingshot or two. What they had, though, was courage, resolve. Well, Maud's boys had that too. You couldn't find a Newfoundlander who didn't, certainly not a Bayman. And yet the Germans at the Somme, entrenched, underestimated, forewarned, had suffered barely a casualty while the Allies were wiped out. What went right for King Henry on St. Crispin's Day; what went wrong here? What went right for David when he slew his Goliath, and what went wrong for her boys?

Could only so many of us be lucky? Why were the Newfoundlanders hardly ever lucky at all?

"I don't know, my dear, I don't know." Et said. *You make your luck* – that's what she believed. But it made no sense here, and she wasn't going to say it to Maud. Harold and Clyde had tried, but they hadn't been able to make their luck.

"There's a park," Maud would go on. Beaumont Hamel Memorial Park. Another one of those *beau* words: *good, beautiful mountain.* She couldn't understand it. Names in Newfoundland meant what they said: Heart's Delight, Harbour Grace, Witless Bay, Exploits. For thirty-thousand dollars the Newfoundland government searched down land titles as far as Africa and bought forty acres near the French village, hiring Rudolph Cochius, the famed designer of Bowring Park in St. John's, to design this one too. The first Beaumont Hamel Memorial Day was commemorated a year after the battle. After Newfoundland joined Canada in 1949, to the dismay of the Island, the observance lapsed into Dominion Day and later Canada Day – where a bunch of kids got together and rode bikes with coloured streamers in the wheels, rang their bells and ate ice cream bars, just damn glad to be off school. Newfoundland was a self-governing dominion during the war, the same as countries like South Africa, Australia, and New Zealand, Canada itself. The Newfoundland Regiment served as itself, not as part of anyone's forces. They'd lost lots, not least of which now was the honouring of their dead.

On the site of the Somme battlefield, the Beaumont Hamel Memorial Park opened at the end of June 1925, nearly nine years to the day of the July Drive, with Earl Haig at the podium. The papers loved him, everyone loved him, even in St. John's. Especially in St. John's. Newfoundlanders loved the Empire – a quarter century later nearly half of them, despite Joey Smallwood's unquenchable efforts to have them join Canada, would vote to love it still. Newfoundlanders hated Uncle Fritz, certain he'd have ruined the world had he and his beast, sprung from its lair, been able to take it. The Newfoundlanders had respect for authority; they believed that the men in charge of the war were good men, smart men, men who led for a reason. As late as the end of 1917 – after Suvla Bay and Gallipoli, after Beaumont Hamel and the July Drive and more hard fighting on the Somme, at Gueudecourt in October and again the following spring at Arras and Monchy-le-Preux, after the long lists of casualties the paper had printed weekly for two years – after all that, the St. John's *Daily News* had, without irony, congratulated Haig on his "brilliant stroke, which has changed the whole aspect of the western front. Developments of the most momentous character may occur at any time."

And they had, for Maud Coish.

As there was at Rudolph Cochius's Bowring Park, at Beaumont Hamel Memorial Park there was a bronze caribou, the emblem of the regiment, to symbolize the boys gone down, a homey touch like the yellow caribou on the bright red Purity hard-bread bag, and when Maud read about it she saw herself transported across the ocean whitecaps to stand at its exquisite feet, shaded from hurt by those broad grand antlers as they caught the sun. She cared not a whit about the field marshal, the earl, whatever he was now. He might have been the king himself for all she cared. He was welcome, she was sure, but she wouldn't walk the length of herself for him.

It was her Harold that drew her. Standing by the caribou she'd be near him, her firstborn and her first gone. There were three other caribou statues in France remembering the regiment, and one in Belgium. The Beaumont Hamel caribou overlooked St. John's Road, the Newfoundlanders' trench on the battlefield. At its feet were three bronze plaques listing the names of the 820 Newfoundlanders who fell at the Somme, whose graves were *known unto God,* and God alone.

"There's a park," Maud would say to Ethel, and Ethel would take her hand, saying nothing back.

~

Harold was buried in a mass grave in the trenches to await a place after the war at Hawthorne Ridge No. 2. With Y Ravine, Hawthorne was one of the two Newfoundland burial grounds among the hundred and fifty or so of the Somme's war cemeteries. Harold's identification disc was removed from his body for shipping to Maud and William Coish, and replaced with a slip of paper that bore his name and serial number. *A Soldier of the Great War,* that's what Harold's white granite marker would say. *Two Soldiers of the Great War* – sometimes a marker said that, when bodies couldn't be recognized and disentangled and all parts accounted for. Crippled with loneliness and fear, Clyde worried about a common grave more than anything. It haunted him. He and his brother had been close. Who was Harold close to now? What corpse, what mangled hand, what shredded flank or lolling head?

Clyde was only seventeen. Like so many of the lads, he'd got into the war by fudging his age. Who would he look to now? Whose hand was Harold holding now, in that mass grave? Who would hold Clyde's hand in days to come?

After Harold, Clyde's life was a collection of dank dugouts or vermin-filled tents in the French countryside, much of it shrouded under snow. He had friends enough, even some Baymen, so cheerful and chatty that they liked to boast they could talk to Hunnybun corpses on No Man's Land half the night with never an answer back and never you mind. But no one replaced Harold; no one held a candle to him; and the nights which were the worst for Clyde were also the time when the vermin flocked. He'd never known so many mice could frequent so small a tent. At least it was better than the trenches, where rats were the constant companions. Later it was gas, which hung around for days in low places, much like the rats. You could jump into a trench or a crater shell for cover and find yourself on a stretcher a few hours later, blistered and blinded. In France that winter, snow seemed everlasting, from late October all the way to the next May. Then, a season of mud, endless rain, and shelling into the soft ground, even a flash lightning storm that flooded the trenches and a sudden freeze that froze it all and the men in it too.

Inland like this, the cold of the winter was worse than any the boy had known on the Straight Shore, not even off the Funks or the Wadhams in March. He had never seen so much white. Not ice, like home: just all-over white as if God Himself, some Great Undertaker, had drained the blood from every living thing.

Dressed in white nightshirts, Clyde's platoon raided enemy outposts in the winter nights. They bandaged their helmets and their rifles with gauze and passed unseen in the snowy dark. Clyde came to like the night raids, to look forward to them, which is to say he liked the day excursions and gas shell attacks and the all-too-frequent attendance at the line a whole lot less. The horror of the line was not even what lay ahead, for at your back you had the short-shooting of your own gunners to worry about as well. You had shelling from your own side too; your own shells could explode right back into your face. Clyde felt tied to the other men, as if they were prisoners shackled together in a dock, and there was some comfort to it. He learned to die daily. At night, though, for a while, at least, Fritz positioned his gas projectors in the dark so that they couldn't be taken out by Allied planes and his own gas exploded right back into his face. At night those few months, except for Fritz firing off his ghastly Verey lights, the open air was clear for once. Clyde hauled it down into his lungs in gulps despite the asthma he had that ran in the Wellons, worsened by cold air and the bouts of illness he'd suffered so far.

So delicious it was, the frosty night air, emptied for a few hours of trench mortars and whizz-bangs and all the other Hunnybun treats. Fritz threw a lot of shrapnel at the Allies too, and once Clyde stooped to pick up bits but flung them down, his fingers seared by the heat. Another time, in daylight, a watch came sailing at him through the air, blown off someone's wrist. He didn't know whose, friend or foe, but something in him prevented him from leaving it where it lay, and he only stripped it off his wrist months later when like a carnival hawker a private in the Scottish regiment showed him a forearm lined with watches he'd "souvenired" from German corpses.

Dead Boche. That's what the British in the 88th called them, giving their report as they passed by the Newfoundlanders when they changed at the lines.

Clyde couldn't see the point of joining in the forced merriment over the enemy body-counts, the harrowing tales of narrow escape, the days' grim accountings, and the nights' too. He lacked the anti-Kaiser bravado, the optimism of his compatriots, because Harold was gone. He lacked whatever it was that made them say "the war's nearly over" whenever they wrote home.

We're here
Because we're here
Because we're here
Because we're here

sang the 88th on its marches. To Clyde it seemed as good or bad a reason as any.

On October 13, Friday the thirteenth, a six-inch Howitzer shattered Clyde's dugout roof, throwing debris at his shaving mirror. Clyde retrieved the largest shard, still fit for the purpose. Matter-of-factly, he tucked it into his kit. Maybe he'd kill someone with it someday. He didn't believe in luck by then, good or ill. He didn't believe in anything.

His battalion spent long weeks making roads. And then, one winter walk on land where the shell holes were filled with snow, dreaming of the cart-tracks of home that were better winter than summer, their breaks and heaves packed with snow, he fell in a hole up to his hip. He tried to save himself with a hand but landed heavily on his wrist, wrenching an elbow.

Days later, the medic looked at it, swollen and hot and red, shiny all over as if something underneath the skin was trying to get out.

"Inoculation reaction," the medic said, opening his teeth and dropping out the hypodermic he'd prepared.

Clyde watched it roll on the little makeshift table. He might have needed it. Hell, he'd take it even if he didn't. "Haven't had one," he said. He'd had shots on the transports with everyone else, and none since.

"Oh." The medic looked tired, sounded worse. He wasn't one of theirs. He wasn't a Newfoundlander. A Canadian borrowed from the next avenue, the next trench, perhaps. "Oh. Well then," he said, "I'll be back."

But he never came back; and though Clyde's arm eventually shrank down once more, it was never the same again, never strong. He had fever dreams for weeks and shivering in the days. Nights he dreamed about the cathedral everyone talked about in the little town called Albert, close by Harold's battlefield in Picardy Province. *Al-bear.*

Clyde turned it over on his tongue, as he did all the French words. The cathedral had a high spire, perfect for observing the enemy and much used for the purpose by the Allies. Throughout the war the Germans tried to shell it. They missed constantly, peppering the basilica walls with craters instead, and the perpetual escape of the Madonna statue at the top of her spire became a sign of celestial warrant, a sign that God had not turned His back on those who fought in France below. In time the Virgin yawed sideways, sticking out just short of the horizontal like a haywire spoke on an old bicycle wheel, but it was said she would never fall down – not on the Allied troops marching through Picardy below, not under any German shell. Not until God let her go – and that would be the end of the war.

I will not let thee go, except thou bless me. In his fevers, Clyde found himself imploring God on her behalf.

Rise, take up thy bed, and walk, the Virgin sometimes said back.

Clyde couldn't make it out a bit, not a Catholic bone in him and all the Orange Halls and Orangemen's parades at home, and here he was all the same chatting nightly with her Ladyship. He tossed in his tent, lifting the corners of his bedroll as if he might take it up, as if he really would rise, sleepwalking, and waltz it away, right into enemy lines. His knees had gone bad by then, too, with all the falling he'd done and the scrambling into bits of wire. They'd swelled and stiffened, and even in his sleep his legs were painful sticks. He dreamed of the Virgin stuck out sidelong from her spire, snagging clouds. She seemed to him like the Hanged Man in the fortune-teller cards of that silly woman from St. John's, the granny everyone talked about who said she'd come from Carbonear but flew into St. John's one night and stayed and set up shop, just flew in on a gust of air that sailed her right smart down the coast. It was said that the Hanging Virgin of the Albert Cathedral was lame, hardly able to hold her baby Christ, and that her debility made her additionally saved by God. Additionally weak, surely, Clyde thought, tossing. It was a mystery. It added up to nothing for him, just his fever dreams in which he took off his bad arm and the Virgin healed it – *if thy right arm offend thee, cut it off –*

and together they rocked the Virgin's stone child and he woke drenched in sweat, wetter than if he'd been dunked in a puddle.

The marches between camps were long. Often he carried four hundred rounds of ammunition in addition to his standard pack. Except for the pain in his knees, he might have staggered through the end of the year and into the next. It was all an orbit of mud, snow, mud. After the battle at Langemarck, it seemed for weeks they went back and forth between Canal Bank and Proven, behind the lines, carrying half the world on their backs. The only thing Clyde was to miss, having tasted all the other deaths, was death by illness. Flu hit the troops early in 1918, to come back in the fall with a vengeance, a new strain called Spanish that would wipe out twenty million souls worldwide. At home, at holding stations and training camps, and on the front itself, populations were ravaged.

The days shortened, lengthened. Another July 1 came and went, and with it the refreshed memory of Harold, lost forever, and then another year's roll call of the days started again. More of the old routine, when they'd been at the line and somehow got back – when someone failed to answer at roll call, the sergeant called him out absent; just like that, as if the bugger'd gone out for a pee and would be back any moment. Clyde hung his heart on the word. *Absent, absent, absent.* After Langemarck, he hardly knew what to write to his mother any more, and he wanted to go home.

For Clyde, the first anniversary of Harold's death would be the only one.

~

Clyde moved on to Belgium, for the third protracted battle in the long Ypres campaign that was, for many, the worst of the war, the worst of anything imaginable. Between the beginning of the fighting in July 1917 and the end of the war, half a million souls were lost at Ypres, the site of Flanders Fields. Two hundred thousand of them drowned in the mud. The Ypres campaign turned to muck for reasons by then all too common, the same ones that had ruined the Somme campaign and killed Harold: bickering between politicians and the military about strategy, and a heavy display of artillery breast-beating at the outset – four and a half million shells from three thousand guns – that not only gave the enemy ample warning but turned the battlefield into a mire of rain-filled craters even before the fighting started. The town of Ypres a few miles south had been a textiles centre boasting magnificent medieval architecture until it was flattened under four years of fighting, its Cloth Hall, dating to 1214, destroyed by shells. The soldiers slept in mud brought on by unseasonal, heavy rains. They crawled in it, fought, and drowned. As the year inched on and the cold set in, the slush was terrible. Mustard gas took nearly eighteen thousand casualties from both sides. For their part, the Newfoundlanders were part of the ongoing attempt to take and keep the Passchendaele ridge. Despite a bad stretch of mumps in the spring – 115 men down and mumps could be trouble in an adult – and a serious rash of measles and pneumonia that killed twenty-three, what was left of the battered regiment from Beaumont Hamel, plus new enlistees, helped secure the ridge in the fall of 1917. They held it over the winter, for the Germans to take back in April. Over September 28 and 29, 1918, the Newfoundlanders helped pull it back one last time, and defend it until the November 11 general armistice. Though half the refreshed regiment had not seen combat before, casualties were relatively low and twelve of the men were decorated.

Clyde Coish was not so lucky.

The 88th Battalion had gone to the line near Ypres on Friday, September 21, 1917; after four days, their reserve battalion, the Newfoundlanders, replaced them. The shelling was the worst anyone had seen, everyone said so. It made Monchy-le-Preux and Arras, even the Somme in the first year, seem a picnic. Or was that just because you forgot, in time? Clyde didn't think he'd forgotten anything. He wished he had; he wished he could – dreadful memories, hideous phantasms paraded before his eyes days and night, even in his sleep. He tried to remember his mother back home, her warm face. He tried

to remember his brother Max, how they'd played with the goats, taken
the little kids bleating one spring to the beach at Ladle Cove and
floated them on a crate end, pretending to send them to sea, pretending not to hold on. Their mother hadn't been pleased with them for
that. He remembered her, angry but still sweet. He tried not to remember Harold. The bombardment was oppressive, ringing in his ears,
shaking apart the trench and everything in it. He grew used to sleeping through it, flinching a little when a shell exploded and shifting
where he crouched on the firestep that ran the length of the trench like
a running board. They were far back from the line, but these were just
the sort of margins of his attack that Hunny liked to neutralize with
gas. The Newfoundlanders sat and ate and passed the time and slept
on the firestep – they did everything on the firestep in order to stay
out of the water in the trench. Even the duckboard that formed a kind
of poor sidewalk was underwater, rotten, treacherous. Only occasionally did someone actually mount the firestep to shoot out through the
sandbags at the top. There was so much air attack from enemy aircraft that you kept your head down, or lost it. Clyde's trench smelled
of the bleach powder the 88th had disinfected it with; there'd been
yellow cross shells launched into it at some point, then, or nearby.
Bleach neutralized them, too late; but it was a way of cleaning out the
trench for replacement troops. The stuff in the yellow crosses seeped
down, sought you out, and you didn't even know till hours later. Then
your eyes would burn, and your lungs if you didn't have a mask, but
even if you did it would burn every other bit of you anyway. Clothes
didn't help. Uniforms were useless. The gas ate right through. *Stay dry,
stay dry*: the stuff loved moist skin: armpits, groin. It was daft. He'd
never been wetter. With the weeks of rain the trenches seemed like the
Yser Canal, or the Yser River itself. Is this the canal? the Aussies would
say. Did we take a wrong turn? We can't tell the difference.

Four days of this. Keep your head down. Jump out when you hear
a warning about yellow crosses. Or green cross three. That was worse,
or better, depending on how you looked at it. The mix of mustard and

suffocator in green cross three would kill you faster, and an exploding shell to bring it would be best of all, taking you out without another thought. You could put your mask on, but what did it matter? You'd gone to law with the devil and held court in hell. The point of the exercise for the regiment now was simply to man the trenches and outlast the shelling, this round of it, until relief came from Essex, the other reserve, or the 88th again. The Newfoundlanders had just seen heavy action at the Battle of Langemarck on the Steenbeek River; not much was expected of them here but to watch and learn. They'd be stand-ins to give the British a rest.

~

"*I* needs a rest," Moores said, next to Clyde. "A permanent one." Moores was from Pouch Cove. He blew out a cloud of smoke; he'd got a cigarette somehow, a match, too, and kept them both dry.

Don't say that – Clyde didn't voice his thought. *Don't even blow your smoke too high.* Fritz had some good gunners, he'd give them that much. He himself, he was keeping just this side of luck. He knew fellows who left addresses and contact names behind at their billets when they went to the line, with instructions: *In the event of my death, If anything happens, In case, just in case.... Dear Mother ...* Often they left entire letters which they held and used again the next time they went up, if they'd been so lucky to return before.

Dear Mother. Clyde closed his eyes, squeezed them.

They went in Tuesday, September 25. It was quiet, briefly. It was Wypers, still Wypers, but at least it wasn't the Trench of Death at the Flanders coast where you got shelled or shot or raided just by stepping inside. Where at first the Allies weren't going to shorten the trench at all for fear of losing ground; the advance had been too hard won. As it was, they didn't shorten it much. All the troops had heard about it, the *Dodengang,* the *Boyau de la Mort.* They'd heard, too, how the campaign to press east and take the Passchendaele ridge

wasn't going well or at least fast enough, and that Haig had cancelled
his raison d'être for the entire Ypres campaign, the sea attack he'd
planned for the twenty-third. The infantry had been supposed to clear
the way for a sea landing, inland and up to the coast, in this godfor-
saken corner of Belgium, in these woods that had once been called
Sanctuary and were now just bombed stumps.

On Tuesday, it was quiet enough for a moment to think about these
things.

Just as the British left Clyde's trench, the bombardment started
again. The Germans were warned by Haig's fortnight of advance
shelling, and it seemed not to have touched them at all. They were
well prepared, and nothing short of a twelve-inch gun could take out
the iron and concrete pillboxes where their gunners nested. The sniper
fire and bombing was maddening, interminable; sitting under enemy
aircraft was like being inside a lightning storm, rocked and deafened
with every strike. Days passed; the Allies never saw the enemy. Fritz
is scared, he's gone into hiding, the troops said. He only comes out at
night. Up the line, other battalions were returning fire.

It was Friday now. A day's journey and a world away in Paris, the
great Edgar Degas lay dying, blind, sad, lonely, bereft of the friends
he'd lost by taking the wrong side in the Dreyfus Affair. Clyde wasn't
lonely. No, he'd have liked to get away. He had a few friends.
Trenchmates. Caines, Clarke, Gillingham, Lawrence – they all crouched
with Clyde, watching Moores smoke his fag with that match he'd
somehow kept dry. They'd had jam for dinner, and tepid cocoa.
Someone had brought rations down the zigzag of the trench. He'd run
out by the time he got to them. He said he'd be back, but they doubted
it. Moores smoked and talked about home, and Clyde's stomach
rumbled. What was it his father liked to say? *A warm smoke is better
than a cold fog.* Where was Pouch Cove, this place Moores was from?
It was still Friday, interminably Friday. They'd be relieved by Essex or
the 88th tomorrow. Clyde had a toothache. He was glad the runner's
cocoa hadn't been warm, though he could have used a warm flask to

hold against his cheek. He smelled of smoke and sweat and mould, and the salty smell of blood that reminded him of Bonavista Bay, when the sealers came in off the schooners. One more day and they'd be out of here, and he'd be one step closer to seeing home again, as well as new places like Pouch Cove. Moores took a deep drag on his cigarette. What a fellow, Moores. He seemed to suck in the air around him with pressure, amazing tension and heat. And light. It was very bright; something had been lit and someone was yelling. There was a distant *something a distant something what was that?* Clyde couldn't hear any more. There was a smell, faint. He'd fallen into the water beside the duckboard; part of him had fallen. Part of him was on the firestep, was that what he was seeing? An arm? A leg? Was it Caines? Clarke? They'd come apart. He might be able to reach it, the thing on the firestep, if he could only see. . . . He wasn't sure where he was. They gave you a map, they said *take the transport to this town, take this transport to such-and-such,* so you loaded up all the artillery, the gear, sometimes on good days a bit of scoff too, you reined the horse, you went down the road jumping off *aah!* and *aah!* and *aah!* for the shells, squeezing your palms together for the sweat, your heart in your mouth and your breeches near filled, or you just breathed hard, prayed, kept your head down and held the horses steady, and you walked and walked and finally you reached a few ruins and went around and around comparing this rubble with your map until you realized it suddenly, *this is it, this is the place. Holy Christ, this is the place.* A smell, faint. *Harold, Harold, Harold. Lovely in life, in death they were not divided.* Who said that? Was it something he'd heard in church? Was the circuit preacher in from Greenspond after all? *I do not ask my cross to understand, My way to see; Better in darkness just to feel Thy hand, And follow Thee.* If only Harold were here, Clyde found himself thinking. He could give me a hand, he could pull me out. But Harold wasn't there. The last thing in Clyde's hand on the afternoon of September 28 was his Lee-Enfield, and when with his arm so weak and the water so cold he could not pull himself up, out of the wretched black suck, he spat a mouthful of mud and died.

There had been six of them that day and now there were none. Now they were just three headstones in Artillery Wood Park, and each said the dreadful thing: *Two Soldiers of the Great War.*

~

"They were brave, Et." Maud always said that. She put her fork down suddenly on her plate. She set the plate down on the grass, too, and unfolded her knees, rising from the makeshift bench Ethel had rigged out of stones and planks in the midst of the half-raised studs. The sisters were sitting on the grassy rise at the end of Campbell's Point, in the open air inside the framing of the new house. Ethel had unpacked Harold and Clyde's picture from her trunks in the store and polished the glass, hanging it for Maud's arrival on the stud which would eventually mark out the head wall of Marion's bedroom. In the new house, Marion wanted Harold and Clyde to stay with her in her own room, smiling down on her in their infantry khaki.

Ethel had been thrilled by Maud's telegram saying she'd come up from Ladle Cove to see the new house. Their father had died the year before; though they'd been born at either end of the family with sixteen years between them, the sisters had always been close and now drew closer still.

What is the secret of your life? Mrs. Browning asked Charles Kingsley. Tell me, so that I may make mine beautiful too. I had a friend, Mr. Kingsley told her.

Ethel thought of it a lot. *I have a sister,* she would have said.

~

She and Maud had erected their father's marker together, next to Fanny's in the Ladle Cove cemetery:

Thomas Wellon

1849–1933

Ever Remembered

Erected by his Daughters

Ethel thought she and Maud would walk up to Campbell's Point from the boat store after lunch, to see the framing-in. But the greeting between Maud and Sidney had gone badly. When Maud pulled her skirts through the doorway and up the stairs of the store, Sidney, on the daybed he'd dragged from the Tickle house and set up here, turned his back to her and put his face to the wall. Ethel hadn't said something quite right to him that morning, so until the woman saw her way to apologizing, no friend or relative of Ethel's was a friend of his. For Ethel's part, she had no idea what she'd done. She never did.

Maud took her dinner plate and walked up to the Point. It was a balmy day, fine for a rebuff from Sidney Wiseman and fine for a picnic.

"They were brave, Maud," Ethel agreed. She looked upward, heavenward, toward the picture of Harold and Clyde. "Max, too." It impressed her, to find such fortitude in souls so young.

"And you. Are you brave?"

Ethel shrugged. *I do not ask, O Lord.* She wasn't one to say yes or no to a question like that.

V

M A R I O N

In her cubicle at the boat store Marion lined her books up by her bed. It wasn't much like her old bedroom at Big Tickle. The books fell over every time someone walked by, even when no one entered the opening between the tacked-up sheets. Ron got at her books too, spreading them open like the peaked roofs he'd seen on churches in books. In Little Bay Islands, there was only one church like that. There was the Orange Hall for dances and weddings and the Salvation Army Citadel on the hill – you had to have good legs and a good heart to get up there! – and the United Church and Strong's wharf and mill, which was a whole lot bigger and louder than any church, and besides that there were a lot of men on their wharves and women in their kitchens and babies and kids and not enough room and no privacy whatsoever. When Grace got hold of Marion's books, she left sticky fingerprints on the pages and wedged bread crusts into the spines.

"My darling," Mom told Marion, "we must all make do. The boat store wasn't made for people. Aren't we fortunate that it's here for us at all."

Marion whacked Grace with the *World Book* and made her cry. Anything these days was enough to make Grace cry, and Marion too.

It had been fun watching the stage and the boat store hauled across the ice in March, and then later, when the ice broke, watching the mantles and the fine mouldings of the Tickle house sailed over across the harbour, load by load. A team of men had dragged the boat store over in one piece, with block and tackle run through anchors lodged into the ice every hundred yards or so. Slipping and sliding on the ice, two men would run ahead to move the anchors forward on either side, and then the team would haul the ropes, straining and singing the heaving song that kept them synchronized. *Sing the poker!* The leader would holler. Then, the others:

> *And it's to my jolly poker*
> *We'll haul the heavy bugger*
> *And it's to my jolly poker, hooray!*

That was the thing about working hard; you could still catch your breath and spit, holler, sing, haul the bugger over and over. Now that everything had been moved, would Uncle Harold and Uncle Nelson still row over every day from Big Tickle? Would the uncles still all do their twine together in the Old Man's relocated store, down below what was to be their summer sleeping quarters? The kids hoped so. When other men were around they didn't get hit so much. To live in the boat store for four months over the summer while the new house was built – that was going to be swell. All the kids thought so, and Tom went around saying it: *swell*. Baby Grace mimicked him, and Ron too. *Swell, swell, swell.*

"Shut up, all of you," Sidney said, clamping his teeth down on the stem of his pipe.

Someone needed to shut him up, Marion thought. The Old Man had been roaring through the boat store again, throwing things at the walls. Tonight it had been an enamel basin, and water still stained the wall down to the floor. He'd thrown it, yelled a lot, stamped around until he found himself in front of the double boat doors. He flung

them open and stormed out. Yesterday it had been Tom and Harry
he'd thrown at the wall. In the Tickle house he used to drag them into
the pantry by the hair and thrash them out of sight, but there
was no pantry here. Or he'd get them in the breakfast room under
the Tickle house table, while they scrambled round and round the
pedestal on their knees, trying to get away. How often had she seen
that, her brothers clambering on the floor with their bottoms in the air,
fending off the split their father had grabbed from the kindling box
beside the kitchen stove? It reminded her of the tigers in *Little Black
Sambo*, running faster and faster in their circle around the palm tree,
so fast finally that they melted into a big pool of butter. The kids in
school loved that story, how little Sambo tricked the tigers and gave
them all his clothes. Giving away your clothes was unthinkable in Little
Bay Islands. What an idea. What was Sambo to do come September?
Besides, no one had anything to give away. Only Marion's mother
gave things away. But the kids at school loved the picture of the tiger
in Sambo's pants, and especially the picture of the tiger who wore
Sambo's shoes on his ears.

But not Marion. Sambo and his tigers just made her sad. Little children shouldn't have to run around like tigers. But the pantry had gone
now, and the big table had gone now too along with the whole of the
breakfast room at the Tickle house. Maybe they wouldn't have a
pantry at Campbell's Point at all. Sometimes Marion dreamed about
the old pantry, about pulling open a flour bin only to have her father
spring out. Here in the boat store they had the stove they'd brought
over from the Tickle. Mom cooked their three meals a day on that just
fine. Surely they could get by in the new house without a pantry.
Marion was willing to eat less. She was sure Tom and Harry would
be too. Could they live in the new house without a breakfast room
too, without a table?

"Can't you make him stop?" Marion asked her mother at
bedtime, behind the sheets that formed her room. As the words
left her she wished she could have them back. Why did these things

come out of her mouth at all? "Why did we move, Mommy?" she said next, quickly.

Her mother pulled her on her lap. "Well, Marion, what is it that Reverend Mr. Davis says? *We have walked to and fro the earth and, behold, all the earth sitteth still, and is at rest.*"

Ethel stroked her daughter's head. Why had they moved, really? Where were they bound? The move was a promotion for Marion. At Big Tickle, Aunt Lizzie had had her own room, and Ethel and Sidney had theirs. But grand as the Tickle house was, despite its plaster mouldings and its decorative ceilings, it wasn't the size the new house would be. Tom and Harry had shared at the Tickle house, and Marion had shared with Jack. Officially the room had been Jack's, and anyone staying overnight went in with Jack while Marion camped out in the bathtub in a nest of pillows and quilts. Not that a place like the Wisemans was likely to have many guests. Certainly none of the children's friends stayed. They seldom visited even in the day: they knew to stay away. Once someone who'd come up on the schooner stayed overnight, in Harry's room, and left bedbugs that bit Harry for nights on end. Ethel and Ede tried everything to fumigate the room; they even stood the legs of Harry's bed in buckets of water. "Them bugs'll be drownded, gettin' up and down," said Ede – but they weren't. They were nowhere to be seen, and Harry was still bitten. Finally Ethel and Ede stripped the room down, wallpaper and all, and that was the end of Harry's bites.

The only other visitor they had was one of Sidney's relatives visiting from Long Island. He'd been storm-stayed, and Ethel and Ede lifted Marion from her bed and tucked her in the tub. She'd awakened in the morning to find herself there. How white it had been, the child had told her mother. How quiet and strange, such great softness within such a hard, hard shell. Like sleeping inside one of the coopie's eggs! At Campbell's Point there would be an official Marion's Room. She'd have to share it with Grace, but it would be her room. It was advancement, but the child didn't feel it.

The move was a strain on Ethel too. She was nearly forty-five, and working all the time. First she'd gone into business with Fred and Winnifred Wiseman at their general store. They were distant relations; they all got along famously.

Too famously. Sidney couldn't abide the pleasure his wife took in the partnership and insisted she depart it. He made her tell Winnie and Fred while he stood back. It was her shop, her business. What did he have to do with it, after all?

Later, he passed Fred on the road. "Old girl couldn't get along with you, then?" he said. "Well, I could have. If it'd been me, we could all still be in business. Women!" He tipped his hat.

Ethel tried again, going on to another alliance with Fanny Anstey at the Ensign, a retail outlet Fanny had going but which needed more capital. Ethel felt close to Fanny. Like Ethel's grandfather Robert Goff Wellon, Fanny's grandparents had come to Notre Dame Bay from across the pond in Poole, Dorset. That made the Ansteys blood, practically. *Whither thou goest,* she found herself thinking around Fanny, *I will go . . .* She pictured her grandfather Robert on the rocks beside his lighthouse, the lonely gulls of the Wadhams wheeling and shrieking above his head. She pictured him surrounded by his children, the fourteen of them who had become her aunts and uncles dead and living, in the centre the one who had married Fanny Whiteway and become her own father Tom. *Martha John Robert Tom George Louisa Joseph Elizabeth Charles Sarah Mary Samuel Caroline Toy,* her aunts and uncles and her father. She could recite them as if they were a verse in a song. The heart was a lonely place, but it could fill up with people if you found them and pulled them to you.

Ethel and Fanny worked the Ensign shop in the centre of town, just above the government wharf, until 1935. Morning and night, Ethel wore a track between the shop and Big Tickle. Sometimes she wished she'd come straight out and asked her father for help long before he died, merchant to merchant. But she wasn't the type to put demands or worry on him. *A woman's place is with her husband; a child needs his father.* Would asking for help with a shop look like she wanted to leave again? But she didn't want to leave. Did she? Her father's death had been a final blow to her in so many ways. Now there really was nowhere for her to go, no family she could replace with her own if she had to, nowhere to take the children.

She had a bafflement about it, more than an ambivalence. She was like an animal in a maze, where every turn was the wrong one and the right one both, for it found something out. "Don't go on about it Et, my darling," Thomas used to say to her in Ladle Cove, whenever there had been a problem. "Your way's set. *For we must needs die, and are as water spilt on the ground, which cannot be gathered up again; neither does God respect any person; yet doth he devise means, that his banished be not expelled from him.*"

It had confused her. What was it to be banished, but at the same time held, pinned down?

When her father died he'd left her something, but by that time Sidney had become accustomed to running the show, or at least owning it. When it came to the Ensign, Sidney thought he owned the place and Fanny Anstey too. A flagship it was, the Ensign, and he a flagship owner. He had his flagship schooner, the *James Strong*, but with his own weak lungs, he'd be off that soon enough. He'd have his flagship shop instead.

And so he took that over too, and ended things with Fanny. Proceeds were disappearing from the till overnight, Ethel had confided to him reluctantly. However she and Fanny decided what they'd divide and take home between them, there seemed too little left in the till in the morning compared to what they'd put there the night before. Sidney knew Fanny's type. Damn woman was pilfering it straight from the till when no one was looking, more than likely. Auger in one hand, Ethel's key in the other, he crept into the shop one evening after closing. He bored a hole in the floor over the counter, ran down and brushed the sawdust from the cash register, ran back up and settled in. He was an expert watcher; peepholes were his specialty. It wasn't long before Fanny came in; and there you had it, her hand in the till. He hardly had to watch at all. All he needed to know about that

Anstey woman he knew by instinct. Sidney had good instincts. Everyone said so. He said so.

Ethel couldn't imagine she'd been betrayed. "Maybe Fanny takes it home for safekeeping," she laughed.

"You think that's funny, do you?" Sidney hit her on the cheek with his auger. "You think I can't do math?" He couldn't, not like Ethel who could add up figures in her ledger at fifteen knots. Sidney was bright enough, but his father Frederick had taken him out of school after grade three to crew on the Labrador, and he was jealous of anyone schooled better – his own children, for example. Ethel had a college degree, and while it had charmed him once he didn't want to be reminded of it now. He was a brutal man, but not stupid. Ethel had it all – grace, dignity, education, and a pure and generous heart. She had the love of her neighbours, their awe, their regard and admiration. She had all the things he would have loved to have, and never would. By marrying her he'd thought it he might touch on it; it might settle on him too. But it didn't. It only made him angrier at his lack, and it made him beat her when he was most angry, most jealous, most disappointed. When the children came along, he saw her love for them and was jealous of it too. He hated it. She stopped calling them *my darling, my dear, my own*. She kept her emotions even, quiet. She called them *my children, my child, my son* just as everyone called children, just as children called their elders *aunt* and *uncle* whether they were related or not. It was terrible to flatten her love, but she did it to spare them.

Ethel sat down hard at the table in the breakfast room, her hand pressed to her face, blood streaming down her fingers. She breathed sharply.

He picked up his cap. Off he went to Ansteys'. Fanny met him at the door, holding up an apron full of potatoes. "You think that's funny, do you?" he snarled, thrusting the drill point at her face. She stepped back in alarm, and her potatoes rolled around her feet.

Ethel never knew what else he said to her. Fanny passed on her part of the business, closed up her house above the government wharf and

moved away, leaving Ethel on her own. She opened Ethel Wiseman &
Co. just a stone's throw down the lawn from the new house on
Campbell's Point. Thomas Wellon & Daughter – how she wished it
was named that instead. In winter the shop would be close enough not
to mind the slope of the lawn; with heavy rope they could tie it to the
house. Sidney never did move the billiards table into his new billiards
room at Campbell Point. He had the men carry it straight from the
schooner into the new shop, where it became a fixture in Ethel's ice
cream parlour. The shop was a true emporium, for kids and adults
both – and, most importantly, for Sid's cronies. It sold yard goods,
hardware, flour and staples, smokes, bottles of Orange Crush with
pulp, candy, gum, chocolate bars, ice cream, games of billiards. The
players paid five cents for a game, and Sidney lorded over all.

"Call 'er Ethel Wiseman and Company, abbreviate 'er to 'Co.'
Everyone does that, it's fancy," Sidney told his wife. But he couldn't
force her to. Her shop was the one thing about her he couldn't regu-
late. He didn't have the schooling or the aptitude to manage a business
like that. He knew it, and he hung back. All he could do was bully.
He swaggered around the new store when it opened, holding court,
deciding who was to get credit and who was not. Ethel was ever solicitous toward her husband. He'd been sick, after all. Might he need
something to do now that his skippering days were through? Might
he need to feel needed? Would he like to help her out, she asked, bit
by bit as he felt able? But he submitted to only a minimum of say from
her about how to do things, and he wouldn't have his name on
the business whether she offered to put it on or not. She didn't – but
he wouldn't have, regardless. That's what he told himself. Who was
Sidney Wiseman, to be a mere shopkeeper? He was still a skipper with
his own schooner, any day now he'd be back to the Labrador or he
wouldn't, it was his damn choice. He was Skipper Sid Wiseman. He'd
made something of himself, after all. His wife was just the damn shopkeeper. He used her precious cake knife from the Royal Stores to cut
the twenty-pound rounds of cheese.

Fan An, Fan An, the children chided when Fanny Anstey's name
came up. It seemed the worst insult in the world, specially constructed
for the woman who'd betrayed their mother.

"You shouldn't be talking about a grown woman like that," Ethel
scolded. She put the big pot of oatmeal on the back of the stove where
it would soak until morning and then be moved up front. She'd set out
Sidney's breakfast of smoked capelin for the morning too – Sidney had
to have a meal every meal, as he put it, none of this gruel for him. A
scoff or nothing, that was how it was to be. What, did she want him to
go hungry? She scrubbed the fish from her fingers and sat, her hands
flaming as they always did when she'd had them in hot water. She
sounded firm enough, but tired. Wistful. "You shouldn't talk about an
adult like that. Nicknames are for children. Aunt Fanny was an adult.
She was my –" *Whither thou goest.* She turned one of Tom's dominoes
in front of her on the table. Ethel had never been betrayed before,
except by Sidney, and somehow what you got used to felt different.
Fanny, oh, Fanny. Alex Anstey, Fanny's uncle, had saved Jack by taking
him to hospital in Twillingate when Sidney had refused. It was all such
a shame. Years later she wrote a little ditty in Grace's autograph book:
Love many, trust few. Always paddle your own canoe. She'd still been
thinking of Fanny, she supposed. Grace had thrust the book in her
hand, and that's what Ethel came up with. For a long time all Marion
had in her book was her friend Net Penney's autograph, over and over
– Net was going to be a tennis star, after all, and Marion thought her
signature would be valuable one day. Marion also had the signature of
one of the pursers on the *Clyde. Hope you will come to see about
freight often* – he'd written that when she'd gone down to pick up a
parcel for Ethel that had come in, and he'd seen her book. He'd been
in his uniform, looking smart; his, too, had seemed to Marion a good
signature to have. Ethel wrote in her own note then too:

> *We live in deeds, not years, in thoughts, not breaths,*
> *In feelings, not in figures on a dial;*
> *We should count time by heart throbs.*

> *She lives most who thinks most,*
> *Feels the noblest, acts the best.*

Ethel forgave Fanny, but she didn't tell Sidney. To forgive much is to love much, Ethel believed. She supposed she could have written that in one of her girls' books too.

"Mrs. Anstey is an adult," Ethel said to her children. She turned the domino back again and laid her hands in her lap.

~

"Why didn't you marry Bert Strong, Mom?" Marion asked next.

The move to Campbell's Point had brought them closer to Strong's, at the other end of the horseshoe of islands. It was a horseshoe, after all. Maybe now, finally, they'd get lucky. Maybe Mom could still marry Bert. Maybe the Old Man could go back on the schooner again and get lost at sea. He could go back to the Labrador and drown and Mom could marry Bert Strong. Bert had proposed to her many times, long ago, and he still hadn't married.

Bert Strong carried a torch for Mom. Marion knew it. It was obvious. Anyone could see it. Why couldn't her mother see it?

Like all the Strongs, Bert was rich, and he had education and breeding too. The Strongs had a tennis court. Bert had built it himself, painstakingly moving a hill of earth by wheelbarrow to level the ground. They called him the Man Who Moved Mountains. He invited all the kids to play there, and they all did, on its worn-down grass. Bert supplied racquets and balls. Marion was only as good as anyone but her friend Netta Penney was ace, born to the game. Bert loved to play with Net, but he didn't favour her. He wasn't like that, and everyone had a turn. Bert was a football star too. He could do anything. Marion liked him. Bert had personally awarded her the cookie jar that would sit on the mantle of the new breakfast room at Campbell's Point. Though its lid had been lost, Mom could not have displayed it better and with more pride had it come from the Olympics. Marion had won it for the hundred-yard dash on Sports Day, last May 24, at the games Bert had set up for everyone around the Bay. The jar had a smashing wicker handle, but without its lid it seemed to Marion second-rate. "It doesn't matter what it is," said Mom. "You won it." And she had. She'd bested even Dot Wiseman, who won everything, and though it was the busiest day of the year for the shop, Mom had run over to see Marion's race. Mom beamed, Bert Strong beamed, Marion thought she'd swoon with delight. On his tennis court Bert Strong had shown her forehand and backhand, chopping the air in little pretend swipes. The only time he had spoken to her sharply he'd been right to be sharp. "Don't lean on your racquet," he'd said, finding her slouched on it, watching a doubles game. "You'll ruin it and it won't work for you then."

Bert looked after the Strongs; he was so capable, so caring. *Let us hear from you:* he'd wired that, just that, to his younger brother Norman in St. John's when the war started, before Norman shipped out. After Bert's little nudge, Norman wrote regularly; he wrote from Stob's Camp as soon as the regiment landed in Ayr. Norman had been killed anyway, a lance corporal in the July Drive, but as far as Marion could see, that was the way things went with wars, and with Newfoundland in general, and at least because of Bert he'd kept in touch.

The Strongs knew what worked. They knew everything and had more. They sent their kids away to boarding school in St. John's and then on to Methodist College. Afterward, the kids came back to work in the family businesses. One of the Strongs, Helena, was way older than Mom – by three years anyway – and not nearly so pretty, but she'd married the Newfoundland prime minister Sir Richard Squires and become the first woman to enter Newfoundland politics. Helena was a grand lady. She'd set up a teacher's college in St. John's, and the hospital for mothers where Marion was going to be a nurse. Sir Richard had even had one of the coastal boats named after him. Sure, Lady Squires, Helena, had run into a little trouble a while ago, when she and Sir Richard had been trapped in the House of Assembly by rioters. But it was *him* the rioters hadn't liked, not her. She'd held her

ground and only left the House when Sir Richard made her. Greatness
was like that, Marion thought – and men could ruin it.

Helena had married the prime minister. If Mom had married Bert
Strong, might Mom be queen now? Marion imagined them in a horse
and carriage. Tom and Harry wouldn't want to sit inside; they could
be footmen, Jack could sit up front and hold the reins and the whip,
and the horses would be palominos and have their tails braided, and
Bert himself would hand Marion his crown to hold while he ran ahead
with a football –

"I didn't love him, Marion." The fantasy exploded like something
out of the boys' twelve-gauges, trailing down cinders on ragged
plumes of smoke.

"Well, he loves you."

"Marion. We all love each other."

"I don't love my father."

Behind her sheets, she laid her head back on the pillow her mother
had plumped. She listened to the wind, the waves in the harbour, the
sound of her father returning. She tried to stay awake for that, in case
he hit Mom and she needed her, but she fell asleep instead. She
dreamed that Bert Strong threw a valentine in a football pass onto
her mother's new porch at Campbell's Point, the porch he had floated
over to Campbell's Point on his new schooner, the *Lady Ethel*. Now
he stamped twice on the porch to let them know, and ran away into
the bushes down the hill to wait and watch, laughing.

~

Below the Tickle house, Back Beach had been rugged, tossed around
and chewed up and windy as the day was long. The Wiseman children had spent a lot of time there, especially that summer the Old Man
had confined Jack and Ron to the beach straight through July and
August for stealing peppermints from the pantry.

"Sidney," Ethel said, "the boys can't stay there. They're too small.
They'll have no one to watch over them. They'll have no food."

"They got their mints. Send Marion there too." Just like that, Marion was banished to the beach as well, but any day the Old Man would be off to the Labrador, and Mom would rescue them all. Jack and Ron were tiny, scared by the roar of the wind and the waves. They cried to go home until Marion sneaked up and brought them back picnics, books from the bookcase too. She read to them while they ate, about Napoleon and his exile to Elba. Napoleon had fought a war for liberty, she reminded her little brothers. For *Liberté, Egalité, Fraternité* – or was that someone else? She wasn't sure. At Elba Napoleon had borne up under his jailer, she *was* sure of that. So bear up, she told them. God had kept the French safe. Mom had said so herself, the time Marion had found that old balloon thrown on the ground by the root cellar and brought it in, started to blow it up. Mom had taken it from her; Mom and Ede had exchanged a look.

You found it where? Mom said.

God, Ede had said, turning away to the sink. Himself. Himself's root cellar.

A French safe, said Mom.

Napoleon had kept the French safe, or God had, something like that, Marion told her brothers on the beach, marching them around like *les soldats* in training.

> *Good, better, best*
> *May you never rest*
> *Till your good is better*
> *And your better best.*

Campbell's Point wasn't like Back Beach. It was tame in comparison, at the centre of town and a hive of activity. Skipper Sid's fish stage and boat store and wharf and privy all were now within a stone's throw of the government wharf. Skipper Sid couldn't exile you to anywhere at Campbell's Point, except to your room. The new house rose up grandly in the midst of all the stages and boat stores and smaller homes around it. A big white pearl, it seemed to be the focus of the town, with Strong's now tossed off at the end of the path toward Mack's Island;

and it was where the Norseman headed and where its two pilots, handsome in their leather, and the young government fellow, handsome enough himself in his suit, got out and climbed up. The seaplane had landed in the North Atlantic just beyond Big Tickle and then taxied through, droning its way on chunky pontoons right around Harbour Rock and across the water to the Wisemans' wharf, where people gathered to watch. It had ignored the government wharf and zeroed in on Campbell's Point. The propeller stuttered and stopped, after all that ruckus suddenly charging the harbour with silence. Then a murmur broke out in the crowd, and swelled. People pressed forward. There'd seldom been so much excitement. Three men, foreigners, dropping out of the sky to have a look at the Little Bay Islanders' small piece of heaven. Everyone ran to see.

The men who got out of the plane talked flat, as if someone had pulled the good out of their voices. "We just had to land," they said. "It looked so beautiful from the air."

Americans, someone said from the back of the crowd.

"You got lobsters in these parts?"

Did they have lobster? Little Bay Islands teemed with cod, salmon, herring, lobster, crab, seals. At the turn of the century, waste lobster, tossed into the twelve-foot depths of the harbour where it edged the cannery, hilled up above the surface. Decades before that, the daughters of George Jones, one of Little Bay Islands' first settlers, gaffed enough to feed the family's three pigs.

"'Course we have lobsters. We're not the capital for nothing." For Harry Wiseman, Little Bay Islands was always the capital. Everything else could revolve around it as it liked. None of this *sin-Jawns, sin-Jawns* for him. He fetched the gaff from the wharf. Who wanted lobsters? Harry and his pals would rather a baloney sandwich. Eating lobsters meant you were poor. Lobsters were practically the Dole diet. The flyers were welcome to them; good riddance. You could get lobsters from anywhere along the shore, just with a gaff, and Harry and his friends climbed down the wharf and set to work. The girls lined up to have

their pictures taken with the men in the leather jackets. They all loved
to get a snap of themselves at the side of something a bit different. Last
winter Marion had walked out on the winter ice on the harbour for a
snap of herself in front of one of the schooners seized by the ice in
November, before it could dock at Strong's. But now she didn't race for
a picture. She stood back and studied the plane. Imagine, an aeroplane
that could float, a plane on overblown water skis. In another ten years
they'd be common throughout Newfoundland as mail planes, but now –

"It's a Norseman," the pilots were saying. "Made over in Canada
there, in Kwee-bec. She's a ten-seater." Oohs and aahs at that.

"You got enough lobster to fill ten seats?" Laughter at that.

The pilots disappeared into the crowd. Marion studied the young
government man in the suit. He'd been quiet, serious, smaller than
the other two; hardly more than a boy, with his hair parted down the
middle and waved back long over his ears. Nod, that's who he was,
and the other two, Wynken and Blynken. Mom used to sing it to her.
The old moon laughed – Mom would laugh there – *and sang a song,*

> *As they rocked in the wooden shoe,*
> *And the wind that sped them all night long*
> *Ruffled the waves of dew.*
> *The little stars were the herring fish*
> *That lived in the beautiful sea –*
> *"Now cast your nets wherever you wish –*
> *Never afeared are we";*
> *So cried the stars to the fishermen three:*
> *Wynken,*
> *Blynken,*
> *And Nod.*

Mr. Nod looked pale; maybe he knew that in this part of the world,
on the water, at least, it wasn't quite true, *never afeared are we.*
Marion was always afeared on water. Even on her father's schooner
at Uncle Harold's, she expected to take a false step every next
moment, and tumble down the hold. Split her head open, for sure.
People were always splitting their heads open, especially kids. Why

not her? The thought left her perpetually uneasy. Perhaps wan Mr. Nod felt that way as well. He was slight, small. He'd hardly take up a single one of the Norseman's seats. He blinked in the glare reflecting off the water. Marion was going to be a nurse; pallor concerned her. Did Mr. Nod have weak lungs too? They didn't get enough light in the government; not enough fresh air, either.

Wynken and Blynken packed their lobster in the plane. They saluted soberly, winking at the girls; Nod studied a clipboard. The pilot seemed to find it hard to squat on his pontoon to scull the plane away from the wharf with an oar. It had a lot of extra weight in the back now: flying lobsters, someone said. The plane pushed away. It taxied back out through Big Tickle, past Back Beach, without a second look.

~

Marion stared out her window of the boat store at Campbell's Point. A plane would never go to Back Beach. Wynken, Blynken, and Nod would never launch their wooden shoe from a place like that. They'd never sail on their river of crystal light there, into their sea of dew. The ragged stretch of sand and rock had a different kind of magic, a drama all its own. At Back Beach the sea boiled in the wind. Harry still talked about how the green punt was torn from its painter, flung right off the shore, and how Marion's pink sun hat blew off her head and far out into the water all on the same day. It was her new Easter hat. Marion always got a new hat at Easter and just as well, the way she was always losing them. Sometimes Marion thought of her hat, imagining a new life for it set on the seat of the punt, pink on green, as if some lady had taken it off for a moment to tidy her hair and fan her face. It made her feel lonely. If her hat ever wanted to come home, how could it find her now, all the way over here at the centre of town? She missed looking out at Goat Island, the rocky little landmark just out from Back Beach where they used to say the punt had gone to live since it had never been found. Their father blamed them for its loss, but he was like that. Everyone knew it had gone away all on its own, and Marion knew that while her hat might miss her, the punt, at least, would never want a way back. At six, she'd been in the habit of gathering Jack and Ron and Grace on the beach to look at them gravely and discuss escape. Grace would plunk her bottom in the sand and muck about, smearing her grainy hands in her mouth. She spit then, like old Uncle Edgar eating his turr and spraying buckshot with every bite. A good thing Grace did that there, on Back Beach out of sight. The Old Man couldn't abide spitting, but still he might have left Grace alone. He seemed to have run out of steam around her. She wore her babyhood like a suit of golden armour, and though it had never worked for the others, the Old Man ignored her.

"The green punt went off to a new home," Marion would say to her brothers while Grace ate sand. "It needed to get away from the Old Man. The green punt has new owners to row around now. It likes them."

"What owners?" That would be Ron. He'd been small then.

Marion thought about it. "Goats," she said. She'd been small then too.

"They won't paint it, will they?" Jack asked. Jack liked things to stay the same. Marion couldn't fathom it.

Campbell's Point didn't promise anything as grand as a Back Beach, seaplanes or not, nor anything as redemptive as Goat Island. When the boys built bonfires at Back Beach they roared in the wind and the flames were sucked away, churning, into the air. They leaned in the direction of Goat Island, and Marion fancied she and Jack and Ron and Grace and Harry and Tom might all make a break for it, fetch Mom and hide out on the island for the rest of their lives. When the Old Man was away they could row over to the beach and walk up to the house to get food. When she was six, she'd had it all figured out. Back Beach had been close enough to the Tickle house to get down to it every day in summer. It was where the first of Aunt Lizzie and Grandfather Fred's Tickle houses had been when they came up from Sulian's Cove with Uncle Nelson and Uncle Harold and Skipper

Sid. Her uncles and her father had all been children then, like Marion and her brothers were now. You could still see the ruins of the first Tickle house's old stone cellar at the rear of the beach. Maybe Uncle Harold was even a baby then, in that old house, and had baby curls like Grace had now. Marion tried to imagine Uncle Harold eating sand. Had he ever been hit, or had he worn a baby suit of armour as well?

Uncle Harold seemed happy. Marion would never be that happy. Tom and Harry neither. Jack might. He had that smile. He had a way of throwing things off. It was forgiveness, Mom said, like in the Bible. To forgive much, she said, is to love much.

Uncle Harold was younger than Uncle Nelson; Marion knew that. Unimaginable, but there it was: that burly Uncle Harold was a baby once, and that he was younger than Uncle Nelson, or younger than anyone at all.

Marion tried to imagine Uncle Nelson eating sand. Nothing came to her; nothing at all.

Marion couldn't account for Uncle Nelson. He couldn't ever have been a baby. A foundling, perhaps, one the fairies judged too grumpy and abandoned. Uncle Nelson seemed sullen, sick, his eyes cast already on the next world and missing all of this one, and with a wife nothing at all like dear Aunt Janet. Uncle Nelson's wife was Aunt Ann. She had dark skin and chiselled features and stood altogether too tall for Little Bay Islands. She usually wore black; she was striking and stylish. Though she said she was from Trinity, Marion wondered if really she hadn't come up from Sulian's Cove as well. That was the tiny place over top of the hill on the other side of Little Bay Islands. It had started out as Suley Ann's Cove. Suley Ann was said to be the first settler here, a Micmac. Maybe Aunt Ann was a descendant of Suley Ann. The kids called her a witch, a hard-looking whore in whore's clothes Uncle Nelson must have picked up off the streets of St. John's in a windstorm. Uncle Harold's boys, Dek and Lloyd, knew words like *whore; hoo-er,* they said, *hoo-er's clothes.* Whenever they played near Uncle Nelson's house, just next to Uncle Harold's back at Big Tickle, Aunt

Ann came out with a witchy shriek and chased them away. Mom was kind to Aunt Ann, all the kinder because she seemed an outsider, and reprimanded anyone who spoke against her.

At Sulian's Cove and then later at the first Tickle house there would also have been all the uncles that Marion never knew – Uncle Plinny with the shrimp eyes, Uncle Good and Uncle Ray with their ticket straight to hell on Grandfather Fred's last schooner. The Drownded Uncles, the children called them.

"Drowned," Marion corrected. Marion was forever improving anyone who would be improved.

"The Drownded Uncles of Skipper Sid," the kids would say anyway.

"The Drownded Brothers of Skipper Sid," Marion would correct them again. Drowned, she meant, not drownded. They were mixing her up. What was it about Uncle Good? She liked his name. What had she heard, now? Something about Mom and Uncle Good. She didn't ask Mom. Somehow it didn't seem like something she should bring up. There were things you didn't mention if the Old Man was around. You got a sense of what you shouldn't say, without ever knowing why. And anyway, you never knew when the Old Man was around, so it was often best to say nothing at all. *Keep your own counsel* – that's how Mom put it. The Old Man might appear to be nowhere in sight, but he had a dreadful way of popping up and stopping your heart in fright.

Once she'd sidled up to Uncle Harold. She loved being around Uncle Harold; he was like a big warm bear. "Uncle Harold," she said, "what was it about Mom and Uncle Good?"

Uncle Harold looked at her, reached over to rub her head until her hair got sparky and stood on end and made them both laugh. "Nothing, my darling," he said. "We all loved ol' Good. I'll go bail for that."

"Hey," the boys would say. "Why didn't the Old Man get drownded too? Everybody knows a proper skipper goes down with his ship."

"He ain't a proper skipper." That was Harry.

"*Isn't*," Marion would say. "He *isn't* a proper skipper."

The Wiseman children excelled in school. They had one teacher there and another at home. Little Bay Islanders spoke the King's English, never mind what you heard in some other places, and the Wisemans spoke almost as regally as Mom, who spoke even better English than the King himself. Marion was sure of that – Mom out-kinged the King in every way. Mom would be just the person to sit in Bert Strong's horse and carriage wearing a crown and an ermine stole and holding a sceptre, whatever that was. Mom went over the business of aitches with them. They would never be dropped in the Wiseman household, though now and then aitches went their own way in town. The Wiseman household was a model of learning. Tom and Marion led their classes at school, what with all the studying they got in at home. They weren't allowed to talk at the supper table, not with the Old Man lying back on the daybed, watching. He didn't eat with them. Ethel put Sidney's supper on a plate in the warming oven, and there it sat while he lay back on the bed, shading his eyes and inspecting the family from behind his hand. "No thumping, Ethel," he'd bark at her before and after. He never spoke to the children directly, and during meals he never spoke to anyone at all. "Tell them not to bump the table. Tell them to be careful with the chairs. Tell them to be quiet." Under their father's surveillance the dinner table was a conversational wasteland, but beneath it, the world of knowledge thrived. Tom and Marion read books in their laps while they ate. They learned the flag of every country, every capital and principal industry, the biggest rivers and the highest mountains. They memorized the periodic table of elements; the planets and their moons.

"Io, Europa, Ganymede, Callisto." Tom would rattle off Jupiter's moons, but only when the Old Man wasn't there. That was the only time you talked; that was certainly the only time you showed off. "Galileo, 1610, thirty-magnification spyglass."

"New moon Barnard, 1892, Lick thirty-six-inch reflecting telescope," Jack would add. "New moon Perrine, 1904, new moon Perrine, 1905, same telescope." Jack did well in school too. Mr. Burden, the grade-six-to-eleven teacher, said Jack should be a lawyer, the way Jack tried to trip him up with questions. The kids hung on Mr. Burden's every word. He was elegant, eloquent. He was *H. T. Burden* – that's how they spoke of him, reverently. One year he wrote an introduction to the high school's historical review which Marion worked on. "I propose in this article," Mr. Burden wrote,

> to give you a mere outline of the History of our early set-
> tlement. The nature of the subject itself makes it apparent
> that it must be a bare outline, as we are dealing with people
> who were pioneers and the Biography of every one of them
> would fill a large book if their life stories were known; such
> men as Philip Wiseman, John Campbell, William Anstey,
> William Strong, George Jones, and a host of others. Perhaps
> some day one of their descendants will write the life story
> of their ancestor and what fine reading it will make, and it
> will not be a mere catalogue of facts as this article must of
> necessity be.

They all wanted to write like that, to think like that, to be like Mr. Burden, all except Harry. Well, there had been Alvin Weir too. Alvin had downright hated school. He was always disappearing. Alvin liked working with his hands. When he asked Mr. Burden if he could shelve his books beside his desk, Mr. Burden agreed; anything to keep Alvin in school. They all watched Alvin bring in his dad's hammer and nails, his bucksaw and some planks, watched Alvin saw and hammer and hang himself a small bookshelf on the schoolroom wall, next to his desk. There Alvin's books sat – but not for long. One day Alvin flew from his seat again. No one ever knew what it was that finally set him off. The lower grades had been doing figures, and the others had been reading about Mary, Queen of Scots. How could anyone object to Mary, Queen of Scots? Unless you were Lord Darnley or Queen Elizabeth, that is. "That's it! That's it!" Alvin cried regardless, leaping to his feet. "I ain't never coming back!" He tore down his bookshelf with his bare hands. The nails yawed from the plaster. Alvin's books went every which way, and his schoolmates never saw him again.

Harry wasn't like that at all. He could do well in school, but he didn't care to; his heart was out in the wide open spaces.

"Melotte, 1908, Greenwich thirty-inch." That was Tom.

"Nicholson, 1914, the Lick again." That was Jack.

"Harry, 1925, Little Bay Islands, sixty-inch about now, a hunn'rt pounds soaking wet." That was Harry, beaming.

~

Through the boat store windows overlooking their new lawn, Marion mourned the Tickle house and Goat Island and Back Beach and her pink sun hat and the exodus from Sulian's to the house that produced the Drownded Uncles. The Campbell's Point breeze riffled the sheets that hung around the bed, her own private compartment. She had privacy because she was the girl. Grace didn't need anything much; she was only three and cried anywhere at all, and when she wasn't crying she got into things. That was why Marion needed her own compartment, to keep out the likes of, well, *everyone*. Mom agreed, and tacked up extra sheets for her, and a few curtains too, to spruce things up.

Mom had spruced up Ede's compartment too. On the far side of her parents' compartment, Ede's had curtains hung like Marion's, between gaps in the sheets. Ede had come to them five years ago on the heels of that winter coat Mom had given her and she wasn't leaving now, move or not. Mom thought Ede should have her own place in the boat store, and that things should be as pretty for her as they could be for anyone else. Mom never called her a maid; she called her Ede, by name, same as anyone called the girls that came to them as help. But not everyone's girls got curtains, Marion knew that. And the boys got nothing, and liked it. The boys didn't want curtains. They had to share together in one long side of the boat store, their arrangements like a dorm partitioned from the rest by a single line of blankets. Ede's compartment was lovely, Marion thought, like Ede herself. Ede's parents lived behind the new place and up the hill a bit, and Ede would be able to see them more often now. Ede had come from lots of brothers and sisters herself – Nina, Margaret, Ralph, Evelyn. She'd come to help Mom when she was only fourteen. Why was that? Marion wondered. To get away from them all? Marion looked at Grace's toffee thumbprint on her good hairbrush, the one with the silver-plated back. Yes, Ede would know what it was like to be in a family like Marion's. Always someone getting on your nerves. Except that Ede's father, Uncle Timothy, was nice, not like the Old Man, and Marion couldn't imagine Uncle Timothy thrashing Ede or Nine or little Evelyn, not like her father thrashed her.

Next to Marion's compartment was her parents', and while being that close to Mom at night made her happy at first, the proximity to the Old Man held terrors nightly. After a day or two she drew her bed away from their side of the space. She hoped Mom wouldn't hear, or, if she did hear, would understand. No one wanted to be close to the Old Man anymore. No one except Mom herself, who assured them she loved their father and would always love him and was standing by him and always would.

No one understood it. Tom thought it had something to do with marriage vows, though Mom said it did and it didn't. "Your father has his faults," she'd say. "You have your faults too. There are good things about your father. He's –"

"A divider," Jack would chime in. "Like these sheets we got here in the boat store to keep us apart."

"A *pro*vider, my darling, yes." She ruffled his hair, still thin after six years as if it, too, hadn't decided whether to stay or to go in a place like this.

This was a summer of mixed blessings; in order to move them to Campbell's Point, their father had stayed home from the Labrador. As skipper, he'd take his cut from the catch the *James Strong* brought in, but he'd sit the voyage out – and be in their hair all year this year, instead of only half of it. They liked it when the Old Man was gone;

they loved it – except for the heartache and anxiety it caused Mom, when they heard about storms up the coast and had no message from the *Strong*. *Don't expect me till I come.* So many of the telegrams people sent to and from the outports said that sort of thing, travelling and schedules were so uncertain. But one summer the *Strong* sent no message at all. She'd been known to be on her way back down, and Randolph Crowell had been trying for days to raise her on the wireless. The weather had soured, but for some reason the vessel wasn't putting in at any of the sheltered harbours. When Mom was troubled, the children were too; and Mom had sure been troubled then. But she'd get over it, they just knew it. If the *James Strong* was lost or just never wired home, Mom would get over it eventually.

And marry Bert Strong.

Then Mr. Crowell came up the lawn again. Mr. Crowell was forever coming up the lawn, and half the time your heart stopped. The telegram had finally come; the *James Strong* had finally *put in Hopedale. All well.*

Oh well.

The Wisemans were a family this once; in this strange place, of all places, this makeshift box of sheeted rooms in the boat store. It was the first and last time they worked together, and there was something to it that was wonderful. In the middle of the night a gale down the harbour blew in the wide door that opened into the second floor of the store. There were double doors downstairs, at the end of the building where the boats were pulled in, and upstairs for direct loading in from the wharf there was a second wide door as well, with its own flight of stairs from the outside. That was the door that blew. In the pitch black like that, tossing them from their dreams, it sounded like the store itself was coming down. Their father came tearing in from his compartment, Mom on his heels in her nightdress. The sheets around the children's compartments blew in on them, snapping at their faces, knocking down the furniture they'd brought from the Tickle, tossing books and papers around, smacking the lot of it against the far wall. They all jumped out of bed, Ede too, and pushed against the door, trying to hold it back while their father ran for long nails and a hammer. No one could see, and Harry thumped Marion in the head while Tom stepped on Ron. It was bedlam. The wind drove at them like a wild thing. It took everyone to close the door, Mom on top of Ede on top of the kids, and then finally their father to bear in on the lot of them in order to squeeze the gap shut and hammer the nails. Next morning, they went out the side door and saw what the gale had done. A boom by Strong's wharf had broken apart; logs strewed the harbour. Already, there'd been much repair. Jim Strong had been out at dawn lashing them together. By morning most of the men had their oilskins on and their punts out, assisting the retrieval.

"Will you look at that," Sidney said, and together they looked, and were a family.

Two days it took for the boom to be rebuilt. Two days while the boats in the harbour still bounced in a stiff wind. It was like Jim Strong to be early, to be first almost before he could see. Years later they would find him fallen over his komatik on the ice, bringing home a load of wood. Jim Strong hardly needed to fetch his own wood, but he did, and he died with his dogs around him and with his boots on. He'd have wanted nothing more, nothing less, his wife, Marge, said. She'd been a Drover from St. John's. Jim had been an adventurer, a go-getter. Hadn't he gone down to find her all the way t'other end of the country, hadn't he just?

During the repairs to their own boat store, Sidney Wiseman had seemed to his children to have had a little of Jim Strong in him. "Good job," he'd called to them when they held the doors shut while he hammered in the dark. "Good job." Two or three days and the glow of it bathed them. But it was gone by the time the gale blew out, and they never saw it again.

On the other side of her compartment was a window, and Marion drew close to it to gaze out. Back Beach was so far away now, way out there at the end of things by Big Tickle. It took her breath away still, to see the schooners sail through the Tickle into the placid oval of the harbour, to do their business from all around the world. *I see London, I see France*. One chilly morning she breathed a wet spot on the pane and polished it off with her sleeve. *Sailor.* The thought came to her suddenly, that Sailor's wet black sloppy nose had pressed against this very window on the last night of his life, looking for a way out. The boat store and all her father's precious windows had been skated over on the ice, and now it seemed that Sailor's ghost had come with them, trailing his ruined tail in the snow.

"Don't think of it, my darling," that's what Mom would say. "Sailor's looking down on us now, even on your father. Sailor would want you to look out his window, Marion, in his place. I think he would. Now, Marion, that that dieth, let it die."

But Marion couldn't look out Sailor's window again even if Mom said so, and she pulled her bed away from that side of the space as well. Back and forth she paced, between the sheets at either side of her little makeshift room. Back and forth, back and forth, like a wind-up toy.

"Back Beach," she whispered to Sailor's ghost. "Go on to Back Beach now, Sailor. My sun hat's there. And the green punt. Go to Goat Island, you'll be happy there."

~

Sidney had an ice house built for Ethel at the end of the lot at Campbell's Point, not because she'd asked for it so many times, but because with an ice house Wiseman's would be the talk of the town. Never mind he had to cut down that white birch after all. Spare that tree now, my darling, Ethel had implored him, and all her yammering made him realize that was just the spot he needed, never mind the damn tree. Never mind she had to have an ice house for the shop; it would be his, and she could use it. He had an ice house! No one else had an ice house, not even Strong's. All Strong's had was a few boats and then the damn nattering mill, shrieking and clattering and rousting everyone from their beds at all hours every morning. And that damn rabbit factory over in South Brook on the mainland, the new plant that packed rabbit and sent it over. It wasn't here, though, not directly, so as far as Sid was concerned Strong's rabbits didn't count. The tennis court, though. What could have been in Hubert Strong's head to move his mountain out of the way by the wheelbarrowful, in order to put in a tennis court, and then let everybody's kids use it? Sidney could barely abide Tom and Marion going over for these doubles, as they called them, or for rounders in the field above, no doubt when they had chores waiting, but at least it got them out of his hair and made his house his own. The Strongs were demented, that's all. Or else showing off. Jim Strong might have beat him to getting in that generator for power, but Sidney Wiseman had been the first to get his Aladdin lamps in, to replace the oil lamps. Ethel had ordered them. People had better remember that, that Sidney Wiseman got there first. It was Sidney Wiseman's children, not Jim Strong's, who knew better than to break the mantles on the Aladdins. They were thin and fine as tissue paper and cost half as much as the lamps themselves, and the girl Marion had had the lecture about cleaning the chimneys Saturday mornings, since her hand was smaller than Ede's or Ethel's.

Sidney loved his lamps. The mantles glowed white. Their chimneys didn't smoke up like the chimneys of the oil lamps. The Aladdins hung on wall brackets during daylight, but come evening you took them from room to room as you went, and Ethel set one in the middle of the breakfast room table to cast its glow on the circle of students at their homework. There were still the old oil lamps in every bedroom – Sid could only get his prizes in so fast on the *Clyde* – and Marion still yammered about the time hers fell over in the night, filling her room with a fearful smell and her dreams with fearful dread. What a scaredy cat the child was! But feral, too. The way she hissed at him, or stared at him at least. Well, maybe she only stared at him, but give her time and no doubt she'd be hissing, he could see it coming. For now, she just tried to stare him down. A savage, that child; a brazen hussy. Couldn't even sleep quiet enough to leave her lamp on its bureau, probably knocked it off by thrashing around in the night. Sid

hated disruption. Why the hell couldn't everybody just be quiet? But
for a while after the Aladdin lamps arrived it didn't bother him when
the kids were noisy with their books, turning pages harder than they
needed to, whispering among themselves, scraping their chairs on the
floor or bumping them into the table legs. The girl Marion rattling
perfectly good paper to fold into her foolish birds or stars or boats.
Normally he'd thump them for that, disturbing his evening and his
Times, but for their first few days in residence the Aladdin lamps cast
a glow of forgiveness. Wasn't there something in the Bible about
lamps? Didn't a good lamp make you a great guy, God's own, a mighty
man of valour? He might ask Ethel, she'd know about anything in the
Bible or in any book at all, but asking her meant he needed something
and was without it on his own.

Yessir, it was progress; you were up in the world if you had an
Aladdin lamp. And now, saints preserve us, Sidney Wiseman had
an ice house. It set him apart. Skipper Sid wouldn't charge anyone
come by wanting a bit of his ice. Not any more than Hubert Strong
locked up his tennis court. No sir, he'd give his ice away so's they could
tell their friends, talk about Sid Wiseman and his ice house all the way
to St. John's. In January when the harbour froze solid enough he had
the men chop out a load of blocks, two-by-twos and three-by-threes,
hauling them up the shore and burying them in the ice house in
sawdust from Strong's mill. With care they'd last all summer long.

The building had a hinged door on its roof that opened up. When
Sid climbed his ladder to the roof he was on top of the world. It was
so perfect up there – a perfect building at the end of a perfect yard,
full of perfect blocks of ice. Atop Sid's ice house, the vantage from
Campbell's Point was unparalleled. Only Pole Hill, where the tele-
graph pole stood, gave you a better view. The wireless nattered on
about that mountain in India, about that Leigh-Mallory chap from
England who died a few years before, trying to get up some damn
heathen heap of rock. Climbing that damn rock, it was all the rage. It
was in the *Times*. *Well, my lads, Everest or no they never saw rock*

like we got here in Newfoundland. We knows our rocks. Come on up, Mr. Mallory, Sidney would taunt him from his roost atop the ice house. *C'mon up, I'll give ye a hand. Mind yer manicure.*

"There's favour in hell if you brings yer splits," Sid's cronies said about the ice house behind his back, drinking his beer to his face. Sid didn't care. Most times, he didn't hear them. The old dog for a hard road, that was Sid.

Ethel wanted the ice house for ice cream. She wanted the white birch too, but that was the way it was with Sidney. Things came in ways you didn't want, things went that didn't need to. You kept walking toward the Lord, your loved ones at your side. You didn't ask. *But it shall be one day which shall be known to the Lord, not day, nor night: but it shall come to pass, that at evening time it shall be light.* At her store Ethel opened an ice cream parlour, stacking the biscuit boxes in the back and clearing a space of floor. The *Clyde* brought her in three glass-topped round tables with curlicued wrought-iron legs, and chairs with scrollbacks to match. She got a bolt of red-and-white checked cotton and hemmed up three tablecloths. She'd never make any money at it – that wasn't the point. She had the idea when Ethel Gates's little girl died of consumption and John, Et's husband, had come in to buy flour and twine. The Gates's little one had died of consumption of the bones, as little ones often did. Maybe they didn't breathe enough in to get it in the lungs, like the adults. They got it in their joints and skin, their nerves, and from there it went up into their brains.

"Twine's not for to hang 'erself," John said, "but might as well be. She's cold and dark, is Et. Nothing to look forward to."

"It's the depression, then, isn't it, John?" someone said.

"Yeah, b'y. The depression."

It was like Nellie Rendell, Ethel thought. Nellie, who'd been so shocked and sad for the longest time when Charlie had brought her home from the war as a war bride. That's how Charlie told it, demobbed with his kit under one arm and sweet Nellie under the other. Ethel imagined Nellie sailing in through Big Tickle with Charlie bouncing, hollering on the deck of the steamer, screaming *helloooooo!* and pointing out the landmarks: *Mack's Island and Little Tickle down there, with Shoal Tickle Bridge over 'er, Strong's empire past there, salt fish for half the world, my darling, and out there in the water his salt warehouse on Salt Rock. Beyond there, my dear, an' just over the hill, the Burnt Woods, and Indian Burying Ground across the bay* – Charlie would have whooped at that and swung his imaginary tomahawk, and Nellie would have gone green. Nellie had been from London; it had taken her years to adjust to Notre Dame Bay, and Little Bay Islands in particular. She felt so alone, cut off. Exuberant Charlie had hardly noticed.

"It's an *island*," Nellie would protest to Ethel.

"Nellie, my dear," Ethel would say. "*Great Britain* is an island."

But Nellie had come round in the end, and now she was Ethel's best friend, each the only one the other could confide in. Nellie had settled in after all; she'd just needed something to look forward to after England, plain and simple.

Ice cream, Ethel thought now, watching John Gates buy his flour and twine. *That* would be a little something to look forward to. Just a little something, but so much better than a lot of nothing. On days she made a new gallon, Tom and Harry raced home from school at lunch time to crank for her, unless she was making a freezer for Education Day. In that case, Mr. Burden let the boys out early. It was his way of helping out another teacher. My, but the boys were strong. Ethel could start the cranking, but she couldn't finish it. She was still tough, but sometimes her heart fluttered and with overwork and her asthma she found it hard to catch her breath. She had a half-gallon freezer – that was for home and parties and the *Clyde* brought it first, for a trial – and a gallon freezer for the parlour in the shop. There'd be rows over the flavour for home. Harry just had to have canned pineapple in his ice cream. No one else liked it as much, and Marion didn't like it at all. But even when there was a batch coming without pineapple, Harry hung around waiting for the dasher to emerge. There was nothing like getting the dasher after a long, hard crank on a hot July day. In the shop, a bowl or a cone – Ethel got cones brought in on the *Clyde* too – cost five cents. A bowl had four scoops and a cone fewer, however many scoops Ethel could fit on, but a cone made the Little Bay Islanders feel cosmopolitan, right up there with the likes of them in New York.

At home, the cost of a dasher was all too often a bit of a ruckus over who'd get the first lick, who got it last time and whose turn it was now, *it is so it is not*, and it often won you a frown from Mom for fighting. Ice cream was supposed to make you gracious. We have enough thugs in the world already, Mom would say. They established a schedule, a rotation for the dasher. They got a dasher a week over the course of the summer, and took turns. Every year the schedule started anew, the little ones up first.

"Mo-om!" said Harry. That part hardly seemed fair.

"Harry, my son. See how far Ron gets through it, or Grace. Do you suppose there'll be a lick left over?"

There always was, and so they learned ice cream making, patience too. Courage came later – or perhaps they'd had it all along.

~

George Rendell, Nellie and Charlie's boy, was high-spirited; sometimes he seemed to have about as much sense as a child. George liked Marion well enough; he was sweet on her, in fact, and Marion, in turn, was bashful. She liked George's sister. "Margaret, Margaret, Margaret," George would implore her, clutching her shoulders, "say a good word for me now with Maid Marion, will ye, lass?" But Margaret said nothing. She was dark, like Phyl Taylor, but quieter. When the girls did their boil-up on the ice in the harbour or in the winter woods it would be Margaret who'd fetch the wood and Phyl who'd pose it for Marion's new camera. Margaret went quietly about the business of the boil-up with Netta, while Phyl and Marion worked the fire. Margaret pulled the sled with the gear. It was Sunday; the girls wore skirts; no one minded the cold. They brought tea, the small tin kettle, cups – the best ones from Margaret's house because her mother, Nellie, was English and knew her bone china. It was one of the many things Margaret's and Marion's mothers had in common.

Winter or summer, they went off after Sunday school on their afternoon excursions: Net, Phyl, Margaret, Marion. The summer Marion turned thirteen, often as not on Sundays the girls walked down to the other end of the harbour. They didn't usually walk toward Shoal Tickle and the bridge at the nearer end of town. There wasn't much to do there. Back Beach was a good long walk to the very end of the road in the other direction, and it had waves and a roar that couldn't be beat. Its thunder was nothing like the clamour of Strong's mill, the way it went on with its shrieks when business was good. It was the end of the Depression; fish markets around the world were back up and there were mouths to feed and money to make. "Credit to pay on our books, my darling," Sidney said meanly, and Ethel looked away. At Strong's mill a huge valve thrust itself out rudely over the grassy shoulder of the road, its great foul breath sucking at anyone going past. Smoke leaked out around the edges of the big steel cap bolted on the valve's end. How could you be sure it wasn't going to explode, that the cap wouldn't fly right off and into you when you walked by? Marion kept to the far side of the road when she had to walk past the mill, and when she got in close she stepped down into the ditch that bordered the road, continuing along in its trench. But for Strong's fence that ran up above, along the far side of the ditch, she would have kept even farther back.

Marion's friends knew she didn't like the mill. Who did? It was loud, impudent, unstoppable. They wondered how Bert Strong and his mother could live so close by, in their house in back of Jim Strong's and next to Bert's tennis court.

"It's how he puts up with us," Netta said. "We seem the peace of the ages compared to the mill." Net was Little Bay Islands' star singles player. They all said she was bound for Wimbledon. Netta went over to the court a lot, practising swings in the air, slicing up and down, forehand and backhand, crouching and springing and jumping. Otherwise, Net was quiet. She'd lost her brother Cyril overseas in this new World War, against Hitler, and she had a quizzical, displaced look about her. Bob Forward's brother Col had been lost too. The Forwards lived in the last house on Mack's Island, on the Shoal Tickle end. The Wiseman kids had been over there many times, playing on the huge swing that Uncle Jim Forward had built so near the edge of his lot that it sailed right out over Shoal Tickle.

Col Forward's death had been worse even than Cyril Penney's; seldom had anyone heard anything so dreadful. Cyril had gone down with his ship when it was torpedoed on the North Atlantic, and Lloyd Wiseman and Frank Grimes had gone down too, but Col hadn't even made it across. He'd been swept off the deck of his submarine in bad weather off the coast of Nova Scotia. His body had washed ashore at Pictou and had been buried in a graveyard there. When the telegrams came to the Forwards and the Penneys, everyone knew, but Phyl Jones took no pleasure in passing them on. Randolph Crowell, the wireless operator and the postmaster for whom Phyl worked, took them personally. It was a man's job to deliver the news, good and bad, of a man's world.

> On behalf of myself and the Government, and indeed, on behalf of the whole of the people of Newfoundland, I desire to tender you sincere sympathy in the great loss which you have sustained: a loss that is not only yours but the whole country's.

That's what the governor wrote; exactly what the governor had written during the last war, to Aunt Maud over Harold and Clyde. You'd think in twenty years or more they'd have had time to come up with something new, something poetic or elegant or just plain to-the-point, like "Nearer My God to Thee." That's what they'd sung on the *Titanic*; that's what the band played and the people sang as she went down off Cape Race, when they sent out the *Algerine* from St. John's for rescue. Or something like *What hath God wrought*. That was the message Morse had sent from Washington to Baltimore in the first telegram nearly a hundred years earlier. Fifty years on, at the turn of century, Guglielmo Marconi had managed to do the whole thing again by wireless, sending from England to Signal Hill, right here in Newfoundland. But Marconi had managed only a *dit-dit-dit*, an s. It seemed anticlimactic. *Dit-dit-dit*: it was hardly auspicious, the start of S.O.S., the *dit-dit-dit dah-dah-dah dit-dit-dit* that pulled your stomach to your knees when you heard it in winter or through the shriek of any summer storm on the ship-to-shore. Why did so many messages bring bad news? Even "Nearer My God to Thee," that was bad news of a kind; the worst, if you thought about it. Often the shore vessels receiving an S.O.S. weren't ready and couldn't help, and even other schooners nearby the emergency were helpless too, because while they all kept in touch by wireless they all also habitually lied about their positions to guard their turf. By the time they came clean it could be too late for a save.

What hath God wrought, indeed? The great transmissions seemed to mean something altogether ungodly, something about pulling up short, reflecting, not about marvels and progress at all. Marion couldn't imagine losing a brother in the war. Bob Forward sat in front of her in school and Marion thought he looked changed. Bob was such a good student, so exacting and conscientious. Bob got everything right. "The area of Little Bay Islands is about four square miles," he'd written in a school project, "A Brief Geographical Description of Our Island,"

and the distance around it is approximately five miles. It is about 2 ½ miles long and about a mile and a half wide at its widest part. Nearly the whole of the Island is an undulating tableland of approximately 100 feet, with a narrow coastal strip around the main harbour and the coves at the back. The highest hills are about 300 feet. The principal settlement has a fine harbour, oval in shape; it is ¾ mile long and ¼ mile wide and the east side of the harbour is formed by Mack's Island which is connected to the larger Island by a bridge about 125 yards long, under which small boats can

enter. The main harbour entrance is very narrow, only about
100 yards wide at some places. The water is fairly deep and
will allow 4,000-ton steamers to enter. About 80 families
live on the coastal strip surrounding the harbour.

I may say in closing that some of these numbers are
approximate and there may be slight errors.

Would Bob get everything right now? Now that his brother was
gone, would he care? Marion's big brother Tom had gone into RAF
training but he'd gone west, to the far coast of Canada, not east to the
front. Newfoundland was the same distance from Italy as it was from
British Columbia, so Tom was putting all that additional distance
between himself and Il Duce. So long as he kept going in the wrong
direction, it was all just fine with Mom and the rest of them.

Marion had gone to stay overnight with Net when Net's mother
got their telegram about Cyril. Net had had a great shock, Mom said.
Maybe Marion would like to go over, and see how she was? It hadn't
been good at Net's. Even Net's remaining brother, Bobby Dude, was
quiet for once. He was forever looking in mirrors to check his hair
and pulling his collar up under his ears in a way he thought fashion-
able. Now he sat, mussed and sullen. Net's sister Ruby had been sent
home from Twillingate to die, and soon there would be two Penneys
gone; three, if you counted Net's father, whom Marion hardly remembered. Marion heard Ruby from Violet's bedroom, coughing through
the wall. It had been freezing cold that night, and lying next to Net in
her small bed Marion was rocked through the night by Net's jerkings
and rearings up. So many summers earlier they'd played Indian, taking
on Indian names and play-acting. *I'm the last Beothuk here on Little
Bay Islands, the one that John Campbell shot on Harbour Rock.
Bang!* Netta would clutch her chest and roll on the forest floor. *I'm
the first Micmac, I'm Suley Ann and I have my own cove. And my
own raspberries and my own burnt woods. I'm the last Beothuk ever,
I'm Nancy April Shawnadithit. Here I am coughing while I scrub
floors for Mr. Peyton in Exploits who caught me, here I am dying of*

consumption in St. John's. They didn't mime Shawnadithit's coughing too much. Coughing wasn't all that funny those days.

They used to climb up into the woods to their special clearing where there was a bed of moss and needles and where the trees hung down to make a perfect camp. A branch had fallen, split from a trunk by lightning, and they sat against it, laying out their hard biscuits and lemonade. Lightning doesn't strike the same place twice, Marion told Net without having any idea whether it did. Lightning was one of the few things that didn't scare her. Holes in the earth, the harbour and the waves, holds in vessels, the prospect of a grave – anything that could swallow her up. . . . She shivered. Even tree trunks; she couldn't sit on them and pulled Net back when Net thought they should. Once when she and her brothers were picking raspberries in the Burnt Woods with Ede, Tom and Harry had informed Marion that stumps were where babies grew until people wanted them. Then they went in and picked them. My, there were a lot of babies in Burnt Woods! Did you know they make babies up in the Burnt Woods? Marion asked her mother once. Her mother seemed surprised. Marion stayed as far away from stumps as she could, so as not to disturb any babies or leave any marks on them that would grow in later life. The Rowsells down the way had a little one with a bright red blotch on his head, a raspberry stain. You could see it through his baby hair and down the side of his face where it had spread. Someone had put a pail of berries down on him in the woods, it was clear, not given it a thought, and then sat down too.

Ah, there was peril everywhere. But in the woods those mornings, with Net, when no one else was up and nothing stirred, it was a magic time. The sun spangled through the leaves of the trees above. If you listened hard you'd hear something more than wind, more than the bushes rustling and the birds tucking into berries the way they did early and late, at both ends of the heat of the day. Net and Marion had their pow wow, their Indian breakfast of pretend tea – lemonade – and hardtack. When someone is lost to the war – Marion considered this now, staring at the ceiling in Net's bedroom while Net shook and Ruby coughed through the wall – we others have to rally around. We have to close the gap, reach for the hand that's been dropped. *To you from failing hands we throw the torch; be yours to hold it high.* She felt for Net's hand in the bed, clutched it. Marion had known Cyril; she'd grown up with him. But Net had been his sister. What the governor had written wasn't true, *a loss that is not only yours but the whole country's.* It was Netta's loss alone, Netta's and her mother's, Violet's, Ruby's, and Bobby Dude's. The rest of them would miss Cyril, yes; the neighbours and his friends and his old schoolmates would grieve, but next to the Penneys' theirs was not a loss at all; it was a confusion, that blank that followed a disappearance. It was a vacuum, a memory. His friends hadn't planned for Cyril like his mother had; they hadn't imagined a future for him. They'd never given that sort of thing a thought. For them, Cyril had just been Cyril, present; and now he was forever past. For his mother, her boy would always be Cyril Future, the perfection of what he could have become, what she had always in her mind's eye seen him become, and now never would.

Oh, it was heartbreaking.

Marion turned her head. Through Net's window the night showed black. On a starless night you'd never seen anything as black as an outport sky. It was black as pitch, wide as the devil's boots. Marion was scrammed, shivering, blue and numb with cold, and outside the night was colder still.

Shawnadithit, the last Beothuk ever, had learned a kind of stiff English from her English captors. She'd told them about Beothuk traditions, Beothuk culture, and one of the white men had given her pencils to draw what she couldn't explain. She said the Beothuk had a Great Spirit called *Aich-mud-yim*, Black Man. He'd be the spirit of the night, Marion figured, in a place like this. Shawnadithit said, too, that there was another Great Spirit, a monster from the sea.

"What do you expect?" Net had said to that, downing the last of her lemonade in the woods against the lightning tree. "We're in Newfoundland."

Shawnadithit hadn't liked any culture other than her own.

"What do you expect?" Net said again.

The first white men who came to Newfoundland had come from the good spirit, but latecomers hadn't. The next white men as well as the Micmac had come from the bad spirit, they said. To Marion, thinking like that seemed bound to cause trouble. Worst of all, Shawnadithit had said that any Beothuk who made peace with anyone who'd come from the bad spirit would be sacrificed to the ghosts of his slain kin. Under Net's bedroom ceiling, Marion sucked in her breath. All this shocky stuff Net was doing next to her – would she die in the night, sacrificed to her slain brother Cyril just because she and her friend Marion had played Beothuk and Micmac in the wood?

It was late, Marion knew. The goblins of sleeplessness were running through her head. She shouldn't think about these things; she especially shouldn't worry about them. What would Mom say? Mom would stroke her head and sing her the song, throw back her head and make her little laugh like the moon.

> *"Now cast your nets wherever you wish –*
> *Never afeared are we";*
> *So cried the stars to the fishermen three,*
> *Wynken,*
> *Blynken,*
> *And Nod.*

Courage took some coaxing; Mom knew that. Mom knew everything. She would never think her big girl was too old for the song.

~

In their Sunday dresses and their patent leather shoes, Netta and Marion and Phyl and Margaret had their long walk and then sat in the sun on Back Beach. Margaret was fanciful; it was the only time she wasn't quiet. The waves, she said, were white horses on the harbour. They were especially high just beyond Back Beach where they were driven through Big Tickle by the North Atlantic, gathering volume and force. After a storm was the best time to go, with the wind still at a screaming pitch and the water raging. The waves are spirited stallions, Margaret said. They're the stallions of the Irish chieftain O'Donahue who was drowned, poor man, in a lake in Killarney on his wedding morn. Ever after could he be seen on any high sea, riding his white horse and following after maidens strewing flowers.

"Really?" the girls said.

"Really," said Margaret. She watched Net. Was it too soon after Cyril to tell stories like this, even romantic ones?

But Net was looking far out past Big Tickle, far out to sea. Marion adjusted her bonnet where she'd fastened it to her perm with a hatpin. There was always a wind in Little Bay Islands, nowhere worse than here at Back Beach. When she was smaller she'd dreamed it could take them all away, leaving the Old Man gaping in their wake. *Long may your big jib draw!* They could yell that back, laughing; but Mom would frown. The trouble they had in the family was no joke. The wind tugged at Marion's hat now, and she put her hands up, too late. Away it sailed, high out over the harbour. There were terraces of rock beyond the beach that the waves hurled themselves against, and she dashed up to the top ledge now to watch it fly. The others climbed up from below, through the undergrowth of blackberries and crackerberries that snapped when you trampled them. They watched Marion's hat until they couldn't see it any more.

"It's gone to Strong's to be salted and barrelled and shipped," Margaret said. "It's going the long way," out over the Atlantic along the far side of Mack's Island and then back in over Shoal Tickle.

"A hat?" That was Net, speaking for the first time that day. She didn't say much.

"You got no soul," Betty said to Net, just when Net felt she had too much of one, crying every night the way she did over Cyril.

Suddenly they all jumped back. The waves had rushed them, seized the toes of their shoes. Here at the beach, the sea roiled in from great boulders farther out. There was a small channel between the boulders that might let a motorboat pass, but only in calm. Here, there was hardly ever calm; certainly not today. There was always a heaviness here, a calling darkness. Back Beach was a part of Marion. She'd always felt it. The tiny channel through the rocks was the beginning and end of life, she could see that. You could save a bit of time coming into the harbour that way, threading your boat between the rocks, but you'd be smashed likely as not and all the smashed bits of you thrown back out through Big Tickle, to drift down eventually and settle on the unimaginably deep ocean bottom. Tom and Harry dared to negotiate the little channel in the punt when no one was around – except Marion and Jack. Tom and Harry loved an audience.

"I'm telling Mom!" Marion would scream, but she never did. It wasn't as if Marion wasn't a daredevil herself, growing up among four brothers. One winter they'd had a big coaster sled from Mom at Christmas that carried the lot of them down the ridge behind the Tickle house. Marion sat up front, to steer; the boys sat behind for weight. It was a fast drop when the snow got icy. How many times had they told her to keep her legs in? Heads bent over where she sprawled on the kitchen daybed. In places down the shin, the skin was sheared to bone. Mom had had her darning needle out, then sighed and put it away. "Watch she doesn't bleed on the linens there," said Skipper Sid. She was up in no time; he wanted his daybed back.

She was more reckless after that, and not always by accident. There was something to prove now, something to win, to outlast.

The water coughed and sputtered and threw itself up against the giant steps of the terraces beyond Back Beach, the steps it had carved out over seventeen ice ages, over all the centuries it had been here in anticipation of all those centuries it would be here after the stone had gone. Paper Scissors Rock, the girls had played that. How had they forgotten water? The sea reared up.

On the highest ledge, the one farthest from the water, where they were standing now, you'd get the spray. It was icy, shocking. It made them squeal.

On the second ledge – *now!* – you'd get a soak. You couldn't always squeal then, with the water you'd be spitting out.

Drenching was next, and utter drenching on the last ledge, where the rock was lowest and closest to the waves. It was always a game, a contest with the ocean itself where you ran back, screaming and whooping and giggling as the water surged, where you ran and jumped to the ledge above, hauling yourself up by your forearms before the sea could get you by the ankles and pull you in. It was a perilous game, and now they were into it without a thought.

Is this really a good idea? No one knew for sure, only that they'd done it before.

Not in our Sunday shoes, we haven't.

The rock terraces were wet and slick. Showers of spray curled around them, dashing up in sheets now, blotting the rocks out and the girls too, and it was almost over before they knew it.

It was Margaret who saved her. Netta holding onto Margaret; Margaret holding onto Marion's hand for dear life. Marion, suddenly, astonishingly, off her feet with water to her neck. Margaret, a couple years older and an inch or two taller, and not much drier. Marion, the smallest, Netta the next smallest and screaming, everyone turning to run and still holding onto the next one, dragging her back. Marion, going under, and Margaret with rubber soles on her shoes. Marion, picked up by the force of the water that swirled around her neck, dragged out and out and out to the edge of the ledge that must be somewhere under her feet.

And Margaret, never letting go.

Back at Net's house, the girls patted themselves dry and combed their hair. Netta was crying; she hadn't stopped. Marion rubbed Net's back and watched Margaret, who'd grabbed her hand and hadn't let go.

~

Aunt Et reads tea leaves! Ede had told Nine and Nine had sent it hotcakes around the harbour. "I'll let you know; I'll send a note," Mom would say when a girl came in the shop with the look. That was how it was with Mom's readings. The girls hung around. They offered to bring their own cups. They mooned – Mamie mooning about some fellow in on the boats, or one of the Roberts girls going on about how she'd come over faint, or what's happened to her letter down to Botwood for the position as maid. The girls didn't pester her, exactly. No one would dream of pestering Mrs. Wiseman. They'd simply bring the little nephews by the shop and get them ice cream, looking downcast, with dark circles under their eyes. *Oh, Mrs. Wiseman.* Or they'd bring a bowl of berries up to the house. *Oh, Mrs. Wiseman, I just picked these for you, thought as how you'd love a berry or two with your tea tonight, and isn't it lucky I got out of the woods at all with the spells coming on me like they do these days, another one just now up t'the woods there, oh my, and if I only knew whether to wait for the Bonnie Nell or trouble Dr. Olds straight to Twillingate . . .*

It was such an honour to have tea with Mrs. Wiseman. You got ushered into the breakfast room – no one else on Little Bay Islands even had one of those! No one else had a Mrs. Wiseman, not even close. You'd drink down your cup so fast it burned all the way down, and then you'd pass it to her. When Mamie came she drank so hard and passed so fast that the Wisemans' good Spode had nearly sailed clear off the table.

Mrs. Wiseman turned your cup over in its saucer and twisted it round three times. That was where you held their breath. One. Two. Three. The girls could hardly stand it.

And then she'd start. "Now you know this is just for fun," she'd say. She had a voice like summer rain. Hearing that voice, whatever it said would be fine with anyone. "Oh look," she'd say, "these little spots here like the Funks off Fogo; someone's coming in to see you, in past the Funks on the next fair wind. Bringing something – this tiny speck here, see? Yes, I'm sure of it. Within a fortnight."

It was safe to say so. In the summer, at least, someone would always be in, westbound out of Fogo. Bringing something? Why, sure. No one ever came empty-handed. The travelling was so hard you carried half of what you owned with you, wherever you went.

"Well," she'd go on, "this shading here where the tea's dribbled down. It's a sign for your circulation, which might be improved if you took a little more of the brown flour."

The girl would make a face. White flour was a badge of honour. Brown flour was the Dole diet.

"Do what you like, my darling," Ethel would say, "but it says so right here."

It was hard for Ethel to find the time. Or the place. Her mother had read tea leaves for her own friends, the ladies back in Ladle Cove, and Ethel, looking on, had got good at it. But Fanny hadn't had to watch that she didn't make too many friends, that she didn't like them too much, that she might appear to like them more than she did Thomas, Ethel's father. Fanny didn't have to have a note friendship with her best friend in Ladle Cove as Ethel had to with Nellie Rendell. Mrs. Rendell was seldom permitted to visit the Wiseman house, and seldom wanted to.

Marion knew it was touch-and-go, Mom stepping outside the Old Man's control like this to go up to the house and meet Delphina. When her father was supposed to be in the store he was up at the house half the time. He was forever going back and forth. She'd seen ants stream on the ground in summer. He was like that, busy, industrious, single-minded for all the world to see – and then the rest of the time he lay on the daybed or on his bed in the bedroom, boots and all, stretched out reading. Today she'd make sure he stayed where he was meant to be, or at least she'd sound an early warning if he moved.

Whatever had Mom told Delphina? Nine Grimes was always dying to have Mom read her leaves but never asked, she was so afraid of what she might hear. Delphi's tea leaves hadn't gone well. Perhaps today Marion's wouldn't either. Perhaps nearly drowning at Back Beach was only the beginning. Yesterday, Delphi had thrown her hands up and run away.

"I told her," Mom said, "that there was a fellow in her cup looking for a beautiful miss." Delphi had been rounding out now that

Evangeline, her younger sister, was seeing to more of the chores. Delphi had given up the washing and taken over the cooking. Maybe she should give it back.

Marion walked up to the house from Net's, where she'd dried off. She could make Mom tea now, perhaps they'd have a leisurely cup together. She took off her Sunday patents beside the kitchen door. They were still damp from the scare at the beach, and she banged them on the door to dispatch the grit they'd collected on the walk home. They were double T-straps, and for all the suck of the waves they'd stayed on her feet. It was hard to believe that those shoes weren't sitting now in a nest of mollusks and sea urchins at the bottom of the ocean. She still felt the pressure on her legs, how they'd been whipped up to her waist and her arms whipped away from her shoulders. Hard to believe that her legs hadn't been torn from her, and her arms too; that the lot of them hadn't been wrenched from the rocks and drowned. They'd had a technique, or thought they did. They waited till the last minute; they always knew just when that was, or thought they did. They held hands. Marion was the biggest daredevil, and she'd be the last to turn and run. *Vanity.* We got splashed at Back Beach, that's what she'd tell Mom. She'd walked slowly home after stopping and towelling at Net's, to dry her hair and her dress in the fresh air. Permed or straight, her hair was always in a French crop and took no time at all to bring back from the edge of disaster. Summer dresses were always getting wet; they took no time to dry. Shoes were always getting wet, too, but drying them was another matter. Marion left hers outside and crept in.

She and Mom weren't likely to have a leisurely cup after all, but she put the kettle on anyway. The kitchen was in slings; Mom must have had a long Sunday afternoon. There was the big treat box of cornflakes that they had Sunday mornings so that Mom wouldn't have to get up early to cook the oatmeal, so that she'd only have to cook for the Old Man. It was still standing in the middle of the table, empty. Marion burned it in the stove and took down the tea. She was shaken by her scare. It made her want to know what was in store for her, for Mom, for Margaret Rendell, to whom Marion now owed her life, for any of them. She didn't want to know any of those things the other girls did – about positions, getting away to St. John's or Gander or Grand Falls, about boys, swoons and headaches. She wanted to know what was in store, what wasn't, what might whisk away what could have been.

Best we don't know, that's what Tom and Harry said.

You make your luck, that's what Mom said.

For we must needs die, and are as water spilt on the ground, which cannot be gathered up again, that's what the Bible said. So often the Bible wasn't very tactful.

Marion believed them all; this was the first time she wanted to know regardless. She was shaken to her roots. Anything seemed preferable to being caught off guard again. Paper Scissors Rock. Now Water, and before that there'd been Fire, too – that time they'd had their Guy Fawkes bonfire at the beach. Harris Winsor hadn't often let them out of school on Guy Fawkes Day but H. T. Burden always did. They'd got to Back Beach late that year, and because the tide was in they'd built the bonfire up above the beach, in the scrub where the blackberries fringed the rocks. They'd put it out carefully with buckets when they left, the way they always did. She'd come back a few days later and *oh the shock* to see a crater burned down at least a foot into the turf and as wide as their kitchen. She'd run all the way to Campbell's Point. "Go back and look," she told her brothers. "You won't believe it until you see it." It must have smouldered for days. It might have burned down the woods for miles around, burned what was left of the old Tickle house too.

It was best to know what was coming, that was clear.

But Mom distracted her. She had sat down after all. "Marion," she said, drinking her tea, "I've got some good news."

News.

"Mr. Burden's just got back, and he's got the CHE results." She held up an envelope. "You've topped the CHE exams for the whole of Newfoundland."

Criminy. Mr. Burden would have come here first, teacher to teacher, to the home of the star pupil. Mr. Burden would be puffing all around the harbour now, stopping at every home with children who'd taken the exams and telling every parent the good news. No pupil of H. T. Burden's ever failed the Council of Higher Education exams. It was his personal honour and undertaking. And now Marion had outdone everyone in the province. Back Beach vanished. She remembered how hard it had been, writing for hours up on the second floor of the school hall where the concerts were put on. The CHEs hadn't been nearly as much fun as a concert. They hadn't been any fun at all. She'd had to keep stretching out her hand and flexing her fingers where they cramped. And now she'd topped the entire province. She would have screamed and stomped and leapt up in her chair and banged the table as hard as Harry did when they played cards with Mom in the evening sometimes, unless the Old Man was around. Harry would hit the table so hard that Mom would say they'd hear him all the way to St. John's. Sometimes they played dominoes or checkers or Snakes and Ladders instead, just so Harry wouldn't forget and pound the table. She'd hit the table that hard now, but she heard a chair pushed back somewhere in the house.

Mom drank down her tea. Marion drank down hers. Mom took her cup, turned it over, twisted it three times in its saucer. "Well," she said, looking in. "These little bars here, with this other bar crossing, like a finger against lips. Perhaps it's best we don't mention this around your father."

Of all her friends, it was Margaret whom Marion told first about the CHEs, and Margaret put her hand out to hold her friend's in it. "You're so smart," Margaret said. "How can you be so smart?"

VI

JACK

S idney wasn't going off to the Labrador anymore. He'd been diag-
nosed by telegram. Rest, Dr. Olds had said. No work.

Sidney Hayward Wiseman. Aged 39. Coughed blood. That had
been Ethel's initial wire. All round the Bay went the news, white lightning, but Ethel tried not to mind. What was important was not that
tongues wagged, but that Sidney got well.

How much? That was Dr. Olds's wire back from Twillingate.

Half a teaspoon. Bright red. She went on to describe the cough and
his weight loss. Ede had pulled on her boots and taken that one down
to the post office, where Gwen Jones's maiden aunt Phyllis was postmistress. All wires went through the post office. These days, Ethel sent
Ede down for the post and wires. Now that Sid had fallen out with
Sid Jones, until then his best buddy, no Wiseman was to have anything
to do with the Jones family. Henceforth, the postmistress would no
longer be called Phyl. All the children were now to call her Miss Jones,
"like you would any half-slack spinster like that who you didn't know
or didn't want to." Even Phyllis wouldn't do, formal as it would have

been. It was to be Miss Jones, spinster, as if there lay in the *Miss* some additional disgrace.

Ethel knew what to do and what not to do. She always did. As with all Sidney's edicts, she set out to make the best of this one: to get around it where she could and to accept it where she must. The children were mortified at calling Phyl anything but that, and so Ethel sent Ede.

"Don't know, Phyl," Ede said to Phyl. "*Half a teaspoon.* Must be some apothecary thing, since it's going to Twillingate, to the Memorial Hospital. Can't be a recipe." Ethel hadn't told Ede anything yet. She hadn't told anyone.

Bed rest, Dr. Olds had wired back. *No work. Patient to attend Twillingate next passenger boat.*

"Ohhhh," said Phyl, passing the wire to Ede through the wicket.

"Ohhhh," said Ede, picking it up.

That was it: six months in the san, whenever the next boat went after the ice broke. Three or four passenger boats went to the hospital a year, in the summer, carrying all the sick who'd waited out the winter at home. Tom, always gaunt, had spent a summer in the Twillingate hospital where Ethel hoped he'd pink up and put on a little weight. Who knows what could be keeping him thin and pale like that? It was imperative to nip things in the bud in summer, to head them off. Come winter, if anything set in, it would be too late. When spring came, Ethel made sure Sidney was on the first boat out.

She got him on board and settled him in, tucking his blankets around him. He was quiet, complacent, cheerful; coddling brought out the best in him. She handed him the lunch she'd packed. It was Roy Jones's passenger boat, after all. It wasn't like the *Clyde* or the *Prospero*, where the porters wore caps and you sat down and ate with the crew, where the saloon was set up like a dining hall and the chairs were shackled down with brass chains. But Sidney pushed Ethel's package away, drawing his blanket up under his chin.

He was sick, yes. He loved being sick. Who could eat at a time like this?

Ethel stepped down onto the wharf and watched the boat pull away. She'd always noticed how these small boats fronted in and backed out. Silly, but it worried her. It was a small thing, but wasn't it just the small things that could worry you most? Schooners nudged into their slips sideways, easing their way up aside the log boom around Strong's wharf. When they left they pushed out from the boom and ahead of it in an efficient choreography that suited their grace. But the smaller boats – *Nothing good to come of backing out of a room unless you've also backed in, yes my darling.* That's what the grannies said. Ethel half believed them, though she discounted their talk of goblins and ghosts. *Don't borrow trouble, my girls,* Fanny had said to Maud and Mill and Et when they were all still at home in Ladle Cove in their pinnies and plaits. *There's enough trouble in the world already, you needn't make up more.*

It was true. Ethel made her luck. Fanny used to say that too: *You make your luck.* Ethel made the best of her luck with Sidney. Backing into a room? Who backed in a room unless it were she, Ethel, backing away from her husband coming at her? Sure, she knew she was not the only one who had this cross to bear, but she had to wonder how many other women actually backed into rooms. Ede's sister Nina, the Grimes' girl, as fearful as the day was long; she suffered from headaches and stuck brown paper to her forehead that she'd soaked in vinegar first, then went walking around backward in circles, as if that would help. Amazing, the things people believed.

Ethel watched the boat retreat. What did she believe? *I believe in the communion of saints.* The Papists said that, the Micks. The Micks said so many pretty things. Funny ideas they had sometimes, though, like the way they'd gone on about the Fisherman's Union oath and how that made it a secret society. And how Sidney had gone on about that, in return! *They can stay out if they like. All the more for us, m'darling, all the more for us.* What would Sidney go on about now, in the Twillingate hospital? How was it possible she cared? How was it possible she missed him already?

She looked up at the sun overhead. She should have worn a hat to shield her face; she didn't do well in sun. It was a warm day on the wharf as the boat for Twillingate pulled out. It was spring again; that was why the boats were going at all, pushing out through the sish ice. But still she shivered. She felt a bit sick herself. Maybe she should try again to get in the bananas she loved. Or tomatoes like they'd had in Ladle Cove, where there'd been time and there'd been soil, not rock. Here, only Phyl Taylor's mother, Rose, had a garden, and it was no bigger than a minute. A little colour in the diet couldn't be a bad thing. She'd tried getting in bananas and tomatoes before, but they'd arrived soft and rotten.

She shivered again in the sun. Such a cold chill on her for such a warm day. She'd kept Sidney warm and sent him off to hospital as best she could. She'd done all she could. Years ago, when Jack had pneumonia and needed to go, it hadn't been that way at all.

~

The wharf at Big Tickle. Jack, a toddler, dying. And Sidney's face as flushed as the child's, though different – pinched, impenetrable, unyielding. Dressing her down for interrupting him while he was getting ready to take the *James Strong* to the Labrador. All around the harbour the men were bringing down the schooners for the new season. Sidney's crew had lowered the *Strong*'s spars to the wharf by block and tackle, tipping her up to lie on her side in the water. Now they'd gone for their mug-up, leaving Sidney to touch up her bottom with copper paint. He brandished the brush at Ethel. *I will not take him. Think of the cost. Who do you think I am, John D. Rockefeller? Let him die. We got too many as it is.*

It had been a knife, straight through her heart. She'd walked up from the wharf to the porch without speaking, shaking with a sudden chill all the while Jack's downy hot head rested against her palm. With the fever he was quiet, though she could hear him rasp as if his lungs

were bubbling. She was eight months pregnant again, and he sat on
her girth. He'd be too heavy for some, impossible to carry. But not
for her. She'd carry him all the way to Twillingate if she had to. On
the wharf, while she and Sidney had argued, the boy's head had glis-
tened slicker than the boots they oiled in winter; now it was hot and
dry. Ethel walked him back and forth on the porch. She hoped he'd
get the air down him somehow, into his tiny chest. It was good air,
healing, fresh and cool off the harbour. She walked. Who would help
her? There was no one to help her. Never, never had she felt so deso-
late. *My punishment is greater than I can bear.* She looked at the
house; she looked at the harbour. She'd swim if she had to, she'd walk
on water to save her child. She looked back at the house. "Ede," she
called through the window, quietly, over Jack's small, hot head. "Ede.
I feel sure Jack's got pneumonia. Go to Uncle Alex Anstey, quickly.
Tell him we need his passenger boat."

Ethel made the arrangements for the children. Tom and Harry were
old enough to stay with Ede here at the house. Tom was nine; he'd
pass the time reading and pretending he wasn't worried. Harry was
seven; he'd roar around outside. He'd be an aeroplane scouring the
country for his mother and his baby brother. *Come in please, Jack,
come in please!* He'd sound official, talking into his pretend aeroplane
wireless. Marion would go to the Lockes'. Ron was just two: he would
go to Nellie Rendell's, and Ede sent Tom running over to the Rendells'
with a note from Ethel to say so. *Well, ask, my darling, don't tell 'em;
just make sure they says yes.* Harry might be the faster runner, but
young Tom had long enough legs himself; he could run far ever as a
puffin flew. Besides, at Rendells' he'd get things straight. He'd present
his mother's note. While she waited for Uncle Alex, Ethel had penned
a note each to the Rendells and the Lockes. Ede had seen the strain in
her, one arm fast around Jack on her lap, the other tracing out the
words in her graceful hand. Ede thought of all she'd have to do to get
Ron and Marion ready and away. There hadn't been time for Ethel to
speak to anyone. Uncle Alex had motored up to the Tickle house
wharf in the *Paragon* and Ethel had held Jack tight to her and stepped

on, like a passenger boarding Charon's ferry across the Styx. She had reached back and hugged Ede with the hand that wasn't around Jack.

"Try not to worry, my child. Put your trust in God," she said to Ede, while the girl bawled into her shoulder. Worse than Nine, she'd been, it was true. Worse than Nine, snivelling at the slightest thing. Just when Aunt Et needed her to be strong. Finally Aunt Et had let Ede go. She stepped onto the boat and looked away into the sky, as if something there might help her.

"Godspeed, Uncle Alex, Godspeed, Aunt Et," Ede said to no one as she watched the boat's wake. "Godspeed, little Jack." She loved all the children, but Jack was the baby who had gurgled and smiled and now, just four, was sunny and spirited and full of beans. Or had been. Oh, there'd been too much sickness and death around, hadn't there just? Ede even counted the dreadful Aunt Lizzie into that. She'd just died, the old witch; all those bloomers and nighties and napkins and sheets Ede had had to wash, and on top of all that the fetching and the running up and down the stairs as if after her spell and her crash into Ron's high chair the old crone could still talk. *Yes Aunt Lizzie* and *no Aunt Lizzie* and *how would you like it then, Aunt Lizzie?* Only the stroke had managed to shut her up. Ede never went in Aunt Lizzie's room. It wasn't that Aunt Et didn't trust her not to smother Aunt Lizzie with a feather pillow or knock her over the head with the chamber pot. It was just that Aunt Et was the daughter-in-law and felt she should tend to Aunt Lizzie herself. Family looked after family, right until the end, no matter how hard the going got. But Ede was right there for Aunt Et, yes she was, standing just back of the door to help with it all and trying not to say a word. *That witch* – Ede had started in on her once, downstairs and out of hearing, and Aunt Et had put a hand on Ede's wrist where it lay on the washboard. *Now Ede,* she'd said, *now Ede,* and Ede was flooded with remorse.

On top of all that there was him to put up with, him moping around in that way you'd like to smash him! Like it was him dying upstairs! Oh, it was always him. Any time Aunt Et was sick, or one of the little ones, all of a sudden it was him bent over the basin, it was him doubled over, moaning, chucking up, pretending to. However sick they were, he was sicker. He wanted the notice. And it was all so silly, really, with his little ones so scared of him they couldn't commiserate or care if they wanted to. *Oh Ede*, he'd say, *this weather, this bronchitis, this rheumatism* – this whatever it was that day, for heaven's sake – *it's getting to me. I'm not good today, girl.* Only Aunt Et could care about the likes of him. How she doted on him! He couldn't get warm in winter, and so Aunt Et sewed carded fleece straight onto the soles and the heels of his socks. He was forever complaining of cold on the small of his back, and so she made him up a felt binder to buckle around his waist. The things she did for that man, the care she took. How she must love him! Well, said Nine, he's got the looks. Nine had seen the men in the picture shows, and Mr. Wiseman had those kind of looks. Ede herself had gone to the picture show with Nine, that afternoon last year when Mr. Crowell down to the post office had arranged for a film and a visiting projectionist to show it at the school hall. They'd let the school out for the day, it was such a big event, then charged everybody a nickel to come back in and see the show. It had been about the Wild West, but even those cowboys were handsome, Nine said, what you could see of them under their hats. Even they had those looks. Where was the Wild West, anyway?

One of the states in the Union, Ede said. Next to Wild East. Like Wild Cove down Twillingate way, or Wild Bight, what?

"Ohhhhh."

Handsome or not, Ede couldn't understand Aunt Et's care for Skipper Sid. No one could. He couldn't stand anyone else to have the slightest attention. It was like he thought there was a limited supply and he had to hang on to every last bit for himself. A limited supply of anything, from Aunt Et! It was ridiculous. She was the soul of charity, her love unbounded. *He* was ridiculous, that Sidney Wiseman. Him with a missus like that, her love a calm, deep harbour without bottom; a cool stream ever-quenching, ever-running. You dipped into it when you needed it, whoever you were – to Aunt Et, there were no strangers – and there was always plenty more. Skipper Sidney Wiseman, a weasel, a chucklehead, a miserly scoundrel with coal and carbon in his heart and below it all a pit of brambles. They all knew he was shamming, lounging his life away on the daybed in the kitchen, his forearm shading his eyes, *oh, oh, oh, I'm sick*. How many times had Ede and the boys stood behind the window and watched him prance up the lawn from the stage or the boat store all full of himself with that man-o'-the-world purpose of his, only to slump and pant the minute he came through the door and found his audience? *Oh, oh, oh, I'm sick*. And then the old bat Aunt Lizzie too, for weeks and weeks and weeks and Blessed Jesus would it never end. Oh yes, how Ede had been glad to see the end of his mother finally, that thorny old bush, but now –

She watched the white wake of the *Paragon* fan across the harbour. There on the deck, as if she had not yet found the strength to go inside, the receding figure of her beloved Aunt Et and, in Aunt Et's arms, her beloved baby Jack. Sickness and death and the way life hit at you, it all seemed so hard. Ede despaired of it. You couldn't look it in the face at all some days, no you couldn't. You may as well give all your troubles to God, she supposed; He'd be up all night anyway. Sometimes she got down with all her worrying. It made her poorly, especially days when Nine walked over to Big Tickle and made it all worse, saying how much Ede was missed at home and how Mom had the aches and pains and Dad hardly had his tea down some days before he felt green to the gills.

"Aunt Et, oh Aunt Et, we're all coming to bad ends!" Ede would moan to Ethel, twisting a kitchen towel between her hands.

"Now Ede," Aunt Et would say. "Thou shalt be buried in a good old age. God has promised you."

But Ede didn't want to be buried, not now, not ever, and she doubted God was much on the watch in any case. Too many Newfoundland boys going out every season, whether it was trawling or sealing or coasting or what, and never coming back except in boxes packed with salt meant for the catch. And Aunt Et herself, forever at the end of the Old Man's fist. But there was something about Aunt Et all the same that buoyed the girl up. Maybe it was just that – that she was so downtrodden but never an ill word for it. It was the effect she had. Everyone said so.

How sad she was to see Aunt Et go now. Aunt Et was Ede's rock, she was at that.

The girl walked back up to the house from the wharf as the *Paragon* disappeared through Big Tickle, untying her apron. If he spoke to her she'd have it in her hands so's they wouldn't tremble for him to see, that was her plan. She'd have something to clutch to steady herself. So often Aunt Et steadied her, and now she'd have to do it herself. Aunt Et steadied everyone, but sooner or later they all had to learn for themselves.

But he wasn't there *oh God thank the Laird ye took 'im off for me,* and she folded the apron and laid it over the back of the kitchen chair, calling to Marion. "Pack some knickers, a sweater, m'darlin, some book that you like. What about that one with the bears? We're going to Aunt Harriet and Uncle Lionel's."

Marion didn't answer, and Ede had to come into the breakfast room and take the child by the shoulders, turning her from the window. Marion had watched the *Paragon* leave, and now she was counting the seconds since it had vanished through the tickle. *One one-thousandth, two one-thousandths . . .* It was the way you counted for the nearness of a storm, between the crash of lightning and the roll of thunder. She figured she'd keep at it; just counting the seconds until Mom and Jack came back. There couldn't be that many, but if there were she could be patient and wait, counting. Last summer, when Uncle Alex had got his boat, Marion had looked up *paragon* in the dictionary, to see if there were other paragons than virtue. She liked Uncle Alex but she didn't know him well. He didn't seem like a paragon of virtue. Marion pictured such a thing as white, alabaster even, with upturned arms holding . . . what? Doves? Marion had seen doves in books. It seemed fitting that a paragon of virtue should have one or two. Uncle Alex didn't have doves; he had gulls circling his boat looking for cod entrails from the pipe out of Strong's; and he wasn't white at all. He was tall and grizzled, and like everyone else come summer, tanned to bronze from working outside. He was Fanny

Anstey's uncle, Fanny's real uncle, not the uncles and aunts they all had, and now and then he came into the Ensign shop to buy things and have a word with Fanny, and Mom too. Paragon or not, could Uncle Alex save Jack now? Marion wanted to go to Twillingate with Mom and Jack, but Mom's look from the porch, where she'd been walking up and down waiting, with Jack in her arms, had told her no. That's all there'd been, a look exchanged between them through the window. Marion hadn't said any words to ask, and Mom hadn't said any words to answer. They had that between them, a bond.

Marion was death on leaving the breakfast room window and abandoning her post, and she was especially death on going to the Lockes. Aunt Harriet and Uncle Lionel, the Lockes, they'd had six kids of their own, but they were so old now that the kids had all grown up and gone away. Maybe now the Lockes were lonely and wanted to start again, have another six. Maybe Marion was just the beginning, and soon Aunt Harriet would be reeling in Tom and Harry and Jack and Baby Ron and then the new baby Mom would be having soon –

Jack. The little girl's stomach turned over. His little arms had flopped like flippers when Mom had stepped with him onto the boat, like there was nothing in them to hold them up. Maybe soon there'd be no Jack to reel in. *Please God, Please God, let there be a Jack.* She'd make a deal with God. She'd go to Aunt Harriet and Uncle Lionel's with gladness in her heart. She'd be good there, good as gold, if only God would let there be a Jack.

~

Uncle Lionel and Aunt Harriet were so *old*, sixty at least. Marion hardly knew anyone that old. They scared her. They were so *definite* about everything. Maybe that's how you got, after that many years and you had time to collect your thoughts. Mom was sure about everything. She just *knew* about things, whatever they were. And she was calm enough, considering the way she just flew from dawn to dusk with all she had to do. But she wasn't particular like the Lockes.

"Don't cut tails," Uncle Harold used to say to the kids disturbing his peace, arguing around the twine store about who was right. Cutting fish tails was how you marked the catch for counting. The Wiseman kids and their cousins were always arguing. Jack was the amenable one. Okay was his favourite word. *Okee-dokee*, he said, from the time he was a toddler. "Okee, Dek. You right. Okee-dokee, Lloyd, you right too," Jack would say to his cousins, taking his thumb out of his mouth. He was too small to have been counted into the argument in the first place, but he didn't know that. He was always so happy to go along. "Okee-dokee, Marion," Jack would say cheerfully.

At the Lockes, everything had to be just so. No wonder the kids had grown up and left! Marion felt quite worn out after her first day. There'd been no point crying for Mom, so Marion had cried for Ede. She felt guilty crying at all. Aunt Harriet was dear, really. Salt of the earth, that's what Mom said about the Lockes. It was true, Aunt Harriet gave her everything she needed, just like Ede had said she would.

When Ede insisted, Marion had gone up to her room at home and started packing. Everything. All her clothes, most of her books she piled on the bed, the kewpie dolls Mom had given her. Ron had chewed the face off one, but Marion loved it still. Into the pile it went. She looked at all her worldly possessions now stacked on the bed. Should she take her pillow?

"Marion, m'darling." Ede was standing in the doorway. "You needn't take the house, now. Aunt Harriet and Uncle Lionel, they *has* a house. While you're gone, you can use theirs. That's the idea, now. You needn't take so much clothes either," Ede said, putting some of Marion's piles back in her bureau. A bundle of socks rolled to the floor. Marion watched them go, her prospects with them. If she left without everything, she could hold on to nothing. Really, she should take her woollen stockings, too, the ones that hung in the back of the closet that Mom had missed packing into the trunks in May, to wait for the fall and the return of the ice. But Ede went on. "When you need more clothes, Muffin, if you need anything at all, I'll bring it over."

"You'll come to see me?" Marion's heart leapt. With Ede there, maybe she'd make it after all.

"I'll come to see you. Maybe I'll bring Delphi." Delphi lived with her mother between the Wisemans' house at Big Tickle and The Bottom, where Uncle Lionel and Aunt Harriet lived. Delphi loved to have Marion over when Mom was busy in the shop. She knew Aunt Lizzie had never liked the child much. Delphi loved her. She dressed Marion like a doll, bounced her on her knee, and thought up games they could play together. Once they took a walk and pulled the petals off a daisy and looked upside down at butterflies and laughed so hard that Marion wet her pants and got to wear a pair of Delphi's knickers home, pinned over in the front with a clothespin. What wonderful things Delphi had, as if she pulled them from some hope chest of the gods! Delphi's knickers were such a beautiful pair, with lace all around the legs. Marion could hardly bear the thought of giving them back.

"Can you and Delphi stay at Aunt Harriet's too?"

"Muffin. Aunt Harriet can't put us all up. Uncle Lionel'd have to come over here to stay then, sure."

That sounded fine to Marion, but Ede assured her everything would be all right. "Try not to worry, my child," she said, trying to sound as much like Aunt Et as possible. "Put your trust in God."

Aunt Harriet had kindly eyes that crinkled, like Ede, and that flour smell that Ede had too, but how she went on about the gate to the yard, the way it had to be *closed just so and kept closed at all times.* She'd showed her over and over. It was for Marion's own good, Aunt Harriet said, what with the water coming right up to the edge of the road beyond the gate when the tide was in. The prospect of a visit from Ede faded, and Marion was really concerned now. How ever would Ede get in the gate? How ever could Marion herself get away and go home to Mom if the gate was always shut? When the time came, she'd have to jump it.

Aunt Harriet served her chicken for dinner. At home, they never had chicken, not since Mom had asked Ron, aged three, to look after the Wiseman flock. Soon there'd been very few eggs too, only pickled eggs in jars in the pantry, because Mom's chicken farming trial ended. Keeping the chickens had been Ron's first big job, and he'd named every one. How could you kill any of them after that? Certainly Ron couldn't. Harry had been in charge of Ron, put there by Mom without Ron knowing, and soon enough Harry couldn't eat chicken either. One look at Rusty scratching away out there in the yard and they all begged for a piece from a side of beef instead, or a ham that the Old Man had hanging in the boat store. *My children, my children, be reasonable,* Mom had said. This was something she felt they'd have to get over, but they didn't. She'd cooked them a chicken and they all lost their appetites, filling up on everything else on the table instead. But at Aunt Harriet and Uncle Lionel's, with Aunt Harriet's roast chicken in front of her, it wasn't hard for Marion to lose her appetite at all.

Aunt Harriet was solicitous. What dark circles the child had under her eyes! "Is there nothing you're not afraid of, my darling?" she asked one morning.

Marion, sitting at Aunt Harriet's breakfast table all alone in the world, kept picking at her fingers under the hem of Aunt Harriet's bleached cotton tablecloth. So it was out – the whole world knew. Goosey Marion. People had seen her, then, pressing along the far side in the ditch to get past Strong's mill when the engine that ran everything there roared so loud. Or they'd seen her walking tightrope, teetering along the cliff from Big Tickle to get past The Bottom, the small inlet on the shore which might have things lurking in the cave in the rockface.

What cave?

Dunno. She'd told Tom once about The Bottom, but regretted it.

What things?

Dunno. How dopey she must have sounded, having to admit it like that: *Dunno.* What guff, that would be what Tom was thinking. She'd told him about how scared she was of the *James Strong* too, the schooner at Uncle Harold's; how it seemed a nightmare ship at the end of the drook, the long wooded path that led there, how she had nightmares of people picking her up under the arms while she wriggled and screamed and how they dropped her down in the dark hold anyway, the one in front of the wheelhouse or the half-hold behind.

"What people? Pirates?" Tom had seemed hopeful.

"Dunno."

Years later, when they lived at Campbell's Point and the *James Strong* was tied up at Strong's wharf, Ron did fall in. He fell in right after the holds had been unloaded of fish and gear and were completely empty. The hatch covers hadn't yet been replaced, and the holds yawned open, bare and hard as the hob of hell. The drop was long, fifteen feet or more. It was a wonder he'd survived. The children could see that their mother thought it was a wonder too. She was white, shaken. How many more accidents would Ron have, and survive? Ethel got out her straight darning needle and her best linen thread and sewed up the three-inch gash in his scalp. She was calm. Ron was calm, too, hardly moving his head in his mother's lap, with just a twitch here and there, and a whimper. How his scalp bled; the skirt of Ethel's dress was red.

"Never mind, my son," Harry said to Ron. The older brother had a soft spot for the younger. "Just imagine you're getting combed for lice, that's all." It wasn't unpleasant to lay your head in Mom's lap for that. She had so little time to sit down with you otherwise. But after Ron's accident Harry could see that his mother was shaken. Marion was shaken too, remembering her dream and her exchange with Tom about the Bottom and the schooner at Uncle Harold's. It was as if her own nightmares had been transferred to Ron, to someone who could make them real.

If Marion hadn't been able to talk to Tom about things like that back then, she certainly couldn't have talked to Aunt Harriet.

"I'm not afraid, Aunt Harriet. I don't think so. No."

She picked at her bread and marmalade, staring at the chunks of grapefruit and orange. Marion hated marmalade, especially any with great chunks in it like Aunt Harriet's had. At home, it was Marion's job to pick through the fruit when it came in off the coastal boats, to pull out anything that had spoiled and chop it up for marmalade. That way, Mom said, they'd still get the goodness of the sun from the south, all that they needed for strong bones and teeth, for rosy cheeks, soft skin, hair with lustre. Still, Marion hated chunks and tried to chop them as small as she could. She swallowed hard now, thinking how she'd resented the job. Oh for home now, all the slops and rinds and chores of home!

"No I'm not afraid, Aunt Harriet," she said again, but with every word she sounded less sure of herself. Her cheeks flamed with shame. She might be only six, but she was fearful, it was true. And was there really anything so odd about that? She was always on the run, that was one thing – from *him*. It was like living with a ghost dragging up on chains from the ocean bottom; you'd never know where he'd appear next, and who he'd come for now. She had a highly developed startle reflex, that was another. That came from years of dodging him, listening for him when he was sneaking around, jumping when he appeared out of nowhere.

Jack was sure the Old Man was a genie. No one could appear like that and not be a genie. "He comes right outta his Aladdin lamp, *shazam!*"

"Dopey. You gotta rub it to get the genie out. I clean the chimneys every Saturday, I should know." She and Jack had been doing a job for Mom, throwing the broken crockery down the outhouse. Jack wasn't helping, really. He was too small to do anything but be in the way, but he wanted to help and Marion didn't let on. All he was doing was dragging the whole stinky business out by being so slow and passing her the pieces one by one, practising his counting.

"Look!" she'd said to him, grabbing a whole handful of china shards to get the job done. "You rub it like this," she said, demonstrating with her palms on half a teacup before she threw it down the hole and stepped away, pushing the two of them back and outside. "Besides," she said, louder now that they were in the open air and she could breathe better, "genies bring favours. They grant wishes. They're good, like angels."

"There are bad angels," Jack said solemnly.

"There aren't." Was nothing sacred?

"There are," Jack said knowledgeably. "Santa was an angel. He fell one day he wasn't looking, stepped offa the cloud and fell right through down into the earth head first, fell straight down into hell, cracked his head wide open."

"Satan."

"Satan. Which is why he's all red, from the blood, I think. He got nasty after that, 'cause his head hurt and he had garden soil in his ears. Couldn't hear God calling him. *Satan! Satan! You come back now! You come right back home this minute and finish your chores!*" Jack reported all this soberly. "Genies is nasty too. Can be."

Marion had gone to the bookcase, looked it up. The evil jinn were hideously ugly, she found, but the good were singularly beautiful, and they all lived in the mountains of Arabia where the horses came from, and the knights too.

"How'd they get here then, from Arabia?" she demanded of Jack. "This is Newfoundland."

"S'pose they can get around on the *Clyde* too, just like anyone else."

"What, they buy a fare?"

Jack shrugged.

"The Old Man can't be a genie. Genies are ugly." The Old Man was very handsome, picture-show handsome. Everyone said so, not just Mom.

"Shape-shifting."

Nothing fazed Jack. Even at four, he was never at a loss for words; he had an answer for everything. At Aunt Harriet's now, fiddling with the marmalade on her knife as if she weren't afraid, Marion felt her stomach twist at the memory of Jack's silence, his utter calm in Mom's arms on the porch. Would she ever talk genies with him again? She wanted to tell him he was right. *Please God, bring Jack home so I can tell him okee-dokee, he was right.* Genies could shape-shift. They could turn themselves into cats and dogs and snakes and goblins of all kinds, people too. But as much as she'd have liked an explanation for her father, this one didn't seem plausible. Why didn't he drink? If he just drank, there'd be the explanation there. Everything about her father was strange. She'd told her friend Net Penney once, when Netta found her crying. "My father hits me," Marion had sobbed.

"Ah now, girl, my father used to too, sure, he used to turn me right over his knee when I was bad." Net had stroked her face.

Marion had dried her eyes. Net's father had had weak lungs and died. The ordinariness of Net's father, dead or alive, the mystery of her own, his sheer unfathomableness – it had cleared her head and brought her back to herself. Her father never turned them over his knee. Most times he ignored them, playing father as if the beatings he gave them had never happened. When he did beat them he laid them up for weeks with injuries that might have killed them. When he came at them that way, it was never because they'd been bad.

Oh, for such cause and effect.

Like a genie, he appeared out of nowhere, that was all. He wasn't likely to appear here at the Lockes, that was true. Still, Marion hated being away from Mom. Later, after they moved to Campbell's Point, Mom would lend her out to Muriel Jones in the next house over, going up the hill. Roy Jones had a passenger boat but on it he often carried freight too, and when he was away on his runs Muriel would get edgy. "She's high-strung, Marion, that's all," Mom would say, sending Marion off to be Muriel's doll for the night. Marion wished Muriel would just get a big dog, a guard dog that knew to snarl. Muriel would feed her beans in tomato sauce for breakfast. Marion hated beans in tomato sauce. She hated everything about being away from Mom, and especially being at Muriel's instead. Sometimes when Roy Jones was carrying freight on his boat he would arrive back in the middle of the night. Muriel would get Marion up, to make way for Roy, and put her in the cold bed in the spare room.

Marion would have been happy just getting up and going home, but it wasn't allowed. She didn't see why not. It was an island they were on, after all; it wasn't as if cougars or bears had made it over across Hall's Bay to terrorize a small girl in the night, going out one gate and into the next, up the stairs and into her own bed. On Little Bay Islands they didn't even have a moose, no wild things at all.

"We got the Old Man," Harry said, but the Wiseman kids would have liked a few real wild animals. On Long Island they had wild horses at least, including a magical white one. Ron especially would have liked a few bears, a moose. He'd never seen even a deer.

"Y'eats 'em, *pow!*" said Harry, pointing his imaginary rifle.

"Ye doesn't. They eats *you!*" Jack said, and Ron ran away, crying.

Jack. Jack Jack Jack. Under the sloping ceiling of the Lockes' spare room, Marion made her plan to jump over the front gate that must be kept closed at all times, and get away. She'd never slept under a sloped roof before, and she'd brought the wrong book for it. *The sky is falling! The sky is falling!* Chicken Little cried, and for the two weeks Mom was away with Jack, Marion stared up at night at the Lockes' sloped ceiling, waiting for it to collapse and bury her.

~

It took the *Paragon* all day to get to Twillingate. It was the worst day of Ethel Wiseman's life. With every throb of Alex Anstey's engine, with every slap of the ocean against the gunwales, her head pounded and her stomach heaved. She'd come away without even a sandwich, but she couldn't have eaten now. She was sick with dread, not seasickness. All she'd brought was a bottle of water, and this she spooned steadily into Jack's mouth. His small head lolled against her palm. He was hot and dry now; his face flamed. Sometimes a drop of water splashed on his cheek, and she watched it evaporate in the heat of his skin. He hadn't opened his eyes in hours. She couldn't hear the bubbling of his breathing for the noise of the boat, so she watched his chest to make sure it still rose and fell. With every lurch of the boat her heart lurched too, and time stopped. Was he dead? Was he alive? By dusk, by Twillingate, which would prevail? *I do not ask O Lord.* She should have taken him days ago. Why why *why* hadn't she taken him days ago? Why had she waited? What could have possessed her? What had she been waiting for? And now, there was only the speck of them out there on the unforgiving ocean. They were alone. There was no one to comfort her, no one to look her way, no one to squeeze her shoulder, to say *it won't be long now. Don't you worry, my darling, it won't be long now.* Alex Anstey was a good man, her partner Fanny's uncle and a family friend – as much as the Wiseman family could have friends, with Sidney so jealous of anyone who looked her way. He was even jealous of the children and *their* friends, poor man. Yes, Alex Anstey was a kind man, but he was busy now, sighting the sky and the waves and attending the wheelhouse. He couldn't stop to comfort her. Ethel was left alone with her thoughts, her crime and her guilt and her panic. She was left alone with sick, sick Jack, dying Jack.

At the hospital Dr. Olds was already gowned. He swept them into the surgery. Dr. Olds was from Johns Hopkins in Baltimore, by way of Connecticut. In the early 1930s, soon after he arrived in Newfoundland, he virtually ate, drank, and slept in his surgery. Everything was epidemic: diphtheria, pneumonia, double pneumonia, seal finger, tuberculosis. Especially tuberculosis. For tuberculosis of the lung, rib-cage excision by thoracoplasty was by then routine. Streptomycin, the only pharmaceutical treatment, didn't make it to Newfoundland until 1947, two years after the war ended, and then only to St. John's. Penicillin and sulpha were available – Alexander Fleming had con-taminated his petri dish with mould as far back as 1928, and mass production of penicillin began in wartime – but against *Mycobacterium tuberculosis* they were ineffective. Rest, fresh air, and sunshine, even folk remedies like cod liver oil which seemed to keep the appetite up – these and surgery were the only treatments in Newfoundland, and with all alacrity Dr. Olds had become an expert surgeon. He removed part of a rib to drain the pus from Jack's lung, but Jack's case was not TB, and it was unusual. He was a tiny child, small for his age, who seemed stunted and bruised and chronically banged about, as if he'd been knocked between the gunwales in a gale all the way from Little Bay Islands to Twillingate. Dr. Olds had seen worse, but seldom. This small patient with pneumonia was more gravely ill than the chronic TB cases Dr. Olds saw; he was on death's door and the door was swinging open. Dr. Olds set Ethel up for a direct transfusion to her son.

Hugely pregnant with a new baby, a child she would call Grace and for whom she would hope for the best, Ethel stared at the tubes in her; in Jack. Under anaesthetic, her boy was still; he seemed dead already. *And the Lord God caused a deep sleep to fall upon him, and he slept; and he took one of his ribs, and closed up the flesh instead thereof.* She looked away, at the surgery walls. The tubes were rubber, from something in nature, a tree: how peculiar it was, then, that they were like no colour she had seen. The infirmary walls, too, were like no colour in nature, a sort of icy green. Except for Dr. Olds there was nothing natural here. It was hell, cool and mint and quite unexpected. She stared at the ceiling too. It was white. *This is now bone of my bones, and flesh of my flesh.*

She and Jack were away for two weeks.

It was an unusual length of stay for a patient at Notre Dame Bay Memorial. Many stayed just the day, lined up at the surgery to be seen and assessed and perhaps reassured; then they turned around and went home on the boat they came in on, or on the next weekly coastal boat. Time was precious, the doctor's and yours; you didn't cool your heels at the hospital if you didn't have to. For those who had to, in the wards or the sanitorium sunrooms at each end, the stay was a season – if they went home at all. Truly acute cases like Jack's were rare. Anyone that sick didn't bother to set out for Twillingate at all. Or if he did, he died before he got there.

Ethel and Jack stayed until the boy was over the worst, and no longer.

Sidney didn't wire the hospital to see how they were; when she returned, he was still home, delayed from the Labrador by weather, but he didn't speak to her. She waited for whatever was to come. No one used other transport when Sidney said no; no one defied him; no one shamed Sidney Wiseman in front of his peers. There would be some dreadful punishment, and she waited. If he hit her, she'd have to protect the new baby in her womb. She waited and waited, and still it didn't come. She waited some more. It didn't come; it never came. Not to her, at least. He saved it all for Jack.

~

"A is for *Argyle*." Marion looked at Jack.

He sighed.

"C'mon, Jack, do try."

"Okay. B is for *Bruce*."

"*Clyde*."

"*Dundee*."

"*Ethie*."

"*Fife*."

They were naming the coastal boats that the railway owned. Jack could never figure out what a railway was doing with boats, but he knew they had all been built at the end of the last century in Scotland and were named alphabetically for places there. Jack memorized things. He had that kind of mind. The old sealing steamers out of St. John's had names like *Terra Nova, Neptune, Thetis, Diana*. Then *Eagle, Ranger, Njord, Bloodhound, Viking, Kite*. He could reel them off, front to back, back to front. But he liked the names of the Scottish coastal boats better. They had symmetry; they went together. Though it was Marion's turn now he butted in with the last two, because he loved their names especially. "*Glencoe. Home.*" He liked that, knowing there was a place in Scotland called Home. He'd tried to find it on the globe at school. He thought his family might have come from Scotland once, and he hoped they could go back, leave the Old Man behind. He was so tired of his room; he'd been here for weeks, not allowed to step across the threshold for meals or even chores – not even to pee. That was the only reason he was allowed visitors at all, why Marion was allowed in now, to empty his slops. In Scotland, at the village called Home, there would be stone walls and vines and hollyhock and a proper outhouse. He just knew there would be. Outside Home, just in the long grass at the far side of the tickle bridge into town, there would be fairies in the night who left a bit of mist in the morning, and his father would be nowhere in sight. They'd leave him behind in Little Bay Islands to mind the fish stage and the twine store and the *James Strong* and look after the house. Jack wished Ede could come to Home too, but the Old Man would need someone to get his dinner into the warming oven. The Old Man's dinner was always served up first, the best of everything going to his plate – the best of the pickled sausage, the best chops, the choicest piece of salt beef, the prime bits of the cod stew, with great hunks of fish – and into the warming oven over the kitchen stove it went, to sit while the rest of them ate and the Old Man lay on the daybed, inspecting them, his forearm shading his eyes but leaving enough clear to see.

Jack was older now. All his life he'd been hit around by his father, and now that his father had weak lungs and had spent six months in hospital in Twillingate and didn't go to the Labrador anymore, it was worse than ever. But for all of that Jack didn't really want the Old Man to go hungry. The Old Man was like the bears in the woods on the mainland; they were just the way they were, that was all, and you didn't want them dead for it. You especially didn't want them to starve, because starving made them plenty ugly and a whole lot worse. Jack knew what it was like to be hungry. How many times had he been whipped and then sent to bed without his supper? He could imagine what it must be like for those starving bears, or for his father if that was his father's problem. What was his father's problem? He couldn't tell, he could never figure it out. His father never did seem to eat much, lying on the daybed in the kitchen until Mom and the rest of them finished up. Maybe that was it – maybe the Old Man needed to eat more. Maybe Ede could teach the Old Man how to put his own plate up, and then she could get a later boat to Scotland and meet them.

Marion didn't mind being scooped with the last two names of the coastal boats, the *Glencoe* and the *Home*. Anything to bring the smile back to Jack's face. She should scramble; the Old Man could appear at any minute. She didn't want to be cuffed, didn't want any challenge about how long a normal person would take to empty a simple slop pail. So what if she wasn't a normal person? She was quite happy to be abnormal, a scut, a slieveen, anything her father wanted her to be, if it meant she could stop for a minute to play a game or two with her brother, confined to his bedroom for two months now. If her father did challenge her, she'd put her hands on her hips and say that to him. She was getting some brave now.

She thought she'd talk back to him, at any rate. She hoped she would. Sometimes, though, it seemed she'd be just like Mom – she'd do anything to defuse him. She'd keep the peace at all cost.

No one could remember any longer just what had been the issue that had won Jack his incarceration for the summer. Jack had defied the Old Man, but no one could remember over what – not even Jack. The boy had said no to him, *no I won't*, and the Old Man had taken a swipe at him. They all held their breath. No one except Harry had ever said no to the Old Man until then, and lately Harry was starting to swipe back. Was the Old Man going to allow it from anyone else? Now there'd be the devil to pay. Their father was like that. He went wild about something that had nothing to do with you and sought you out just the same to lay it on you, on Jack especially. Jack didn't seem to have the instinct the rest of them had to look out and hide, to watch and get away. *In a leaky punt with a broken oar, 'tis always best to hug the shore* – Jack didn't think like that. There was something different to him. He bowed his head and took it. And when it came to Jack, there was something different about the Old Man too. It seemed to the children that there was more going on than the Old Man's usual devilment, that whatever happened to Jack at the hand of his father was, Mom believed, in some way her fault. They wanted to get to the bottom of it, but Mom just stroked Marion's head.

"Why does he do it, Mom?"

"Why does anyone do anything, my child? The secret things belong to God. Maybe He'll tell us one day."

"Who? God or Dad?"

It was a good question. They were both in charge, weren't they? When Sidney had passed sentence this time, Ethel hadn't said a word. If she'd said anything at all he would've hauled off with a few more blows and doubled Jack's sentence. It was as simple as that. He could come out at the end of the summer, Sidney said, but only to go to school.

"What does that mean, Mom?" Harry was out of school by then, off to the Labrador whenever anyone wanted crew, and he was ready to smuggle his brother out to gainful employment if his sentence was to be open-ended. Would Jack be allowed out in the fall and winter but only for school? Harry was sick of it, sick of it. Many a time he'd been sent to his room and imprisoned there himself, but never for as long as this. It was like the Old Man had got bored with him and Tom. With Jack, though, the Old Man never got bored. When Harry had taken his own last lick from the Old Man, he'd given it back double. The look there'd been that day on the Old Man's face! But now it seemed he was taking it all out on Jack, everything he had left.

"Let's hope, my children," said Ethel, "that it will blow over." All summer long, when Sidney wasn't looking, the others sneaked Jack the best plates that any of them had. Ethel's asthma kept her off the stairs now, but she would never have risked getting caught anyway. Who knew what would happen to Jack then? She had no excuse to be upstairs. Her room and Sidney's was downstairs; only the children were upstairs. Whatever could she say she'd been doing? Sidney might pop up at any time, just when he'd made a big show of going out. Marion carried the contraband up and down. From June to September, she cut the heels off all the loaves she made and spooned molasses on them in heaps. Or jam, raspberry jam. The summer before, she'd picked enough raspberries from Burnt Woods to buy a red hat. She ordered it out of one of Mom's books and counted the weeks till it came up on the *Prospero*. The year before that, raspberries had got her the red coat the hat was to match the following year. Ede had helped with that. Ede had a nose for where the best berries were, and for what ungodly time you needed to rise in the morning to get them.

When she pulled the kids out of bed before dawn, they moaned. *Out dogs and in dieters*, Ede would say, just like the men did at Strong's wharf as the season approached and they got the schooners ready for the Labrador. Or, *Get up now. Let no man steal your lines.*

Ede would pull back their sheets in the pitch dark and sit them up, her hand against their backs so they couldn't slouch down again. They whined, but later they thanked her. There they'd be, the troupe of them at high noon coming down from the Burnt Woods, the Sulian's Cove road way, just as the other berry pickers were coming up, already struggling in the heat of the day. After the Wisemans had been through the woods, would latecomers find a berry left? Ede carried a big bottle of lemonade and filled the kids' pockets with hardtack. Once there had been potted-meat sandwiches, that time after the first fall frost when they'd gone to Long Island to pick partridge berries and Mom had come too, and spotted them a partridge right in the middle of the berries. Mom was magic like that. Mom said that eating hardtack was what gave them all such beautiful strong teeth, straight and white too. That, and the marmalade, and the lime that went into the well twice a year to clean it. The well filled from a spring under the Salvation Army Citadel, high on the hill overlooking the harbour. Some job to get up there, the kids said, but some job to get to the well below it too. It fell to Tom and Harry to go, down past the shop, through Oxford's property and down a lane, where finally they stepped into their hoops and carried back buckets of water. Marion took a turn of water when she had to, so that the Old Man wouldn't find out when the boys were late with their chores. A child of Ethel Wiseman's did not fail to close someone else's gate behind him, and so fetching water was an arduous process of opening and closing Oxford's gates, one on each end of the lot, on the way down to the well and again on the way back – and then climbing the painful grade to the back of the house. By the time the boys got back they were ready to drink up half of what they'd brought. Their shoes were full of water. Sometimes on the steep hills they would fall flat on their faces, buckets and all, despite the engineering of the hoops, birch saplings from the mill which Strong's also supplied to the cooperage for barrels. In winter it was worse. As soon as the Old Man tapped his barometer and forecast the storm coming in, Tom and Harry were off, running, to haul extra buckets. Afterwards there was always the interminable track to shovel from the house, through Oxford's, to the well. A simple stamped track wasn't wide enough to accommodate the hoops and the buckets. A small shed stood over the well to keep it clear of snow, but the boys had to break the ice on the surface with the pickaxe kept there in winter.

The hardtack Ede gave the children for berry picking was easy to keep, easy to nibble on, and it didn't make a mess. It kept you full, too. Once Marion ate all of hers just waiting for the sun to start its climb behind Bert Strong's house. They'd got to the cliffs too soon, past Strong's football field at the back of the tennis courts, and still couldn't see in the dark. What a murky hour, with everything charcoal, forming itself into life – the roofs of the houses, the stones in the walls by the football field, which they sat on to watch the games. A roof peak, a mast rising beyond it on the water like a paladin over the deck of someone's livelihood. Here at the wall, a stone and a stone and a stone all emerging in the dawn as if none had ever been before and, for the very first time, now became itself. It was magical. Some of them found it so, at least; munching their hardtack, they fell quiet and thoughtful. Harry just fell asleep in the grass.

Soon enough Harry and Tom lost their taste for berry picking, but Marion and Ede were diehards. Ede had a nose for the best routes over the island, too; the quickest, and to get up into the Burnt Woods she took them the route behind Strong's. Coming down was another matter but going up was a fierce climb, straight up the rocks through brambles. They hung on to the alders to pull themselves up, pushing off against the rocks. My children, my mountain goats, Mom said. You couldn't come back that way, though, not with your bucket full. What if you tripped? The thought was terrible. They protected their berries, never ate them, never even sampled them – that was unimaginable. Everyone had a bucket, and a smaller cup to pick into. When the cup got full they walked back to the bucket and dumped it in. Tom and Harry were fast pickers, Harry the best by far, but Marion was no slouch. Jack was an utter failure, and when the others were finished his bucket usually stood half empty. And so they filled his. *Many hands make light work*, Ede said, as Mom would have. They all finished Jack's bucket with him, even Jack picking up steam again, and then they all went back down the long way, down the Sulian's Cove road.

Marion had a going concern with her raspberry picking and with Mrs. Adolphe's endless demand. Mrs. Adolphe would buy gallons and gallons, every single berry that Mom didn't want herself for jam or desserts. But this year was different. This year Marion didn't have to worry about Mom's alarming habit of piling up the raspberries for Mrs. Adolphe, twenty cents a gallon, five cents a quart. It was Mom's idea of a quart that was so alarming, and Marion watched mournfully as she heaped the berries in a jug, hilling the top.

"Aunt Annie's got to have full quarts," Mom would say. "Uncle Dolphe likes his pie and his jam. And anyway, we must give good measure." Maybe, Marion hoped, Mrs. Adolphe would sometimes like a jug of chopped citrus instead.

None of it mattered this year. Mrs. Adolphe would be getting her berries from somewhere else. Marion's weren't for sale; this year, they were all for Jack. She pulled on her shorts and her sunhat every morning and climbed up into the Burnt Woods alone, where she picked and picked and picked. It all went into jam and sweets and then on up the stairs, and the Old Man never knew. It'd be a wonder that Jack didn't come out at the end round as a ball, bouncing down the stairs. Once Marion had sneaked a chop off the Old Man's plate in the warming oven. A choice one, on a heap of potato. She took some of the potato too: that went to Jack. It was bliss. She'd hummed as she'd carried that tray up the stairs. There was nothing like trumping her father at his own game. She carried Jack's water in basins and made his bed. Boys didn't make their own beds, Marion knew that.

Not even when they were in jail. Marion didn't mind. She was practising making hospital corners. In nursing school she'd be faster at
hospital corners than anybody. She'd be faster at giving injections too.
She'd be so fast the patients wouldn't even know what was coming.
"Why, Miss Wiseman!" they'd say, incredulous, still grimacing for the
catastrophe to begin when Nurse Marion, already stoppering her
syringe, told them it was over. She'd be quick as lightning winding
bandages and setting bones and applying plasters and especially
pulling them off, all at once, without thinking about it, like Mom had
shown her.

Things hurt a lot less when you got them over with. That was the
pity about Jack in his room here. It would go on and on.

She held up his sheet by an end. "See, you fold the corner up like
this, straight up, it's geometry, really, and then you tuck it under." She
talked to him in whispers. No one was supposed to be talking to him
at all, and Mom wasn't even allowed to see him. The one time Mom
came Marion kept watch, looking in on them, Jack with his head on
Mom's lap while she stroked his hair. Any other boy might have been
too old for it, but Jack wasn't any boy and Mom wasn't any mom.
Jack called Mom "the Mother." She's my best friend, he'd say, the
Mother and my best friend.

"Jack."

But he was looking off in the distance, wistful. He wasn't interested in hospital corners. Tom had written from RAF training out west
that the way the drill sergeant checked your bunk-making was to
throw a quarter on and see if it bounced. If it didn't bounce, you
hadn't made your bunk up tightly enough and you remade it until
you did. Imagine, Tom had written, having spare change to throw
around like that! It was like the time he'd seen his first shower, as a
medical student at Memorial University in St. John's. Though he'd
described it in exacting detail, they still couldn't make out quite what
it was. Tom hadn't had the word for taps. "Water comes down over
you," he had written, "and runs through a hole in the floor."

"Jack," Marion tried again. "What's a shower?"

"A shower," said Jack, "is rain."

Marion folded and cornered and tucked. "Jack. Remember when you said the Old Man must be a genie?" Marion's mind never left the inevitability of her father. He was like doom, always coming.

"I did?" Jack turned away from his window, the one that overlooked the lawn. He could only spend so much time lying on his bed, so he paced between his two windows. Sometimes he looked out, sometimes he didn't. Often as not it just plain hurt to see what lay outside, with him inside. Now he took hold of the curtain of his closet and swung it back and forth on its rings. How often had he done that these months, out of sheer boredom? He was allowed no books, nothing that would help pass the time – not even his school books, since school was out.

"Sidney," Ethel had said casually, "with a school book or two Jack could get a start on next year, or a better grasp of last."

"I believe, my darling, that a better grasp of last year is exactly what he is getting, without your damn books." Sidney hated school and everything in it. Doing well in school was just showing off, that was all, and he never did. Why should his kids? His week's supply of the *New York Times,* seven issues, came in a huge bundle off the *Clyde* every Thursday, with the mail. He saved them until Sunday when he read them in bed, picking sideways from the meal trays Marion brought in while he draped the papers on his lap. When he finished, he threw them in a heap. Ethel saw that they made their way to the children.

Jack occupied himself with the times tables and with memorizing things backward. If she listened closely, Marion could hear the "Ode to Newfoundland" winding its way down through the ceiling backwards, on Jack's wheezy tenor, half sung and half whispered so the Old Man wouldn't hear. *Thee GUARD God, thee GUARD God, thee guard God, smiling land.*

Jack turned back to the window again, looked out. Clouds were stacking over Shoal Tickle. There'd be a downpour soon.

"I said the Old Man was a genie?"

"Yes. You still think so?"

"Nah. I think he must be like a bear. The way he's worse around us. If we weren't here, he'd be fine. Maybe he'd even be nice to Mom. They say that about bears, Marion – they're worse when there are cubs."

"Oh Jack, that's because they're protecting them and someone gets in the way."

Jack didn't turn from the window. "Oh," he said. "Well, the Old Man does provide for us. You mustn't be hard on him. You mustn't forget that."

"So he does. So he does provide." *Rubbish. Without Mom's shop, they'd all be back on the Dole diet.*

Jack craned his head to see past the window frame, out as far as he could toward Mack's Island and Shoal Tickle. "Shower coming in now." He'd like to run out into rain like that, just to feel it.

"Pity the Old Man didn't just put you in the root cellar," Ron said from beyond Jack's door. Ron was afraid of his father and to some extent observed his law. "Remember how Brer Rabbit begged Brer Bear not to throw him in the briar patch?"

Jack remembered. He remembered that the briar patch was really where Brer Rabbit wanted most to be. Jack would have loved to have been banished to the root cellar, among the half barrel of apples, the potatoes, turnips, cabbages, and carrots. But no one was ever interred there. The way to Sidney's soul was through his stomach, and his children were to have no part of his provisions. Jack thought of it every time he was whipped, how he'd like to be sent to the root cellar instead. He would have smuggled down books and a light, would have basked in the sweet smell of mellowing apples all day long. Any one of them would have savoured a day off from the Old Man, locked in underground.

~

Sidney was holy about his food. He loved it, had to have the best of everything. It was a measure of his worth. The kids were not to go near the larder in his boat store. Marion had to once, the year Mom had Dr. Olds take out her kidney in Twillingate, and Gillingham, Ede's replacement, traipsed around in Mom's dresses instead of looking after the family and promptly got herself fired. Ede had gone off to get married; Gillingham was supposed to have held down the fort. She took jewellery as well; it had been awful. Marion had rounded the newel post of the stairway into the hall to find Gillingham standing there in Mom's green dress. Marion had sat down in her shock, right in the middle of the hall on the floor. Gillingham had been sacked, and Marion had to cook until Mom came back. It was the only time since she'd been a tiny child that her father was civil to her. He'd almost been warm, coming up behind her at the stove to make sure she didn't splash the Gillett's lye for his handkerchiefs into the peas, where they soaked for the next day's pudding.

In winter, the Wiseman boat store housed more meat than fishing gear: bacon, turr, rabbit, sides of beef, halves of pigs, huge whole hams hanging by their shanks. It was a creepy place. The kids were glad only Mom and Ede had to go down and get things. The one thing they liked there was the barrel of pickled sausages which pulled out on an everlasting string. It was amazing, once you took the barrel lid off and pulled out the link on the top, to find it was connected to the next, and the next, and the next, like that story about the angel disguised as a man who made the kind old couple's pitcher pour milk forever. *Good morrow to you and get out of there before I come in and get you out*, Sidney said when he found them at it once. And once it was; they never went back.

Ethel baked bread daily and got in wheels of cheese. She put up jars of mussels, salmon, lobster, seal, moose. The corned beef they had, from tins, came in on the coastal boats. There was always brace upon brace of snared rabbits and several pairs of turrs, and a competition among the children to see who could get the first turr plucked without tearing the skin. One day a neighbour brought a puffin he'd shot. Ethel was uneasy about Sidney's cache of provisions as it was. Did they need to be eating exquisite birds now too? The puffin had a dear little face, with downcast eyes like a sad old man's, and a bright orange bill that seemed to have no end to it, matching its orange webbed feet. "My son," Ethel said to the neighbour, "there are enough turrs out there that you might leave the puffins."

There was soup in a tureen, and potatoes, turnips, carrots, and cabbage served from vegetable dishes on the table. There were baked beans and pickled beets and macaroni and cheese; there was brawn and headcheese and there was fish, too: fresh fish in summer and, in winter, salt fish and smoked fish stew with onions. Sidney ate that. He had smoked herring or smoked capelin for breakfast, and sometimes steak. For everyone else there was oatmeal or cream of wheat, and on Sundays cornflakes, with evaporated milk and white sugar on top. Brown sugar was no good; it got hard and lumpy. They drank evaporated milk, too, with water added from the barrel by the kitchen door which the boys filled from the well. On Sundays there was a percolator of coffee; other days they had tea. Mrs. Adolphe would send clotted cream from Uncle Dolphe's cow, but that went with dessert. There was stewed fruit with cream, and on Sunday a layer cake with Mom's jam in the centre and frosting on the top. There was hot chocolate and sometimes there were bakeapples from the Labrador, which Mom bottled and kept in the pantry. "You don't bake them," she explained. "Nothing like that. They're a berry like any other, only better. Our French forebears in Newfoundland gave them their name. '*Bais qu'appelle?*' they asked the Beothuk. '*Bais qu'appelle?*' What berries are these?"

The children stared at her. How beautiful their mother was, how accomplished. She spoke French like she'd been to Paris.

~

"I saw where you were, with Mom and Dr. Olds in the surgery," Marion told Jack another time. "Do you remember when they took your rib out?"

"Nah."

"You don't?"

"I was a kid then."

He was down in the dumps, that was clear. Usually it was easy enough to get Jack to show his scar, so she didn't press him. "You were lucky that time you went, lucky that the Old Man wasn't there too." Imagine, getting miles away, only to find him there after all. That was how it had ended up the year before last, when Mom had sent Ede down to Phyl at the post office again, with another cable for Dr. Olds: *Marion Wiseman. Ten years old. Gaunt, run-down.* Ethel hadn't been sure whether she should spend the extra on *Wiseman,* or just say *Marion* and sign it: *Ethel Wiseman.* Dr. Olds would know the family by now. *Marion Wiseman,* she wired in the end. Where her family was concerned, where she had a say, she took no chances.

Considering the history of your husband, Dr. Olds had sent back, *I think this child should rest for six months.*

There it was: somebody was always sick at the Wisemans. With that many kids and the Old Man too, it was just what the day brought; it was simply the law of averages. The Old Man's daybed was in the kitchen, but for the children, for whichever one it was now, Mom had one set up in the breakfast room too, where she could keep an eye out. Marion waited out her time on the breakfast room daybed until Uncle Clem Locke could take her, and then she was off to Twillingate. It was grand, riding the passenger boat in the fresh spring air. Uncle Clem wanted her to stay inside, out of the weather, but she clung to the rails and stayed out. Inside made her seasick. Any cabin of any boat smelled to her of peanut butter, ever since someone had made peanut butter sandwiches in a cabin once and left the reek of it to make her sick. Uncle Clem wanted her inside, fine. But his boat was newer and bigger than most, and he was used to taking Aunt Dorothy and her folks around to the Labrador with it, not going down to Twillingate. He was too used to the Labrador, that was all. Going to Twillingate was nothing like that. Twillingate was south. Twillingate was practically the tropics!

Marion tried to reassure him, her teeth chattering, the wind whipping her protests out of her mouth and Uncle Clem's out of his too. Nothing much sick about this girl, it looked to Clem. *Women!* he mouthed finally, throwing up his hands and returning to the wheelhouse.

The wind whipped Marion's hair all the way to Twillingate. It was mops and brooms for days afterward while she tried to untangle it. It had been a glorious, glorious trip, out on the sea like that, out in the open air. And then – her father. There he was too.

Come day, go day, God send Sunday – what did he want now, another half-year siesta? All winter he'd hardly gotten up from his daybed in the kitchen. And now here he was at Dr. Olds's san. Mom hadn't said. Marion wouldn't have gone herself if Mom had said, and Marion needed to go. The Old Man had left home a week ago. Hadn't he gone to the Labrador? No, he'd come here instead. Where there wasn't room for both of them, that's how Marion saw it.

Did Dr. Olds think people could fake things?

"With some folks you just never know," Dr. Olds said casually. "These things come and go. With some people, we catch things early enough that they're not on death's door." He peered at his new patient over his glasses. This was the sister of the toddler years ago, the one who'd been so banged up and whose mother had been so white, so silent. He'd done a direct transfusion; he wouldn't forget that soon, nor the condition of the child or the look on the mother's face. In another year or two he'd find himself taking a kidney out of the mother, an emergency. Luckily it would be in the summer. She'd come in quickly on a schooner, saying she'd fallen from her wharf onto the rocks below and the next day started bleeding. He'd wonder then, as he wondered now.

"Yes, these things come and go," said Dr. Olds.

How Marion wished the Old Man would just *go*, never come again. He was in his element in the hospital, singing to the patients on his ward whether they liked it or not. No trouble with *his* lungs. Couldn't Dr. Olds see that? Trouble was, the patients did like it – the Old Man had a stage voice to match his looks, fit for gaslight, vaudeville, the wireless. Charming, he was charming. The smart people here were like the shell birds at home – you only got one shot at them, then they knew. They knew Sidney Wiseman's type. But the rest hung on his every word, held court at his feet. He'd start with Harry Lauder, work his way through a medley of hymns and Italian arias, and wind up grandly with songs from the war. *Roses are flow'ring in Picardy, but there's never a rose like you!* He'd warble that one to the nurses. Or "My Belgian Rose," another of his favourites. *My home shall be thy home, and all my treasures thine!*

Marion pulled her pillow around her ears. His treasures, yes. What the nurses didn't know about Skipper Sid's treasures, now. "Abide With Me" rang in her ears. "Keep the Home Fires Burning"; that was best of all, a surefire crowd pleaser. It was what the Newfoundland Regiment had sung on its marches in Belgium and France, over and over, straight into the bullets of the July Drive. Sidney would croon it in his tenor at the end of the day. Years after the Great War and nearly on to the next, the entire ward off the Old Man's sunroom would join in. Voices would trill all the way out over Twillingate Harbour, calling home to points west around Notre Dame Bay. The patients would get up out of bed, tie their robes and push their feet into their slippers to shuffle over to the windows and gaze into the sunset. They'd sit on each other's beds, maudlin, pining, craning their necks toward the windows in the direction of home. *There's a silver lining/Through the dark clouds shining/Turn the dark cloud inside out/Till the boys come home.* It wasn't a song any more; it was a promise.

And interminably, always always always at the end of every day like Taps and the beginning of the next like Reveille, Sidney would render his "Ode to Newfoundland." *When silvern voices tune thy rills, we love thee smiling land. We LOVE thee, we LOVE thee, we love thee, smiling land!* He'd hold the line for effect – and invariably Mrs. Rowsell, the old lady with the gout, would shrill down the ward from the women's side. "Oh Mr. Wiseman, what a silvery voice you have!"

It made Marion twist in her bed, made her long for Mom and Harry and Tom and Jack and the faces the boys would pull. *Thee LOVE we, thee LOVE we, thee love we, smiling land!* Women on her ward found out soon enough that Caruso was her father, and passed along their requests to her. She'd have to call them through the wall to him. How could she say no?

It had gone from bad to worse. They'd put her on the ward, first, when she'd arrived, where there was safety in numbers. Then, soon enough, a nurse stood over her with a clipboard:

"Wiseman, Marion. Are you the wee one, now, whose dad's in the sunroom? Elsie, darling," she called to another nurse. "Help me move this little one closer to her dad, he's down the way in the sunroom."

At least they were separated, even in the sunroom. The hospital had a long men's ward and parallel to that a women's ward, but the prime sunrooms on either end were reserved for weak lungs. On three sides the sunrooms boasted great windows that were thrown open to the elements daily, except in winter. Sun and fresh air were always good for TB; aside from Dr. Olds's rib shears and bone nibblers, there was, in fact, little else. Cool air and stiff breezes didn't hurt either. In the warmth the bug would grow faster; that was the theory. The sunrooms were divided down the middle with a wall of double doors that swung to and fro when Dr. Olds came in. The doors were wide enough for beds and stretchers to be ferried in and out, and on the other side of the double door, by the head of Marion's bed in the women's sunroom, lay Sidney Wiseman in the men's. It was the closest Marion had been to her father in years, with a wall and a double door and the great doctor and all his staff and all the patients to keep them apart, if it came to that. She could spit at the Old Man if she wanted to; she'd just bound up out of her bed and run through the doors in the night; he'd never know what hit him. She could be gone in a flash. Soon she imagined doing it in the day, in broad daylight. She'd never spit at anyone in her life, and there was a first time for everything. She thought she might, at any rate. She hoped she might.

Sidney abhorred spitting. Sure, no one did more spitting than he, but he did it at home, properly, into his spittoon, and he had the girl Marion there to empty it. But for all the snake oil peddled to the outports for the weak lungs that seemed rampant there, for all the calabogus rum and all of Dr. Chase's Nerve Beans and Dr. William's Pink Pills for Pale People and even the respectable preparations from St. John's, like Stafford's Liniment & Ginger Wine or Phoratone for coughs or whatever else ailed you, the one thing Sidney Wiseman knew for sure was if you had weak lungs, you didn't spit just anywhere. Lord only knows what you might spit at someone else! No, b'y, Skipper Sid was no casual spitter. And now here he was, trapped for six months in a sanitorium where his neighbours coughed and spat and retched and horked into their sputum cups insistently, day and night. How close the beds were, with only narrow washstands at their heads to keep them apart! How cramped the whole place was, sixteen beds to a ward and four more beds in each sunroom. The place was swimming in spit.

Marion propped her pillows against the wall her sunroom shared with her father's. Was that him groaning? He'd be apoplectic, beside himself. Spitting, spitting everywhere – and here, not a thing he could do about it. Here he couldn't hold anyone down for spitting, couldn't put a knee on a chest and punch and slap and try to wrench out a tongue as he'd done to Marion that time Harry had said she'd spit at him. Harry was so so so sorry ever after – how sorry he was, how stricken, how guilty. Any lie, any ratting on her would have been better than that. Years had gone by and Harry still looked at her like that: *forgive me, Marion, forgive me!* Marion had forgiven him, but he still looked at her as if she hadn't, as if she never could. She wondered that she had lived through it. If she were really to turn out to have weak lungs now, it would be the Old Man's fault. He'd knelt on her chest to pin her down and nearly broken her ribs, trying to choke the breath out of her. Or if she turned out to have brain damage, like Bertie the mongoloid up the hill. Mom had had to check her head again; had had to check her all over for broken bones. He'd slapped her face, smashed her head time and again against the boardwalk. Blood had streamed down her neck onto her dress. An eye closed up, swelling around the contusion there. Mom and Ede had taken all the mirrors down for a week after, to prevent her from seeing her face.

She couldn't walk at all the next day. Her new black patent shoes for Easter went unworn, and her new straw hat too. She didn't go to church or Sunday school the next day; she didn't get out of bed for a week. She lay there in her makeshift cubicle at Campbell's Point staring at the ceiling of the boat store, shifting painfully when she needed to get up for the chamber pot. After a week, when she was sure he was out, she crept down the stairs of the boat store one step at a time. When she got to the bottom she missed the last step altogether, falling on the floor in a heap with a little scream. To work enough air through her lungs to yelp properly hurt her chest too much, and to keep her face as still as possible she barely cried either. Besides, it pained Mom to see her cry. Mom might hear her from the shop if she cried. Mom was white as a sheet over her as it was, running up to check on her every minute she could get away. She could barely speak. Marion wouldn't let on to Mom that she felt so bad.

Marion had been eight years old. She and Harry had been fooling around on the boardwalk on the way to the store, that's all. Marion had gotten the upper hand and Harry resented it. He ran down to the shop. "Marion spit on me!" he screamed at the Old Man.

So, so sorry. The Old Man had run out after Harry along the boardwalk, kicking him so hard in the seat that the boy nearly fell into the harbour. In saving himself he split all the fingernails on one hand. Sidney jumped over Harry where he sprawled. He flew at Marion and pinned her down, slapped her face back and forth on the boardwalk until it rang. She'd writhed and screamed as well as she could without breath, trying to get out from under him to run to the store, where she could be seen and saved.

"Marion," Harry had called to her from his cubicle some weeks later. Sidney had heard him swearing and had beaten him till his back was bloody, in ribbons. Rather than lie on it Harry sat up in bed for the week he was banished upstairs. Gordo Gillard had hit him in the back with a rock once, between the shoulder blades. It was the last time Gordo Gillard ever did anything like that to Harry Wiseman. Mom had put on her coat and gone over to talk to Gordo's mother as soon as she'd tended to him, but he could have fixed things himself. Harry was in the habit of fixing things. That rock had been bad, but nothing like what his father had done to him now. He wanted Marion to see; it was his penance. Marion didn't want to. Nothing made any of it better.

She heard him now, their tormentor, turning over in his hospital bed with a sigh of disgust. He must've given the spitter a look. It was the man who'd had his foot taken off; a TB foot, Dr. Olds had told a nurse. Nobody kicks a crippled dog, that's how the saying went, but her father did. Just look at what he did to Jack, routinely. Her father would be kicking the man with either of his own two good feet if he could be bothered to get out of bed.

"I gotta get it offa my chest, b'y," Marion heard the man say; she heard her father's harrumph. "Jaaaaay-sus!" She smiled.

Marion was in Twillingate Memorial to put on hospital weight. But it hadn't worked for her brother Tom before her, and it didn't work for her. They were skinny, gaunt, ghostly white, and destined to remain so; there seemed little that Dr. Olds's extra plates of porridge could do about it. Tom had been sent to Twillingate by Dr. Olds himself, come by Little Bay Islands one summer on the *Bonnie Nell*'s rounds along the bay. It was the year the family had moved to Campbell's Point from the Tickle. Marion had rowed over to the government wharf to meet the clinic boat. "You should see my big brother," she bragged to Dr. Olds, who seemed unimpressed with her infected toe. "He's sick. In our boat store." Dr. Olds remembered the Wisemans, Ethel and the baby Jack, and rowed back with Marion to make a special house call at the store. The *Bonnie Nell* was going farther north, Dr. Olds told Ethel, so the boy should take another boat to Twillingate – the first boat available. He needed to rest for the summer because he had weak lungs. And he needed to bulk up.

Tom didn't bulk up, but at least he came out of Twillingate alive. Some people didn't, and fear of the hospital competed with everyone's awe and love for Dr. Olds. Some people took their chances and stuck it out at home. Tom had had a hot appendix out at Twillingate that summer and had awakened in the dying room. That's what the men on the ward told him when he was brought back. They'd been surprised to see him. But Tom hadn't needed to be told; he'd known on waking. People all around the bay talked about the dying room. It was legendary. You knew it right away. It was a private room, to begin with, and no one had those. It was small, dark, without windows. Waking up there wasn't a good sign – Tom recognized that immediately. The last thing he remembered, he'd been very ill. But there was Dr. Olds in a chair beside the head of his bed. He had his hand around a coffee cup that rested in his lap, and he looked tired. Whatever time it was, it seemed the wrong time to Tom – too late, too early. His head swam.

"Tom, my boy, how are you feeling?" said Dr. Olds.

Tom opened his mouth. Nothing came out.

"Well then, you'll have coffee?"

"Yes." This time, Tom croaked it out. You didn't say no to Dr. Olds.

Dr. Olds went out and returned with a second mug. He wasn't gone long; he hadn't sat all night with a youngster in that condition only to lose him on a trip for coffee. First the telltale chest, now this. Dr. Jacobs had seen the boy when he arrived, in Dr. Olds's absence, and had let him lie around. Then his appendix ruptured. Dr. Olds was just back, and Tom went to the OR right away. It hadn't been too late then, and it wouldn't be now.

Tom drank down a few sips. He couldn't believe it himself. He was eleven, far too young for coffee. Maybe with surgery, he'd graduated. Drinking the coffee had started out as a matter of pleasing Dr. Olds, but it turned out to be the best thing for his intestines. Had Dr. Olds known that? Dr. Olds just smiled, and pinned a tube to Tom's pillow. It was Twillingate's version of IV fluids, connecting to a water pitcher at the bedside which Tom would have to empty hourly. Dr. Olds would prove to have been right about Tom's chest in the long run, too. Years later, during the war, Tom's RAF admission X-ray showed a calcified lesion on his lung.

Dr. Olds would make his rounds by seven or eight every evening, standing at the end of the bed with the head nurse. He palpated

Marion's abdomen. Her mother had told him the girl had intestinal flare-ups, some right quadrant pain.

"Does it hurt here?" Harder. "Here?"

But it didn't hurt here, not now at least. She wished it did. She didn't like to be up in the air. What was it the oldtimers said? *Praise the weather, when you're ashore.* It worried her, the way Dr. Olds walked back to the end of her bed and stood there staring at her, rocking on his heels. He was making up his mind. The child had a classic island appendix. Dr. Ecke used the spiffier term: a geographical appendix. So much medical treatment in Notre Dame Bay was a pre-emptive strike. If she went home at the end of the season and sickened in fall or winter, if her appendix burst then when he could have taken it out now, peritonitis would carry her off in a day or two. In the end, he scheduled her for surgery and took it out. The following year it had been the same, for island tonsils that time. She went in still scrawny and rundown; came out after six months still scrawny and rundown, with two tonsils gone.

Tom had returned to Twillingate two years after his appendectomy, for tonsils as well. That time Dr. Olds had brought him a rubber ice collar for his throat.

"How long they let you keep it?" Marion had asked her brother.

"Days. As long as I wanted. Not long, though; I was brave."

"I was, too." But she hadn't been, and when her turn came she'd cried when they'd taken her ice collar away after only two days. The nurses didn't have time to keep emptying it and filling it, that was all. Her throat was as raw as ever; couldn't they see that?

But she got over it, and then her stay became boring. Her stay this time had become boring too. She prayed for the mail that came in weekly on the *Clyde* or the *Prospero*. Mom had a letter and a package on every boat. There'd be books, and little games you tipped just so, to sink a tiny steel ball in a hole. For sure there'd be a Mr. Big bar with peanuts, and chocolate-covered marshmallow bars as well. Marion liked little so well as the taste of chocolate and marshmallow; it blotted out the liquid yeast and the liquid iron she had to drink at the hospital twice a day, for being rundown. The yeast tasted viler than the iron but the iron left a rough film on her teeth. Mom's chocolate whisked it all away. A friend of Mom's came to visit her and brought two more books. The Twillingate patients seldom had visitors; three beds down from Marion, the woman with the bandage seemed to resent hers. Never mind. Marion missed her *Lorna Doone.* Mom's friend had brought little kids' books, but Marion could make do. One book was on Shirley Temple, the big star who was getting bigger daily; it teemed with glamorous pictures. When she got out of Twillingate Marion thought she might invite Shirley Temple to Campbell's Point. Mom would help her with the invitation. *This is to let you know that I am well and hoping you are the same.* It was Mom's example of how not to start a letter. They could script something together with Mom's fountain pen, on a lovely card. Maybe Delphi would let Shirley stay at her house; Skipper Sid wouldn't be likely to welcome her at his. Marion thought Shirley Temple might like Little Bay Islands. Mom had a candy shop of sorts, and Mom had better than bonbons: she had ice cream. *Shirley, girl, will you have a dish or a cone?* The harbour wasn't any Peppermint Bay, likely, and Marion thought Shirley didn't have Little Bay Islands beaches in mind in her song. Strong's would never name a schooner the *Lollipop* – Newfoundland vessels weren't the type. Shirley's boats might be made of sugar and melt dead away in the kind of real water they had out here. Still, she might like the place. It was one of the most beautiful spots in the world, after all, and Delphi could keep Shirley's hair in spills like that, however she liked it.

The second book was a biography of the Dionne quintuplets in Canada. That one had exclusive pictures. Marion thumbed them and peered and squinted, knew every corner of every snap and every word of every caption. Whenever she got really lonely, she pulled out her books and turned the pages, reading them again. She knew them backwards and forwards.

At her most bored, she got up in the evening and went to visit the patients in the women's ward. She'd stay clear of Dr. Olds's final rounds with the nurses, setting out before he came. She carried a clipboard she pinched from the nurses' desk, stood tall and scrunched her shoulders. "Good evening, Mrs. So-and-So," she said gruffly, officially, peering down as if she had glasses to peer over. Usually she didn't know the patient's names; Mrs. So-and-So they were. She was Dr. Olds. They thought her cute. "With some folks you just never know," small Dr. Olds said. "These things come and go. Carry on," she said, as if there was someone who might not unless she said so. She knew enough to leave patients alone who were just back from surgery. The grumpy ones too. That woman three beds down, for instance; the testy woman with the bandage who glared at her. Marion wondered whether she'd done something wrong. Or did they know each other, perhaps? The woman seemed familiar. Mom's letter came soon enough: *Aunt Mae is in hospital just now*. Marion folded Mom's stationery tightly and tucked it inside her pillowcase along with the games and the Mr. Big wrappers, smoothed now and folded. Nothing Mom had touched was discarded. Marion sneaked glances at Aunt Mae. Humourless, as always. The world owed her. Aunt Maud would never complain about Aunt Mae when she came to visit, bringing news of Ladle Cove, but she didn't need to. They all knew.

There was one emergency. The sunroom was listless that night, the crickets sang outside the windows in the deepening evening, Marion thought about the little Dionne quintuplets in Quintland – Annette, Cecile, Emilie, Marie, and Yvonne; no Marion – and their father, Oliva, who loved them and missed them and was telling Canada's Commission of Government, who stole them, how he wanted them back from Quintland right now, *right now*! How he must love them! It fascinated her that a father could so love his daughters. And then, beside her, *whoosh!* The girl in the next bed vomited so much blood that it spilled all over the bedding. She wasn't conscious, yet a red torrent poured from her mouth, all over everything. The girl still didn't move. She'd drown in it, for sure. The girl had been in surgery that afternoon for a T & A, tonsils and adenoids; she'd come back pale and had got paler by the minute. Marion had been looking at her most of the afternoon to make sure her chest still rose and fell. It had seemed to her the girl should be waking up, and yet she didn't. Now this. Marion scrambled up, pushed the girl's head to the side and held a K-basin under her mouth. "Nurse! Nurse!" she screamed, but she and the girl were soaked in red by the time she heard the footsteps, running. The girl had swallowed so much blood that her stomach was full – and out it was all coming now like the tide, nowhere else to go, and darker bits in it like the lolly ice that formed mid-afternoon off the wharf at Campbell's Point on cool October days. Handling her was the strangest thing. She was so, so heavy, asleep like that with all her insides coming out, and Marion having to save it all.

Quintland was never like this, whatever Oliva Dionne thought of it. This was revolting; this was thrilling. Marion had saved a life; she was going to be a nurse and save more lives and the Dionne girls too. Her neighbour was returned to her side in the middle of the night, back from resuturing in surgery, still under anaesthetic and unable to say thanks. Marion didn't mind. One day, she'd have other patients who would thank her.

~

"Anyone ask for me?" Jack looked out his window, studying something. It had been a long time since he'd been in hospital, been anywhere at all. Marion wished he could get sick, just a little sick with a sliver gone to seal finger or something, and be in hospital now. It was a means to get away. And their father wouldn't be there, not this time. Surely their father wouldn't follow the boy there. The Old Man had been well for a long time – well enough to keep complaining and gallivanting with his cronies and never working again and doing nothing, except torturing Jack. What did he think Campbell's Point was, some sort of resort? When the Old Man had come home from Twillingate that October, Mom had made the breakfast room over into a convalescent suite. She'd pulled the daybed in from the kitchen and removed the carpet and the drapes, anything that might harbour dust, and he stayed there until he got bored and moved the daybed back to the kitchen, where he could stare down the children at their meals. Rest, Dr. Olds had said, and rest the Old Man was to have. Mom couldn't take Dr. Olds's orders seriously enough. She knew people who'd died of weak lungs – Net's dad and her sister Ruby, one of her own brothers, and Max, Harold and Clyde's little brother. Aunt Maud's husband, too.

"Every day," Marion assured her brother. "All the kids ask for you every day." It wasn't true, though – all their friends knew. They knew enough not to ask, at least.

"What you tell 'em?"

"That you're feverish. Soon's the fever breaks, you'll be down at Strong's."

Jack walked across the room and sat on the bed, his hands between his knees as if he might raise them and pray to God. "Fevers can last a long time, can they?"

"That's certainly what I said to them."

Jack put his head in his hands. It broke her heart.

"They know I'm going to be a nurse. They know I know about fevers."

Jack's head nodded in his hands.

"They suspended football in your honour, you know. Can't play without you on the team."

It was partly true. But then they'd gone and got one of Strong's grandkids home for the summer from private school, and he made do.

~

Long arms, man arms. Hefty, fat, red arms. White, furry cuffs. Lovely cuffs, smart-looking, and they'd keep out the cold. Fat hands, mittened hands. Gloves, really. Nice gloves. Mrs. Satan would have made them. Mrs. Santa, Mrs. Satan. Those hands, those gloves, they were picking her up under the arms now. She began to wriggle, to scream . . . This had started out well, and now doom crept in like a bad smell. In her sleep, her heart began to pound.

There's a long, long trail a-winding
Into the land of my dreams.
Where the nightingales are singing
And a white moon beams!

There's a long, long night of waiting
Until my dreams all come true;
Till the day when I'll be going down
That long, long trail with you.

Someone was singing it in the san, someone with a golden tenor down in the men's sunroom and everyone joining in from the wards, and then they sang "Jingle Bells" too. *Dashing through the snow . . .* Dashing. Dashing! Marion woke with a start, her heart pounding as if she'd been running the hundred yards for Bert Strong's cookie jar once more. She'd been dreaming about the schooner at the end of the drook to Uncle Harold's again, its holds of hell fore and aft, about being dropped down them by those smartly gloved hands, having walked in so innocent down the long wooded path. She had had the schooner dream for years but somehow Santa had got into it lately, and she knew why. It was because Santa had dropped off the face of the earth.

If there wasn't a Santa Claus, what was there any more? Marion would have liked to discuss it with someone, but there was no way she was going to tell anyone what she'd seen the night he disappeared. If she told Tom and Harry it might eventually find its way back to Jack.

Jack lived for these things. The Jesus, Mr. Christ. Santa Claus, who filled their Christmas stockings and sometimes brought presents too, who had brought Jack his coaster that they'd all piled on to hurtle down the steep grade behind the Tickle house. The genies, the good ones with their singular beauty. His best friend, the Mother.

All these things Jack hoped would save him, Marion would guard with her life.

Santa Claus was a mystery to them all, and no one more than Jack. Santa was a logical problem, to say the least. Here's where he had to get to in an evening, just around Green Bay: *Little Bay Islands, Long Island, Nippers Harbour, Smith's Harbour, Burlington, Middle Arm, Jackson's Cove, Birchy Cove, Rattling Brook, King's Cove, Harry's Harbour* (which Jack's brother claimed to own), *Beachside, Little Bay, Coffee Cove, St. Patrick's, Shoal Arm, Springdale, Port Anson, Miles Cove, Roberts Arm, Pilley's Island, Brighton, Triton* (it was easy to remember those two, since they rhymed), *Card's Harbour, Locks Harbour, Cull's Island, Leading Tickles, Fleury Bight.*

Jack recited them all. Memorizing and reciting and figuring out things was his specialty, and after this list he couldn't even begin to think how Santa could ever make it to the rest of the world, all those countries with the flags Tom had memorized. It was too much. There was, additionally, the problem of chimneys. The house at Campbell's Point had two. How would Santa choose? Going down the wrong chimney would lose him time. Who else had two chimneys? Let's say Santa lost two minutes every time he went down the wrong chimney, either getting back up it and out onto the roof again and then across the roof and down into the right chimney – here, Jack would take a breath – or tracking through the house from the wrong hearth, to find the stockings at the right one. Let's say every second house had two chimneys, every second house in *Little Bay Islands, Long Island, Nippers Harbour, Smith's Harbour, Burlington, Middle Arm, Jackson's Cove, Birchy Cove, Rattling Brook –*

"My child," his mother said, "it's why we believe in things not seen."

Santa Claus had disappeared the night Mom had been sick. Christmas Eve and so much to do, but Ethel couldn't get out of bed. Ede had already left to spend the night and Christmas Day at home. The children ran for Mrs. Rendell, never mind a note at a time like this, and she came and held the basin under Mom's chin. Marion was fascinated, appalled, a dread upon her. They were going to have to get Uncle Dolphe's cow in and hooked up to her to drag her from her mother's side.

Jack hung on too. "Mom! Mom!" He pulled at Ethel's quilt. There was nothing worse in the world for Jack than for the Mother to be down and out. Mrs. Rendell could get not a budge out of him, to get him up the stairs and into bed. He'd been in his room so much this year anyway; now that he'd been let out he never wanted to go back.

It was Marion who finally got him to go. "Jack," she said, "however is the Mother going to tuck you in if there's nothing for her to tuck? Go on now, run up and get in bed and Mom will be up in a minute."

Jack nodded dumbly – he was already half asleep – and then there remained only the problem of Marion herself.

"Marion, darling, how's Santa going to come with you up and roaming around?" Mrs. Rendell had tried to coax her up the stairs to her own room and into bed.

It was late. The kitchen swam before Marion's eyes, the flowers in the wallpaper blurring above the wainscot. "I have to stay and help Mom." She was already straying back into her mother's bedroom. She'd been wearing a path between the bedroom and the kitchen, fetching cool, wet cloths. She was anxious, she was going to be a nurse one day, this was shift work, this was Mom.

"Marion, darling, I can stay up and help Mom." Mrs. Rendell stood behind her now, in the bedroom doorway. She was tall and sparse and so refined the children never called her Aunt, like they did most everyone else. "I can stay all night, and I'm going to," said Mrs. Rendell in her accent. "You'd be helping Mom best if you went up to bed yourself."

"She won't leave me, Nellie, not Marion." Ethel had turned her head on the pillow, shifting it an inch so that in the gloom of the lamp they could see her dry, split lips. Her hair was down on her face. It wasn't like Mom; she was always so beautiful. "Marion," Mom said, "I'll be fine if you just lie down on the daybed in the kitchen and get some rest."

With that, the child lay down. It was hard to stay awake and watch over Mom, Mrs. Rendell or not. But she managed it. Or did she?

What was this, now? A dark figure leaning over her on the daybed, poking at something hanging from the picture rail. Stockings. Their Christmas stockings – Tom's, Harry's, Jack's, Ron's, and Grace's, and the third down the line her own. The long wool socks, their Christmas stockings, and Mrs. Rendell's hand at the top of every one. Hankies, apples, a few candies going into them; a toy plane with a propeller into Harry's, hair buckles into Grace's at the end of the row. Bending over Marion on the daybed, leaning in, Mrs. Rendell was filling the stockings with gifts. Quietly, painstakingly so as not to wake her, ever so slowly the hand crept up to each sock, again and again. In Mrs. Rendell's hand now – what? A kewpie doll with a celluloid face. Mom had given Marion one just like it for her birthday. Mom had dressed it in satin ribbon, gathered at the waist to make a skirt, with a narrower width of ribbon for the bodice. Was this a Christmas sister for her birthday doll? There it was, dressed in pink satin ribbon, its fat little arms atop the mouth of Marion's sock. How did Santa know? What was Mrs. Rendell doing with it?

Marion snapped her eyes shut again. She couldn't watch. She was shocked. For a moment she even forgot that Mom was sick. And then when she did remember, the whereabouts of Santa swam away, of no consequence now.

It was Marion who went up and checked on Jack. She lay awake until the house was quiet, then crept upstairs. He was fast asleep but she tucked him in anyway, crooned as Mom would have crooned. He needed so much care. She stroked his cheek. *Ho ho ho, Jack*, she whispered, leaning in, *Merrrry Christmas!* Mom had had to take the night off, and Santa Claus too, and someone had to see to Jack.

ESCAPE

VII

HEROICS

Marion raised her head from the pillow. Her hair was full of lumps and ribbons of linen. She'd been trying a new look, achieved each morning by wetting her hair at bedtime the night before and tying it up in strips she'd torn from an assortment of old cloths she'd found in the storage room at the back of Mom's shop. Jack said they looked just like the blankets that used to make up Sailor's bed. Marion knew they weren't, and she knew Jack had been too young to remember much about Sailor anyway. It was just that they all missed him still. All these years later and she still thought of the spot behind the stove as Sailor's spot; still remembered that old doggy tangle they'd dismantled so carefully, bit by bit lest her father notice the disappearance. How dreadful it had seemed, lying there behind the stove without Sailor every time she walked into the kitchen at the Tickle; she'd cast her eyes away. Her mother hadn't the heart to throw it out, and her father had decreed against it anyway.

"Just leave it moulder," he'd said. "Maybe I'll get another dog now, shoot that one too."

"My darling. Sidney. Oh no." All those years ago, and Marion still heard the dismay in her mother's voice. Dismay was the most Ethel ever offered in protest.

"Maybe I will, maybe I won't," her father had said. "Serve everybody right."

Marion pushed a rag out of her ear. It had hardened into a lump in the night, and she'd been lying on it. Was that what had wakened her? She peered down the length of her bed through the gloom, through the enamelled rails at the foot of the iron spool bed. "Aunt Janet," she said.

Aunt Janet had her Sunday suit on, the navy one with the white Peter Pan collar and cuffs she wore to church and on the *Clyde*, too, when she went to Twillingate or down to Springdale. She didn't wear it on the *Prospero*. The *Prospero* was old; it was too drafty for a fine wool suit, and sometimes the seats were damp. Aunt Janet had her white gloves on, too, and carried her handbag, her right arm looped through its handle. Her gloved hands clutched and picked at one another, as if she had had a ticket for her passage but had lost it suddenly, just now. Perhaps it had floated down to the floor at the foot of Marion's bed.

Should she get up to help her aunt look? What in the world was Aunt Janet doing in her bedroom in the middle of the night anyway?

"Aunt Janet," Marion said, raising herself up on an elbow. She was conscious of the sight she must be, her bedhead of hair knotted up in doggy rags. "Aunt Janet, are you travelling?"

"Yes, my darling, I'm off," Aunt Janet seemed to say, but Marion couldn't be sure she'd heard the words. It was as if she'd seen them instead, as if something had moved from her aunt into the darkness around the small spool bed, around the whole of the girl's room. Aunt Janet had brought the fragrance of summer, and the room smelled of washing. Marion was transfixed. How pretty her aunt was, her cheeks blooming like that. She was always so pretty. If Marion hadn't wanted so much to be just like Mom, she'd have wanted to be just like Aunt Janet. Aunt Janet bloomed like a rose, Mom said. Her chestnut hair framed her pale face and her cheeks bloomed like a rose.

"Well, where, please?" Marion asked, as much to have an answer as to hear that voice again, to see it ripple the air.

"Well, where," said Aunt Janet. "That's a question. Where?" Her lips hadn't moved, no they hadn't. Her lips bloomed red too, another rose, but they hadn't moved. Marion hoisted herself up higher on her elbow. It was beginning to strain under her weight, but she didn't want to make a production of sitting up in bed. If she did, Aunt Janet would go. Somehow she knew that.

"Could we choose?" said Marion. Maybe Aunt Janet needed help. She'd known her aunt to be indecisive in the past. She was gentle, girlish. Uncle Harold was just so big and smart that no one around him needed to be, and Aunt Janet liked to defer to him.

"Choose?"

"Where to go."

"Oh my darling, I know where to go."

"Where, then?"

Aunt Janet seemed to think about this. "I've got a friend in Fleury Bight. She grew up here, you know, moved away. Married a Budgell."

"Cottrell's Cove, then. New Bay."

"No. Harold had a telegram last year, said she passed on. Well, strange, isn't it? Usually it's us going fear and trembling, waiting for the telegrams. Every time the men are up to the Labrador. A storm blows in, you hold your breath and wait. You pray it will come. Then, finally, Randolph Crowell comes up from the post office. He doesn't send Phyl up; this is important news, and he's got to get it out himself. He's got it in his hands, your scrap of lifeline. '*Got into Hopedale last night. All well.*' You don't know whether to hug Randolph or hit him, he's been so long coming. But he's been all round the harbour with wires for everyone. Out at Big Tickle, we're always at the end of the line. 'Janet, my darling,' he says. 'I would have run the length of myself and back if I could have got here any faster with yours. It's news from your Harold.'"

Marion was feeling strange. She should offer Aunt Janet a chair. She'd heard her mother and Ede talking about the veins women got from standing all day. Maybe if Aunt Janet sat, her circulation would improve, her head would clear some and she'd make more sense. Behind her aunt, Marion's bedroom door yawned open into the gloom of a hallway. Marion always kept her door open at night, listening for her mother and Jack. If her father went for either of them in the night Marion would hear. She could be there in a flash. Aunt Janet must have come in and seen Marion's door open. How did she get in and up the stairs without anyone hearing? Without Marion hearing? Marion heard everything.

She stared at the woman in the travelling suit.

"Won't you have a seat, Aunt Janet," she said. "You could sit here on the foot of my bed." Aunt Janet would be close enough then to really get a good look at the mess of Marion's hair. Her own hair was always so pretty, shimmery, the colour of palaminos in a meadow of clover. Oh well.

But Aunt Janet demurred. "Well, my darling, no time. You tell your mother for me, all right? You tell your mother –"

Marion thought of her mother then, how her mother would miss Aunt Janet. A tear stung her eye. "Aunt Janet, you could tell her yourself, sure you could. She's just down below –"

"Can't. Your father, my darling."

It was true. Her father was in the bedroom too. No one wanted to be near her father, that was certain. Only Mom. Marion looked at Aunt Janet. She'd got thin in her travelling suit. It was only the beginning of the summer and no one had been out on the *Prospero* or the *Clyde* since last fall, before the harbour closed in. Aunt Janet hadn't worn the suit since then, and over the winter she'd lost a bit of weight. Maybe they could all go along with her now, have her eat a little something they'd pack to have on the boat to go with the hot bread the crew baked and served right there on board. Maybe they could all take a trip, and get away from the Old Man for a while. Marion could go ahead first, and her mother could come along once she'd collected Tom and Jack, and packed up Ron and Grace. Maybe Harry could meet up with them later, after the schooner got in. He'd gone to the

Labrador again with Uncle Harold on the *James Strong*. Now that the Old Man no longer went, lying home on the daybed instead while he tried to look sick, the job of skippering the *James Strong* had gone to Uncle Harold. He skippered while Uncle Nelson and Harry crewed. The rest of the crew came from Little Bay Islands and all around, all up and down the coast. Harry loved going up to the Labrador, even when the Old Man had still been going. It was an adventure. Tom had gone once, with the Old Man, and come back white as a ghost. He never talked about it.

Marion pushed back the covers. "I'll come too, Aunt Janet, shall I? I can help look after Cedelle and Wilson." Aunt Janet had her own huge brood. Wilson, the youngest, all mouth and tummy, and his sister, Cedelle, hardly bigger than a minute herself.

Where were Cedelle and Wilson now? They were really too small to be left. "Aunt Janet –"

"Miss Hynes Parsons from Lushes Bight is coming to help your Uncle Harold with the children," Aunt Janet said. She frowned. "But she'll have a little trouble of her own." And whenever in years to come Marion thought of how Maggie Hynes Parsons, the merchant's daughter, did marry Uncle Harold the next year and take him away to Lushes Bight where she lived. . . . They never saw Uncle Harold after that, and Uncle Harold and Aunt Janet's kids got broken apart and went to relatives. Dexter and Lloyd, the older boys, and then Sheila, Joy, and Josey, and then the little ones Marie and Hope, and then the really little ones, Chesley and Cedelle and Wilson. Hope stayed with Marion and her family for a few weeks, but it wasn't safe, that was clear. They ran interference, and Uncle Harold sent her to relatives when he got back. Seventeen then and barely married to Ross Vincent off in Triton, Sheila came back long enough to get Cedelle and little Wilson. All that suffering, and out of it only Sheila and Cedelle and Wilson managed to stay together. Mom wanted all of her own children to stay together with her, to make a family. Even the Old Man, if he could. *Hope springs eternal,* Mom would say when she talked about keeping the family together. It's the most important thing.

What, hope or staying together?

Both. It's the same thing.

They heard that Maggie Hynes Parsons had a miscarriage right away and was very sick, though she didn't die. *She'll have a little trouble of her own.*

And then Aunt Janet did the strangest thing. She clenched her hands by locking her fingers together, the way Dr. Lidstone used to tell you to when he banged your knees for reflexes with his little rubber hammer while you tried to keep your feet together to hide the bruises on your ankles. Aunt Janet clamped her hands together like that and pulled her arms hard apart, just like Dr. Lidstone told you to, but her fingers didn't come apart. They just held tighter for all the pulling.

"You lie back now, my darling. But you tell your mother," Aunt Janet said again. And then she walked to Marion's window, overlooking the moon now where it was starting to fall again in the sky, and she set her handbag down on the sill as if she were staying after all.

Marion looked at it sitting there, and then up again at Aunt Janet, and she was gone.

~

Janet knew she was in trouble when the pains came on. This time she'd had them a day or two, and Ethel had been over and then she'd gone back to work in the shop after sending for Nellie Rendell to help her raise the foot of the bed. Ethel came again at the end of the day, with Granny Gert this time too, because for all Ethel's learning this looked bad to her, not much she knew how to do. Janet had had the pains before, but never mind. It wasn't as if the doctor could know. You'd hardly take yourself off to Twillingate on account of a miscarriage, even if it was summer and you could get there on a coastal boat or on Sidney's passenger boat, the *Traveller's Convenience*. Imagine it now, having to explain your trouble to the likes of Sidney Wiseman there at the wheel. Your hands over your middle, pressing down hard to keep your innards from dropping clear out of you, trying to explain anything at all to the likes of him. You'd be a sorry sight indeed to get the time of day from him, let alone get passage to Dr. Olds.

Anyway, it was forty miles to Twillingate, a journey that would take the most of a day. And then there'd be Dr. Olds himself at the other end. Setting bones, drying out lungs, tying off amputations. It wouldn't be right to bother Dr. Olds with some trifling woman's problem. That was just the way things went around here. It was just the way things were. In the outports during the off-season, women got pregnant. During fishing season, with the men gone to the Labrador, they died alone.

Died. Had she thought that? My, how her mind was running now. It must be the pain. The summer outside in full bloom, and here she was with something ending. Granny Gert had told her to stay in bed with the feather pillow under her legs until the blood stopped, but she'd had to get up for Wilson, and while she was up she came over queer and sank down to her knees.

We'll just take little Wilson for overnight, Granny had said, and keep an eye on him so's you don't have to, but no, Janet said, she'd be fine, she wasn't that bad really, there needn't be any fuss.

"Now girl, we'll just take the child and stick a bottle into 'im and g'wan, won't be no trouble."

"No, no." For some reason, Janet couldn't bear the thought of giving up little Wilson. Maybe it was just the way the last little boy had been there and then he'd got that cough and been gone, so sudden. Little Alfred, that had been, before Cedelle. Gone, just like that. "No, Granny now, no fuss."

Nothing worth a fuss now, that's what they all said every day of their lives, and nothing was. Janet lay herself down on the floor of her porch, clutching her middle, feeling the spreading, warm wet now under her bottom and down her legs. She turned her head on the worn pine floor. Still a lot of dust at the feet of the old painted chest there, and she thought she'd cleaned it. Never, never, never ending, all this cleaning and fetching and washing and feeding and tending of kids, and Harold, too, when he was home, all of it neverending – but something was ending now. Summer or not she was cold, freezing, and she shivered. Where'd her cardigan got to, the one with the elbow she'd just darned over again last week? *I believe in the communion of saints I believe in the communion of saints.* Her feet were half out the porch door, pointing out at the maple that had begun budding only a while ago and now flung its leaves out toward her impudently, the sign that frost had flown, summer was here to stay. *Stay, stay,* they seemed to say, and the wind ruffled through them with a word of its own that she couldn't make out. Something rushed in her ears; she seemed wetter than she'd ever been before, as if there was some tide taking her now. Taking her to Harold. Was Harold on some tide now, pulsing along by her side because he'd want to be there, *by God my darling by Jesus I'd want to be there,* or was he so far out by now on the Labrador banks that the water seemed just a block of grey, impenetrable, endless, unmoving?

Harold, now, her Harold. Warm as the brick in the bed. Huge Harold. The way the hair was beginning to go from his head and spring up in his ears instead. The way she rocked on the sea with him, on the sea of her own unstaunching blood, the communion of saints.

"Mommy," Wilson said, standing over his mother in his undershirt. It had been summery enough for that; Janet had just been going to pull a pair of shorts up over him. "Mommy?"

His mother stared at him, eyes wide, never to answer again.

~

Ethel went through her latest delivery from the Royal Stores. The ice had broken and the coastal steamers had been back in by June. Crates of goods had just come in for her on the *Prospero* on its first run of the season. Mail was weekly, except in winter, which lasted six months a year despite what anyone said, and then mail never came at all unless the ice was good enough for a komatik and dog team; sometimes even horses and sleds came across. Cargo and goods and groceries and occasionally an order of clothes from the Eaton's catalogue came with the coastal boats. That was every week but more likely every two, and often as not your things weren't on it, or only some of them were on it, or they were the wrong things or someone else's things and there it was. What could you do? Often as not you made do. Ethel never had enough of anything, and there she was trying to run a shop to provide for the whole town.

What she had a lot of now was heavy cardboard. Things came in wooden boxes still but more and more in heavy cardboard too, and she cut two large, wreath-sized circles from a box side and for a double thickness wrapped them together with purple ribbon all the way around, the same purple ribbon for a sash across it in a diagonal, with vees scissored into the ends, a bit of gold paint. A little glistery, the gold, but it would have to do. Lastly, some small bunches of artificial flowers she'd been keeping in a drawer, from a hat she'd owned way back in Ladle Cove. Little use for it now; it may as well go to Janet. Janet should have some flowers. Small things, all small things. *Who hath despised the day of small things?* She'd tie the flowers on somehow. It would be fine. No one would look up close. *Leave well enough alone* – how often she'd said that to the children when they struggled to master something well after they had, without even knowing. Ethel's wreath would be placed in Janet's casket, buried with it long before Harold and the men got back, long before he ever even knew. Randolph Crowell at the post office would wire Hopedale on the coast of Labrador to leave the message. HOPE THIS IS LITTLE PLS ADVISE HAS THE JAMES STRONG PUT IN YET WE HAVE URGENT TRAFFIC FOR HAROLD WISEMAN.

Hopedale would pass it to Holton Harbour, Indian Harbour, to find out who'd seen the schooner. Morse code passed around like typhus, everyone listening in, everyone wanting to pass it on, throw it from his hands before it stuck with its foul luck. Finally, it would find Harold. And then Harold would stagger and sit with his hurt the rest of the summer, casting nets that for him would evermore come up empty, and then in the fall Ethel would see the schooner come in, its flag at half mast. The schooner would come in when the rest of the world would have already forgotten – when the rest of the world had gone on for weeks now, months, getting on with its life.

Ethel's eyes filled. What a shock. *Shock* – there were so many shocks, who could bother to use the word? The new Reverend Mr. Rowsell, now, what had she heard him say? *The Lord be with us, for we never know what lies beyond the next bend.*

Well, yes we do, Reverend: a pit o' doom the size of all Conception Bay.

The pastors were always a bit green, the people said. It was why they were in the outports at all, paying their dues, rather than in St. John's or Grand Falls. The schooner would come in and the Reverend Mr. Rowsell himself would be gone, off to Bell Island for the next year without even a word for Harold Wiseman on the loss of his wife.

Ethel went outside. Through the trees, a nice breeze. Janet would have liked it, had she lived to see it. Yes, the wreath would be fine. There was no one at all to inspect it up close. There was hardly anyone to see it at all. Mostly women and children would be there at the service, those who could manage. Sidney would lie on the daybed in the kitchen, shielding his eyes and complaining how the spring sun made them water, but that was fair enough, for Sidney had had consumption and wasn't his best.

"Jack!" Ethel called up the stairs. "Are you boys ready?" She needn't ask about Marion – Marion was ready before she ever got started, so on guard the girl had become.

The boys stood in front of their mother in the kitchen. How small the family had shrunk, with Harry on the Labrador and Tom away now, working for Dr. Olds, taking X-rays on the hospital boat, the *Bonnie Nell,* or meant to be. There'd been some trouble about that, he'd written. The *Bonnie Nell* was needed for the diphtheria epidemic up the coast, and poor Tom was having to use the coastal boats, or passenger boats as he found them. He'd have to pack up the gear each time and take it along to each stop on the coast on whatever steamer came by. "Ron, my child," said Ethel, "step away a little from the stove, now, or you'll be dressed in soot." The boys had on their blue worsted suits with the short pants and the belted jackets, and Jack had scrubbed Ron's face till his cheeks glowed red. Fine, Ethel thought. People won't notice how his socks forever capsize around his ankles. What people? she thought again, wanting to shake her head as if some sense might enter and settle into it. But she didn't do such things in front of the children. Ron had on Jack's suit from last year, big on him yet, and Ethel folded back the cuffs. Jack's breeches so swamped him he looked like he'd filled the seat.

In the doorway, Marion hung back, holding on to Grace by the hand.

M O T H E R, Ethel had lettered in gold on the wreath's purple ribbon. Ethel had a calligraphic hand second to none, but she hadn't scripted the lettering. It was printed in large block capitals so that the smallest of Janet's children could read it. She held it out to Marion.

"Mommy, it's beautiful," Marion said.

"It's for Aunt Janet, my children. A beautiful wreath for beautiful Aunt Janet. Marion, you give it straight to Sheila." Sheila Sunshine Fanny Wiseman, Janet's oldest girl, had arrived the year after Ethel's own Tom. Sheila had been the oldest girl but for Edna, Harold and Janet's first, the little girl who'd died in infancy. Sheila Sunshine, born at the height of a sweltering August, bringing all that happiness. For Harold and Janet a girl again after little Edna had been lost. Ethel saw a basin brimming, a lake, something full and flat and overflowing that held all the world's tears. She could hardly breathe, thinking about it now. Her eyes filled. She kept them on the wreath, fiddling with the flowers. "Have Sheila take it up to the front with Josey," she told Marion. "Reverend Rowsell will help them lay it. Joy should go up, too, behind Sheila and Josey. Have the boys go a ways behind her so that she can been seen." Joy was so short Ethel was afraid she'd be swallowed up. "And Marion, dear, straighten Chesley's jacket when he stands to go up – just give it a little tug in the back. And when they go up, you sit Cedelle on your lap, my darling, and sit Wilson on Grace's lap. Sit Hope and Marie by your side. Cedelle and Wilson needn't go up to the front of the church. Hope and Marie should go up if they want to." Ethel blinked back her tears. So many children Janet had had, like steps in the stairs. All these little ones left motherless now, and then there'd been little Alfred too, the child before Cedelle, who'd died before he was a year old with something in his chest.

Marion looked at her mother wide-eyed, committing the instructions to memory.

"And when Reverend Rowsell says pray, you pray for your Uncle Harold on the Labrador."

"Not Aunt Janet? We won't pray for Aunt Janet?" *That that dieth, let it die.*

"You pray for Uncle Harold and Uncle Nelson out on the Labrador, and your brother Harry too. And your father, here at home. They need our prayers now."

"Pray for our father?" How odd. He was home, on his daybed in the kitchen, everything he needed well within arm's reach. What did he need praying for? It was Aunt Janet who'd gone away – she'd *died*. Yet it was the Old Man who got the prayers. The Old Man got everything.

"He's a part of our family. He's had his troubles."

Marion supposed she believed it. Dr. Olds had seemed to believe it. People could come down with weak lungs and not seem sick at all, just whiny, while other people coughed blood and got thin and died. Her older brothers weren't so generous about it. The Old Man was just a goldbricking slacker, they said, a malingerer.

"Mommy, where did Aunt Janet go?" Ron asked.

"Aunt Janet died, my children."

"Marion said she was going to New Bay," Ron objected. "Aunt Janet has a friend in Fleury Bight. Mrs. Budgell."

Ethel turned the wreath in her hands. The funeral would be starting soon, and the day was running. She needed to get down and open the store. "Only the *Northern Ranger* goes there, Ron. She couldn't have got on it yet."

"She said so," Marion piped up, mustering her courage to object to death, to squandering her prayers on her father.

"Mrs. Budgell died too, Marion. She died last year."

"Was Aunt Janet picking Mrs. Budgell up, then?"

"Maybe she was. Maybe she was, after all. You pray that Aunt Janet gets there safely, to pick up Mrs. Budgell. She's far from us now." *Asleep in Jesus*, the old hymn went, *far from thee,*
> *Thy kindred and their graves may be;*
> *But there is still a blessed sleep*
> *From which none ever wakes to weep.*

She went off then, to the shop. There was no need to keep it open today, nothing pressing, but she went anyway. She should go to the service to fill out the ranks of mourners. She knew she should. She couldn't bear it, that was all. She sat in the shop with the door locked, and wept.

Marion took the wreath. How light it seemed, as if it might blow away in the spring breeze. All on the way down the road to the church she hung on to it tight, as tight as she might have hung on to Aunt Janet in the night.

~

Many a time the Jones's had been Marion's storm stop, but now that her father had had a falling-out with Gwen Jones's father, Marion considered staying in the schoolhouse overnight. But Mom would worry. Besides, however bad fording the snow was, being alone in a drafty old school would be worse. A night at the school would be cold, too, for fires were forbidden in the stove except in the teacher's presence. During the day, at least, there was a fire. It wasn't like the church, where the Old Man never went, where for many years there was no stove at all. "Freeze my backside in my own privy before I'll freeze it in the devil's," Sidney said. Ethel would have gone but her one day off was too busy. With the books and the sewing machine out on the

kitchen table long before the Sunday sun rose, she was already overwhelmed. She sent the children in her place, and years later when the
boys didn't want to go any more, she cried. There was so much to
regret. "Instead of sending you I should have taken you by the hand
myself," she said.

Church, schoolhouse, fire or no fire, storm or not, for Marion,
though, it was all beginning to seem better than home. There was no
safe haven at home, that was certain – not since she'd defied her father
and gone off to the NGIT meeting anyway. On her return home in the
midst of a blizzard she found he'd locked her out. It was getting more
and more dangerous trying to get around the Old Man, to have a little
fun and wrest herself out of his control, but it was Newfoundland
Girls in Training (Nicest Girls in Town, they all said) and she wasn't
about to be left out. The meeting had begun after supper at half past
six up in the parsonage, and it got blizzardy outside as the evening
went on. Inside, the girls took no notice. It was Newfoundland: if you
worried about weather you'd have your mind on nothing else six
months of every year. The NGIT leader felt differently, and sent them
home early. *Day is done, gone the sun, from the sea, from the hills,
from the sky: all is well, safely rest, God is nigh.* They raced through
Taps, and yelled the benediction at each other into the gale as they
plowed down the snow already drifting on the parsonage steps: *the
Lord watch between me and thee, when we are absent one from
another.* Snow spat in Marion's face when she stepped outside. The
Old Man had been right after all. When he tapped his barometer
he was seldom wrong. Storm coming in, Skipper Sid said. No one was
to go out, and Marion went just the same.

Most of the girls lived closer to the parsonage than Marion did,
even at Campbell's Point; heading out, they dropped away soon
enough, leaving her alone. Head down, she charged through the gale.
Already the drifts along the roadside were higher than her head, the
snow up to her knees, and her walk even the little way down to
the Point was an ordeal. As soon as she could see the house, she
headed straight to the closest door. Most outport houses had doors

that opened out, dysfunctional in even a bit of a storm once snow piled against them. But the Campbell's Point house was built right, sound in every way.

Only its inhabitants were not. Marion kicked snow away from the door and pushed. Something pushed back. She pushed again, and this time the door flew open.

His face appeared.

"You turn around now and go to the back door," he said. "Look at you. Looks like you, my girl, have been out in the snow without permission. Anyone that wet can't be entering a house by the front door. The back door for you, missy."

She could hardly see him, could hardly make out the icy words. The snow drove in her face. Shrieking, the wind whipped everything away.

She was stung by it all: the elements, the evil, and her father the most elementally evil of all. But she had some wits still, and as she struggled through the snow on the steps to go down again and around to the back, she studied what she could see of the line of the house, determined to keep it in sight. They all went on ropes between their buildings in weather like this. In winter, there was a rope strung permanently between the front steps of the house and the shop, down the slope. You went hand over hand, gripping hard lest your feet gave way. Tom had insisted on that rope, for Mom. He'd tied it to the porch rail back in November. Last summer Mom had fallen off the wharf on to the beach, quite a drop, and it sent her to Twillingate, an emergency. She came home without a kidney; Dr. Olds had had to take it out.

Did she fall, did she now? Tom said, ugly, his head down over the rope as he worked it, something more than the words coming out of his mouth.

It was easy enough to get lost, buried alive within a few feet of your own front door. The ropes gave you a chance. Marion wished Tom had strung one from the front of the house to the back, but who could have foreseen needing that? Who could ever know what the Old Man would come up with next? *Levi Joe, here we go.* As she groped her way to the back, she lost sight of the house. An avalanche couldn't drop snow faster than this. From what she could tell it was high to her waist, but really the way it raged it was over her head, into her mouth and down her throat, stinging her eyes, blowing her off her feet. Oh God, the cold. It was stunning. *Courage, fortitude. Onward. Onward Christian soldiers*, she told herself, panting. Walking in a storm was nothing new. What was a little snow anyway? A little cold? Before they'd moved to Campbell's Point her mother had walked with her lantern in every kind of weather every morning and every night of the week, hiking the rut that passed for a road between Big Tickle and the Ensign at town centre, or over the ice in winter. Marion might not have a lantern tonight, but there now, rounding the corner, she had the windows of the house and the light behind them. Not much of that light was thrown out for her now, so heavy was the snow in its descent and already so deep against the windows, but it was there so long as she believed in it.

She slammed a foot hard into the door of the root cellar. Pain flashed up her shin. She took her bearings. It was hard to believe anything with the gales of snow slapping her in the face. She felt like she might die. She on one side of a wall, her mother on the other. A few feet between them. A world between them. Her mother helpless, watching her die. For what?

It was like the fellow from Sunday school, the fellow in the Old Testament. The punishment people got in the Old Testament! The children they had – enough to populate entire nations. And never very happy for it, all the same. Always having to move or to go to war or outrun famine, loaded down with all these kids, or else having to leave them behind where they got into it sixes and sevens and grew up and wore each others' clothes and stole each others' wives and blessings and curses, or what have you. The trouble they got into, and really, for all that, God not very nice about any of it.

Marion blinked through icy lashes. What little light there was haloed in front of her eyes now, and she couldn't see at all with snow crusted on her face. Suddenly the ground rose up in front of her – it was the slope up to the back of the house that she was climbing now, but she hadn't seen it for all the snow, the wind full of snow like an explosion – and she fell flat on her face. She got up, half defeated. Now there was ice frozen into small beads inside the cuffs of her mittens. She spat the snow from her mouth, knocked it from her face. *Levi Joe* – oh, to hell with Levi Joe. She was panting now, could hardly get a breath. The fellow in the Bible, Jonathan, had got into trouble. She knew his name was Jonathan because she won all the Bible tests at Sunday school while Ralph Weir forever had to put up with second place. *Do all that is in thine heart,* Jonathan's friend had told him. And Jonathan did, and look where that had got him. *I did but taste a little honey . . . and, lo, I must die.*

And, lo, I must die – just for doing what was in your heart. For heaven's sake. Marion struggled on. The wind shrieked down into her ears, whipped into her throat and hurled away her breath. She'd have to believe it, that she could reach out and touch the house, follow a light through a window and make it inside to warmth and safety. And then, suddenly, what little light there had been went out, and she was pitched into total darkness.

From his perch at one of those windows inside the house, Tom had breathed on the glass and wiped a circle clear. He'd been watching her until the lights went out. He was amazed. He wasn't concerned his sister wouldn't make it in, even though the Old Man was hissing *no helping!* He was like that snake in the Bible, *the serpent, more subtil than any beast of the field.*

It was like the Old Man, to hover in the hallway and not face what he'd done, to do it and pretend he hadn't. Looking out at the small, dark figure of his kid sister, overwhelmed by snow, Tom had no doubt that Marion would survive. He admired her. At eleven he'd broken down in tears when his father had banned him from Scouts. Every one of his school friends went to Scouts. It was so unjust, to be denied something only because he wanted it so much. Marion had been made to go through the same thing, over a simple pair of skates.

"Skates? Yes, my darling, the girl can have skates," Sidney said to Ethel. Marion hadn't asked him directly. She hardly spoke to her father. Mom had asked on her behalf. That was how it went. Marion and her brothers asked Mom, and Mom tried to clear it with the Old Man. At first Ethel thought it would be good to have the children look to their father. It would be good for him, too, off from the Labrador, now, with nothing to skipper and no one to steer. It had been a mistake, though; she saw that immediately, but couldn't backtrack. She could get them what they wanted – and often did, through her orders for the shop, under the guise of what they needed. But she could only go so far. Treats were out, without his say-so.

"She can have black skates," Sidney said, because he knew Marion wanted white ones. Laced into black ones, like the boys had, he knew she'd die a thousand deaths. She knew it too. It would be worse even than the Depression, when she'd had to wear Mom's boots. Mom knew what was important to her. Mom knew she'd have to have white skates. You never had to tell Mom; she just knew. The boots had been something different. That was the Depression. Then, you had no choice.

"Sidney, my dear, I believe Marion would like white skates." Ethel kept her voice even. She was making jam on the stove, and she kept her eyes on it, her back to him.

"Who does she think I am, John D. Rockefeller?"

"Well, she doesn't, Sidney, I don't think." Mom was so reasonable. "I don't think you'll find white skates cost any more than black."

"I don't think I will either, Ethel, because I won't be looking. Black skates are practical. Black skates are what the girl can have, and if that's not good enough, she can stay off the ice."

It was the same as when Marion had wanted five cents to send in to the radio so that she could get her cardboard Howie Wing plane. Tom would never forget that. First it had been the Singing Lady, something about elves and gnomes who sang a lot – way too much if anyone wanted to ask *him*. The Singing Lady had gone on for years, and all just to sell Kellogg's Corn Flakes. Tom would have eaten Kellogg's Corn Flakes day and night to keep Mom from having to cook. As it was he'd tried to help her by plucking the turrs and cleaning the rabbits – and then his father had made sure to shame him about that. Tom had left a pellet in a rabbit back, a browse button – well, no one was perfect, and he less than anyone. "What's this?" his father had said over his plate where it had come from the warming oven, his face going grey. "What's this?" And then, ever after, whether it was cod or ham or salt spare ribs or the pickled sausage that Ede pulled in strings from the brine keg in the boat store, "What's this? Did Tom clean this?" With that little laugh of his, his sneer. Even brawn, headcheese, he said it over that too. "Well, I don't suppose we got any buttons in this." Tom went white inside, in a rage so hot no colour could survive. No one needed to sell Tom on cornflakes from the battery radio. And now that the Singing Lady had finally piped down, it was Howie Wing, his Howie Wing flying adventures, his Howie Wing airplane. Phyl Taylor's father, Uncle Jim, was going to get one for Phyl, and Marion wanted one of her own. She cried about it. By the time she got her five cents they'd be all sold out; she knew they would.

"We'll ask your father," Mom had said.

"Who do you think I am, John D. Rockefeller?" the Old Man had said.

The kids had no idea who John D. Rockefeller was. Would Mr. Rockefeller give Marion five cents?

Harry thought a cardboard plane from Howie Wing was some chucklehead thing.

"I'm a chucklehead? So I'm a chucklehead?" Marion wasn't in a good mood about this at all. She eyed Harry. It wasn't like him to let her down. Tom eyed Harry too. They should all stick together against the Old Man, for Howie Wing or anything else.

Marion didn't like her brothers to disagree. She loved them to pieces. In winter she'd walk between them, a hand in a patch pocket on each of their coats.

Tom was sorry for Marion. He liked her friend Phyl. What a pretty girl, eyes black as the harbour under the ice pans in May. She was deep like that too, and lively. Tom liked it when Phyl came over for Marion when the Old Man wasn't around. Except that they listened to dumb Howie Wing week after week after week, their ears pressed to the fading battery radio, he liked it a lot.

Ethel had worked on the Old Man for days over Marion's white skates, and finally she had won. God only knew what she gave up, what leverage she used. Marion was careful not to wear her new skates in her father's presence. And so it had turned out – one of the few times things did. When Tom had been denied Scouts, it hadn't turned out. He'd felt such rage, such shame. He'd broken right down in front of the Old Man, and hated himself for it later.

And now here was Marion, told *no, missy, over my dead body*, and there she was, off to the NGIT meeting anyway. Here she was making it through the blizzard their father hoped would kill her. Tom ran back and forth between the windows, silently rooting her on.

And then the lights went out. Sidney had extinguished the Aladdins throughout the downstairs, and herded everyone into the kitchen on the other side. No one was to watch. No one was to shine a light to help her.

In the dark, Marion fell flat on her face again. Her knees were torn out of her stockings by this time. If there was blood it would be staunched by the cold, and except for the cold she couldn't feel a thing. Small mercies; God always provided them if you cared to notice. She climbed the steep steps to the back door. Her chest heaved with the effort. In the time it had taken her to round the house the drifts had doubled at the back door; it was work to kick them away. She pushed the door in gently, determined to be graceful. Staggering into the porch, she pulled off her coat and shook the snow from her middy top and her navy skirt, its pleats now waterlogged that had been so smart and sharp up at the school just an hour before. She sat heavily on the floor, biting her lip hard to keep the tears back while she peeled off her snow boots and stockings, taking care where they'd frozen to the scrapes on her knees. Her eyes were wet anyway, where ice had crystallized on her lashes. She blinked it away and knocked the crusted snow from her eyebrows.

"Mom," she called quietly, through the back pantry into the kitchen where she knew her mother would be waiting, under orders not to assist, not to move, not even to answer. "Mom, the meeting was good."

~

George Hicks was back, Grand Falls George, her mother's George, the one who sent her mother postcards of camels, postcards of the pyramids all the way from Egypt where he had been an army officer in the Great War.

"The African Campaign," Tom corrected.

"Gallipoli," Marion said. Ethel Wiseman & Co. was always getting international mail with exotic stamps from foreign countries, the countries Tom and Marion could rhyme off the capitals and flags for. Ethel had kept them to show the children, and Tom decided to be a stamp collector. A *philatelist*, said Marion. Laboriously, painstakingly, the philatelists worked night after night one winter, all of them around the table whispering because of the Old Man, soaking the stamps off Mom's envelopes, drying them and ironing them out. Mom and Ede kept the water hot in the two enamel basins between them on the table. Finally, they were done, and Tom packaged them and sent them off for his accreditation. The letter that came back was dreadful. "It's kind of sad news," said Mom. Stamps were not collectable once they'd been removed from their envelopes and cleaned of their cancellations. Tom was crestfallen. "Never mind," said Mom, "we'll collect something else." But they never did, and so when George Hicks came by he seemed almost as good as a cancelled foreign stamp.

Mom said George Hicks had been famous at Gallipoli, but he'd survived it anyway, and then he'd been in the July Drive in France where he'd been hurt but recovered. He'd been famous there too. He'd become a major. It was a thrill. The only major Marion knew was the bear in the sky. Everyone else was a minor or worse – the other bear, too; he'd been a minor. Marion guessed George Hicks had only been vacationing when he was in Egypt during the Great War, though perhaps they didn't call it that. In a war, they called it leave.

"Gallipoli's in Turkey, not Africa," Marion said.

"Turkey?" Tom wasn't sure. Marion did read under the supper table a lot. She knew all those flags, but he could still beat her at national capitals.

"Turkey."

"Chicken," Ron said.

Wherever George Hicks had been, it didn't matter to Marion. He was here now, even with the war on. If someone could leave the war once for Egypt, for a break, he could leave it again for Little Bay Islands, for good. He was her mother's George Hicks, the George Hicks from Grand Falls who had been counted out by geography; and now, perhaps, it would be geography that would count him back in. Ethel had kept the postcards; Marion brought them out now and turned them over in her hands. How stately the pyramids seemed in the gauzy Mediterranean light. How unlike Grand Falls. Everyone said Grand Falls had no light at all, the belching smoke from its pulp mills forever blotting out the sky. Special things happened around the pyramids. You put a rusty old dressmaker's pin inside a pyramid and celestial forces made it grow sharp. Marion had read that in one of the books in the bookcase with the glass doors, though she couldn't remember more. Why would anyone take a pin into a pyramid in the first place? Could you even get in? Weren't they all tombs, death chambers? What if you stumbled on a mouldering corpse, its mummy bandages all awry, dried up and peeling off with age? What if you stumbled on a grave robber? And what were celestial forces doing anyway, in a structure so earthbound as a pyramid? Still, the names – Nefertiti, Tutankhamen, Imhotep, Ramses, Cleopatra; especially Cleopatra – these were the kinds of names that made things possible, made it possible that George Hicks could enter their lives now and her father could exit. George Hicks was a war hero; if anyone could, he could make her father go away. Marion didn't really want her father dead. Maybe he could start another life with a family in Egypt. Maybe his new family would even like him. They could all wear robes and sandals. White; a lot of white. White was good for the desert. No one wore much white here at home; it was too perishable, as Mom pointed out. The Old Man could go east and wear white and George Hicks could stay here. It would be a good swap.

"He's recruiting for this war," Jack said. "He's going back. He has to. It's his job."

Marion's reverie sauntered on. He *was* back, right here in Little Bay Islands, and how handsome he was. Better still, he was on his way to see Mom.

~

On the coastal boat steaming into the government wharf, George Hicks was lost in his own reverie. He was up the coast recruiting again for the war effort, as he had for the first war between tours of duty in Europe. That first time had been quite a success if he did say so; he'd signed up 270 men on the east coast, from St. John's to Little Bay Islands. Why, that was more than half of the First Five Hundred over again. And when he thought now about what happened to most of his recruits, and what happened to most of the First Five Hundred before them . . . Well, he wouldn't think about it. He'd think of Ethel instead. He'd seen her in Ladle Cove that first time, and now, twenty years and a few scars and medals later, he'd see her again. He looked forward to it, to say the least.

He did say the least, far too often, and that had been his problem with Ethel Wellon. He'd seen a lot, but none of it compared to her. He'd been around, but he had often wished he hadn't been, that he'd made his intentions clear instead, that he'd stopped, merely stopped, put the question and stayed.

~

Major George Hicks of the Royal Newfoundland Regiment hadn't been on leave in Egypt in 1915. He'd been on the job, interminably on the job and hard at work. A sergeant promoted to lieutenant, in 1918 he was made a captain, and his "great energy and fearless devotion to duty" won him the Bar to his Military Cross. By then, it seemed, he'd been anywhere and everywhere in the war. After six weeks of camp at Pleasantville near St. John's, where they trained, drilled, and got a taste of the years of tent life to come, the first contingent of Newfoundlanders sailed on the *Florizel*, the Bowrings' flagship that with the *Stephano* three years earlier had attempted rescue of the crew of the SS *Newfoundland* during the great sealing disaster on the ice off the northeast coast. The *Florizel* had a checkered past and a dark future which, in another three years, she would smash into headlong. Ferrying passengers to New York from St. John's, she would mistake breakers for ice and change course straight into coastal rocks. The skipper was seasoned, a pro; why was he so far off course? He would be censured and stripped of his papers until the chief engineer admitted to having run the engines at half speed. The chief engineer had wanted to arrive late to Halifax, a stop on the journey, in hopes of staying the night with his family there. Because of him, the Bowring family of St. John's lost a little granddaughter and her father in the tragedy. As if in the chief engineer's memory and not for their loved ones at all, they erected a statue in Bowring Park of Peter Pan, leader of the Lost Boys who wouldn't grow up.

Afloat for most of the Great War, however, the *Florizel* carried George Hicks and the rest of the First Five Hundred overseas, rendezvousing with a convoy of Canadian troops at the French-held island of St. Pierre, off Newfoundland. Then she was on to Plymouth. The voyage took ten days; disembarking, nearly another week. She sat at Plymouth while the regiment waited for orders, and the self-appointed Florizel Glee Singers tried to keep their colleagues entertained with renderings of "My Bonnie Lies over the Ocean." For six weeks thereafter the regiment camped with the Canadian Division on Salisbury Plain in the south of England. The ominous monoliths of Stonehenge looked on silently, their long view taking in the white tent tops on Salisbury and all the world beyond. They were prehistoric, all-knowing, and, gazing back at them, it seemed to George that something could now be proved, or should be. But nothing was, and it was on to Fort George, Scotland, to train under Imperial Command, and then on again to Edinburgh Castle to meet up with the second contingent of Newfoundlanders. From there, Stobs Camp, near Hawick; then Aldershot in Hampshire; and then finally, after ten months in England, came the regiment's wait at Alexandria, and the postcards to Ethel back home. The SS *Megantic*, with eighteen hundred troops on board, took them down to the Mediterranean in August. She was the liner known for having returned Dr. Crippen from his Canadian escape to his accounting in Britain a few years earlier. *Megantic* postcards were sold on board; Dr. Crippen postcards too, and the men sent them home. *This is a spooky ship,* George wrote on the card he mailed to Ethel. In Ladle Cove, Maud and William Coish had one from Harold. *Megantic* was the vessel that had been the lead ship in the convoy out of Newfoundland nearly a year earlier, part of the famed thirty-two-troop-ship convoy from Gaspé to Plymouth which had been escorted by the warships *Charybdis, Diane, Eclipse, Glory,* and *Talbot*. She was nearly five times the size of the *Florizel*. The Newfoundlanders felt good to be aboard her. They spread out, relaxed. But then there was Gallipoli, and then back to Suez.

The contingent returning from Gallipoli was rather smaller than the one that had gone out. The Gallipoli campaign had been another debacle, with some 215,000 Allied casualties. The first Newfoundlander to fall in the war fell there. Private Hugh Walter McWhirter was gone on September 22, 1915, but not forgotten, as his grave marker at Hill Ten Cemetery in Turkey attests. The twenty-one-year-old son of Henry and Lottie McWhirter of Humbermouth near Corner Brook, Hugh had an aunt in Quebec whose cousin was Lieutenant Colonel Dr. John McCrae, who also died in the war – after surveying Ypres and writing "In Flanders Fields." Hugh shared a birthday with the British anti-war poet Wilfred Owen, author of

"Anthem for Doomed Youth." Owen, fighting for England, outlived Hugh by sitting out most of the war in an Edinburgh hospital where he'd been invalided, but he'd had to return to France in 1918, where he won the Military Cross and was killed on the Sambre Canal a week before the Armistice.

Hugh McWhirter had been among Newfoundland's second Five Hundred recruits. Relieving the Royal Scots Regiment on September 20, the First Battalion of the Newfoundland Regiment came ashore at Suvla Bay, an inlet on the Dardanelles Strait. Young Hugh was a shelling casualty; at Suvla he lasted little more than a single day.

The rest of the regiment stayed three months. Twenty-nine more became casualties, falling to nighttime shell and sniper fire; twenty-two were killed in action while the rest succumbed to their wounds. Being wounded usually meant death, sooner or later, for conditions in general and trench life in particular took the worst toll by far, with disease felling half the regiment and killing another ten. The men suffered typhoid, dysentery, diarrhea. Trenchfoot led to gangrene and amputations. November turned the constant trench flooding to ice, and the Newfoundlanders suffered exposure, frostbite, and more amputations.

It was the beginning of the end for most of the Newfoundland regiment. Over the course of the war 846 were killed or reported missing in action; 253 died later of wounds; 146 died of illness; two were the victims of accidents; one took his own life. Of those who managed to survive, 2,314 were wounded. Of the 5,482 who served in the regiment (another three thousand Newfoundlanders fought in the Canadian forces and others fought in British battalions), the casualties totalled 3,565.

The war was the worst single disaster in the province's history. By comparison, in 1982 the drill rig *Ocean Ranger* dragged eighty-four men down with it into the stormy North Atlantic. There are those who will argue that the whole province – man, woman, and child – disappeared kicking and screaming into her Smallwood-engineered confederation with Canada in 1949, but the SS *Newfoundland* sealing disaster of 1914 is generally remembered as Newfoundland's worst moment. It took seventy-eight lives. The loss of the *Southern Cross*, also in that same dreadful sealing season of 1914, meant the deaths of all its 173 hands, mostly green boys on their first mission out from Conception Bay.

Dying in the war was noble. Dying at sea was not; it was expected, common, a way of life.

~

Private Hugh McWhirter's father, Henry, had come back to Newfoundland with his Corner Brook wife from the English settlement of New Richmond, Quebec, one of a string of Scots-settled towns on the Gaspé with names like Black Cape, New Carlisle, Hopetown, Port Daniel. Harry, as he was known to the family, continued patriotic despite the loss of Hugh and the ongoing prospect of losing his remaining son. He told the Corner Brook *Western Star* that he was too old to fight for the Empire, but was happy that the boys had gone to war.

Hugh's death did not weigh on Major George Hicks's conscience. George hadn't recruited him. Sometimes George even reminded himself that young Hugh hadn't really been a true Newfoundlander; he'd been born on the Gaspé and moved down with his family. George had to wonder about himself, had to wonder about everything having to do with this war, when he caught himself thinking like that.

By November, after most of a year, Gallipoli was judged lost (and reported to the homefront as an orderly, tactical withdrawal), but the Newfoundlanders stayed until January of the new year. George Hicks was one of the last Newfoundlanders and one of the last of the Allied Forces to exit. To make the enemy believe the Allied posts were still defended after they had been evacuated, George, as head of the Newfoundland rear party, rigged a few tricks. He attached cans of sand to rifle triggers with other cans hung above them, dripping down water. When the waterlogged cans on the bottom hit seven pounds, the triggers would move and the guns would discharge, ghosts firing upon the enemy at Gallipoli about as effectively as had the living.

It was the kind of trick George learned from the boys under his command. He loved kids, and for George at thirty, that was what his men were. Years later in Bonavista Cemetery, George saw a monument to one of Hugh McWhirter's friends, another kid called Roper who'd grown a bad moustache to make himself look older and who went down at Gallipoli too. George stared at the stone. He couldn't get the inscription out of his mind. It reminded him of Ethel Wellon. Over the years they'd written back and forth, and he could read between the lines.

> Thou dieds't for honour's cause at duty's post
> Thus passing hence thy life has not been lost.

Another of the Bonavista lads, John Reader, a mere child with the most angelic of faces who couldn't have grown a moustache if he'd wanted to, hadn't even made it to Gallipoli. *Thank Christ,* George found himself thinking when he stood at Reader's grave in Cornwall, where the boy had died of measles in training camp. *Thank Christ.*

All of the First Five Hundred – Reader, Roper, McWhirter, George Hicks himself – had enlisted for "the duration of the war, but not exceeding one year." They'd been wrong, the three boys. They'd signed up for life.

How strange it had all been, the way events unfolded. A few weeks into the war, in September 1914, a citizens' committee chaired by the governor raised the "Newfoundland Regiment" for war service. The regiment would have to earn its "Royal" title, which it did after distinguished service at the otherwise inconclusive Battle of Cambrai in northern France in 1917. The Newfoundland Regiment was the only regiment to win the designation from the British War Office before the war's end. The citizens' committee that had mobilized the regiment early on in 1914 had been just that – private, sanctioned but not supervised by the Newfoundland government, which became more interested only after Canada's conscription crisis in 1917. After

George's efforts, that was. The first contingent of the regiment, formed privately and funded poorly, arrived in England in October 1914 without rifles, ammunition, equipment of any kind, or even proper dress. They were the Blue Puttees, khaki being in short supply. Lacking even hats, they wore stocking caps.

So many things had been in short supply. Even for George, too, when he came back for the recruiting tour after a bullet to the shoulder had invalided him out during the July Drive. His energy had been down, his spirits forced. His wound was substantial; in October he'd still had his arm in a sling. On that first visit up the coast, he'd had to grasp Ethel's hand with his good hand. He'd seen her at the family home in Ladle Cove. It had been awkward. He wasn't sure of himself. She'd lost a nephew in the Drive, Harold Coish. He didn't know what to say to her; what condolence to convey to her sister Maud. Should he, George, have died instead? Had he died, he wouldn't have lived to recruit another day. He'd never have been able to trot out the Martin letter, the one that ran in the St. John's *Daily News*. It could never have worked its terrible magic on more of the precious sons of Newfoundland, at least not in George Hicks's hands.

> Father, it is not all hell over here, but for sure when we get into the thick of a shindy with Fritz you would think that you had been transferred to Hades with everything devilish let loose, but that don't stand long. It don't take much persuasion at the point of the bayonet to make Uncle Fritz cry "Kamerad," or to show you a clean pair of heels if he could get the chance. We are giving him a hard time of it. He is getting more than he bargained for in 1914 when he started out to make a football of the world.
>
> Well, father, I note by your last letter that recruiting is nearly still at Burin the past winter. Why, there must be quite a number of boys left in Burin with nothing to hinder them from doing their "bit." There must be 20 or 30 between Bull's Cove and Ship Cove. I have them in my

mind's eye as I write, fine strapping young fellows. To them and all others who are shirking their duty, give this message from me. Tell them to put away every excuse for there is none, and come over and help end this War, and not to stay home and enjoy themselves as if they did not care a hang if the Hun smashed us all up and won this fight, in which so many have given their noble lives. I should be ashamed to be at home now enjoying the comforts purchased by the blood of the brave boys who are fighting over here.

But, father, I know that in some cases the boy is not to blame, it is the parents who use their influence to keep them back, but the mother or father who hinders their boy does not realize the cruel position in which they place that boy. The world does not blame the boy's parent, but the boy, and says he has not the pluck.

The copy George had in his uniform pocket was designed to look like the original, old and worn, and when he pulled it out and unfolded it and read it to the upturned young faces in his audiences, it worked every time.

What should he think about that? Best not to think of it at all. He didn't know how these things happened, how young lives were cut off by a depravity like war and then the whole thing celebrated; no one understood it, and yet he thought he should have said something to Ethel, by way of explanation. But there had been nothing to say. By that time, in St. John's Road at Beaumont Hamel, he'd been a lieutenant; he'd seen Harold down the line in the trench, his younger brother too. He'd seen Ethel after Harold's death but before the younger boy was killed, a year later. That had been after Langemarck – having survived Langemarck, had the boy thought he was safe? After that, had they all thought they were safe? – and just before all that mess at Menin Road Ridge, Polygon Wood, Poelcappelle, Broembeek, Cambrai. Battles one after another like rounds out of a Lee-Enfield, coming at you and at you, it made your head ring. George Hicks didn't remember Ethel's nephews much. It had been his intention not to remember anything much, nor anyone. You tried to watch the middle distance, on the battlefield but in the trenches too. You didn't want to fix on anything in particular, on anyone. What you fixed on had a way of going.

~

His sun went down while it was yet day – that's what young John Reader's stone said, the gravestone of the boy with the angel face. George had stared at Fred Roper's marker in Bonavista Cemetery and in England he'd stared at Reader's too. Little John Reader had been so loved, so babied, that this early monument had been erected by his colleagues, the other regiment boys, a modern, slight stone to call to the parent monoliths on Salisbury plain, *Thou dieds't for honour's cause at duty's post.*

It became a song in George's head, its rhythm taken up now, more than twenty years later, by the *Northern Ranger*'s engines. But George himself hadn't died. Might he have, just as well? What had he lost at duty's damn post? Had his sun gone down? All this time gone by and some light still hung in his sky, thready, lemony and washed out, the drained shades of regret. And now here he was, another war, more talking the lads into it all over again. New lads, new blood for new mud. A new Martin letter would surface soon enough, he was sure of it.

Great energy. Fearless devotion – these were the qualities George Hicks had been honoured for with the Military Cross and Bar. That was what he brought to his work still, after all these years. Was it wrong? No. It was a life, it was valour, it was honourable. What else was like that any more?

Ethel.

The *Northern Ranger*'s engines hummed. George Hicks straightened the collar of his battle dress. The government had authorized it for training and drilling under the new Auxiliary Militia Act. Twenty years past the last war and nearing fifty-five, George was the new

commander of Newfoundland's militia at home, the Home Guard out
of Grand Falls. He was on tour again, he was dressed for the occasion. He was off to see Ethel once more.

~

"The common raven, Mom, mates for life," Marion told her mother.
"When they're courting, ravens fly with their wings touching." The big
birds were common enough, easily distinguished from crows by their
size. Their tails were wedged and their beaks heavier, too; they croaked
instead of cawing, and they made a practice of hopping once before
taking off as if there were so much to them they needed a bounce.
Marion had seen lots of ravens along the rocks and cliffs of Little Bay
Islands. On the cliffsides and along the streams she'd seen their bulky
nests, knitted up from dead branches and lined with hair and bark.

"Mom, don't you think that's wonderful?" She spoke with the
effort that came from lacing up Ethel's corset. Ethel had had six children and some abdominal surgeries since she'd seen him last – her
kidney and gallbladder as well as a hysterectomy – but she was going
to look nice for George Hicks.

"It's wonderful, Marion." Ethel's mind was divided. It wasn't like
her; usually she could focus. But now she was thinking about George
Hicks, long a major, long out of his khaki jacket with that bullet hole
in the shoulder. She was thinking about the shop, too; she needed to
get down and open it. Time was running. She'd told Sidney she was
expecting an old friend in on the *Ranger*, for just a half an hour or so,
and asked him if he might mind the store. She'd have to get it open,
though, and get the cash set up. He'd never wanted to learn things
like that.

She told the children about her old friend, too. "I'll want to see
Major Hicks in the breakfast room," she'd said.

Oh.

"Alone."

Oh.

Marion had been thrilled. She shivered. This was the George Hicks who sent the postcards. Mom kept them in a drawer. The kids were allowed to go through them any time, asking questions about the first war, about history, the Empire. It got them an education. Mom was always hoping to get them an education. Mom must have had a letter from George Hicks, in Thursday's mail off the *Clyde*. Another post-card, perhaps? No, a sealed letter, and it must have been a letter, not a telegram. If it had been a telegram, everyone would have known. Mr. Crowell would have got it in on the wireless; Phyl Jones would have walked it up to the house, breathlessly. How Phyl would have gone on to Ede about this one at the Wisemans' door. *Major Hicks, in the Home Guard from Grand Falls, Ede, if you please. That war hero, what? Imagine, him coming to visit our Aunt Et.*

G'wan wit' you, Ede would have said. *G'wan.*

But Ede wasn't here any more – she'd left them and gone off to marry Fred James – and neither had Phyl arrived at the Wiseman's door all bottled up with no one to tell, but breathless nonetheless.

It had been a letter, then. If you didn't have a box, Phyl or Mr. Crowell, one or the other, just passed you your mail through the wicket. But the Wisemans had a box. Mom must have picked up the mail herself that day, along with the Old Man's newspapers in their weekly roll. She hadn't said a word, though, until almost the last minute.

Now she was a bit flushed. That good kind of flush, not the kind that flared her face and made welts on her arms. Not the kind that shot red up her arms whenever she put her hands in hot water.

"Don't you think it's romantic?" Marion said now, pulling the last lace tight. "The ravens?"

"It's romantic, yes it is." Ethel had pins in her mouth now, for her hair.

"Mom, why didn't you marry George Hicks?"

Ethel stopped, turned, a hand to her head. She took the pins out of her mouth and thought a while. "Because, Marion, I married your father instead."

～

And there he was, in uniform. Mom had gone to the door herself. She had said she would. She'd been firm about that. Major Hicks was to arrive in the morning, and she'd go to the door. The children were to make themselves scarce. She'd open the door, she'd take him into the breakfast room – she knew the way, thank you – she'd see him in private.

When Mom was firm, that was it. But Marion had had her glimpse. Major Hicks was a handsome man. She strained to see a sign of the bullet hole in his uniform shoulder.

Mom had closed both the breakfast room doors – the one that opened straight into the kitchen, and the one into the hall. Marion went outdoors and waited until Major Hicks came out. It wasn't long. He walked away smartly. Perhaps he'd learned to walk that way during the last war, to get out of the way of bullets. She watched him walk right past Gordo Gillard and her own cousin Dek, who was in off the schooner that day. He didn't even stop to pull out a clipboard, hand them a leaflet, nothing. Was he really doing any recruiting here? He didn't seem to be staying. From the wharf below the house, she saw Major Hicks walk to the government wharf and jump up on the gangplank of the *Northern Ranger*, just as it finished unloading and prepared to leave. He'd been here all of a half an hour. The Old Man would know exactly how long. The Old Man would have timed his visit to the minute, she was sure of that. Her father, going back and forth between the house and the shop, would have seen him leave too. Was Major Hicks here to recruit, or was he here for something else?

Her father went in the house right after Major Hicks left; he came out a few minutes later. Marion waited until he was far down the lawn, returning to the shop. She dashed in to see her mother. *How did it go? What's he like now?* The words formed on her lips and died.

～

Ravens were black as ink. The whole of the breakfast room was black as ink. Someone had thrown the inkwell. Him, he'd thrown it. Her mother would never do something like that, not even in self-defence.

Her mother never lifted a finger in self-defence. It only made things worse. Marion didn't see her mother at first. All she saw was the ink. Then she saw her mother crumpled on the floor between two chairs that had been knocked over. And then she saw her mother's neck. She would never have believed that if she hadn't seen it herself, however many times she'd read about that sort of thing, strangling, in mystery stories. Her father's fingers had left deep red oval marks on her mother's throat. They'd pressed there in her mother's neck and held. Marion could see that, even with her mother thrashing and coughing in front of her, choking. She'd open her mouth, cough as if the life itself was coming up out of her, so much life that it couldn't pass. Her mother's face was turning purple with the coughing. Mom was crying, holding her neck, hauling in breaths.

"It's all right, I'm all right," she said.

Marion jumped. How long had she been standing there, gaping? Where was George Hicks? Why couldn't he have stayed, fought the Old Man off? He was a soldier, wasn't he, a major? Hadn't he had a gun? Hadn't he had a uniform on, battle dress at that? She'd seen at least that before Mom had closed the doors.

The doors. Closed. That's what had done Mom in. The Old Man must have sneaked in from outside and hidden in the pantry, staring at that closed door to the breakfast room, and thought about it. His wife and George Hicks. An old boyfriend. How dare she leave him down there, with the drudgery of the shop, to go and sit with some old boyfriend, some fancy pants from Grand Falls? Was there no end to the woman's gall? A teacher, a colleague from Normal School at Methodist College. A learned man, educated. From St. John's, even. Fancy. Done up. A major, now, a war hero, all done up in his uniform. Festooned, beribboned. Sidney would have paced the hall, silently, leaning down to the keyhole of the hall door to the breakfast room. He would have crept into the kitchen, too, and watched and listened at that keyhole. He would have heard the affection in George Hicks's voice, after all these years. He would have heard how Ethel was loved, much loved, as she was by everyone she met. No one loved him like that, no one loved Sidney Wiseman at all, and it was more than he could bear. He would have flown into his rage the minute the breakfast room door opened and George Hicks left to resume his recruiting tour.

George Hicks, on yet another stop doing damage again just when he'd meant to do good.

~

Marion snapped. "He can't do this to my mother any longer," she thought. She ran for a drink of water and a cold cloth for Mom, and then her legs took her in a quick march down the hill to the shop. "He can't do it to her. He can't, he can't, he can't. I will not let him do it to her. I won't, I won't, I won't." She entered the shop from the back, through the long storage room. She flung open the door opposite, into the storefront. It was a busy day in the shop, as busy as any May 24 Sports Day. The room thronged with men off the *Ranger*, which hadn't left yet, and men in on their own boats to check on orders and pick up provisions. Someone was buying yard goods and soap to take home to his wife on Long Island, where the pickings weren't so good as they were at Ethel Wiseman & Co. He was just replacing a bolt of good linen on the shelf. Black Bob Wiseman was just pocketing a plug of tobacco. Though Ethel had posted No Smoking signs which the customers respected, they all bought their tobacco from her. In the midst of the throng – there was her brother Tom, too, behind the counter, helping out with the customers – Marion marched up to her father, drew a breath, and screamed at him. "*You're not going to beat my mother any more!*" She wanted to hit him, but thought better of it. "Now you've gone and nearly choked her to death," she shrilled. "You choked her and left her for dead in the shambles where you threw things." She planted her feet on the floor and reared toward him, all five feet of her. She was on a roll now, like the train off the tracks that had been washed out by tides at Kelligrews and wouldn't be stopped, and only gradually did she become aware of the silence in the shop which her screaming was slicing through. Every conversation, every greeting and transaction between visitors had ceased. They were all staring at her, with shock on their faces – that a child would come and face the father like that, with all the world to see. It wasn't done.

She might have gone in and gone up to him quietly, she supposed. In a tiny mouse voice she might have asked *May I see you outside a moment please?* But inside, in the midst of this great crowd, there was safety in numbers. If he killed her he'd at least have to wait a bit to do it. There was safety in knowledge, too – in the fact that a lot of these men were regulars to the shop who knew her mother and her father. And if she was wrong, and he did kill her on the spot, at least there'd be witnesses.

She rocked on her feet. The silence stretched. Then, finally, Sidney broke it.

"That child's a liar," he said. He'd flushed bright red. "Always going around telling lies, you can't shut her up. I never laid on a hand on her mother. She's got an imagination, that one!" He was almost stuttering. He looked at one dumbfounded face in the crowd, then another. All these people who knew him. And who knew people who knew him. This would travel faster than a trap gone off on a sea in a gale.

As he protested, Marion shouted back. It was a symphony; it was a cacophony; it was a contest for Marion to raise her voice over her father's. She threw her words to the rafters of the shop. She was angrier, more outraged by him, than she'd ever been in her life. "*You're ALWAYS beating my mother, you damn well stop, now!*"

She didn't know a word like *damn*. No one said damn. Not even her father said damn much; he was all manners, in his way. Where had that come from? Who was this, speaking? What was coming out her mouth? Was she possessed? Was it the voice of blind fury and vengeance and lunacy, or was it the pronouncement of deliverance, her own and her mother's too, something come, finally, from the heavens, to rescue them?

He grabbed her by the collar of the red pullover Ethel's sister Mill had knit for the girl and sent out from St. John's. Still she shouted. He dragged her through the door to the storage room, and still she kept it up. Once he'd slammed the door behind them, he twisted the neck of the sweater into a stranglehold; it was that, finally, that choked off her voice. Her words died in a gurgle; froth surfaced on her lips, and at the end of his ferocious grip her feet left the floor. She knew she'd die then, strangled and hanged in her own sweater from Aunt Mill. She may have saved Mom from strangling but now she was to go down herself. She kicked, flailed as he held her in mid-air by her collar, trying to spin her with his free hand to twist the ligature tighter. Her feet swung and knocked over some boxes of Mom's, oh dear; on top of everything else today she didn't want Mom to have to clean up any mess. Could she die quietly? But her legs kicked as though they had a mind of their own.

Tom, out front, had gathered himself. Through the door he had heard the abrupt end to her rant, and he heard the boxes crash down now. He burst in. Throwing himself on his father's back, pounding and flailing with all of his own five feet and a few inches, he hauled the Old Man off her.

Marion and Tom stared at one another. The Old Man had been murderous. It was clear in another moment that he would have killed her. That was what he was capable of, brother and sister seemed to say to one another, when he was shamed in public.

Marion stumbled out the back door and up the hill, coughing, to find her mother. She composed herself in the hall, outside the break-fast room, and went in. The two of them sat, not speaking. Her mother seemed defeated. She was still breathing heavily; her gasps were laboured. There was a small choke at the end of each intake of air, as if her mother wanted to cry and with each breath thought better of it. Shortly Marion would find her a scarf, something to put around her neck to hide the marks. It was the sort of thing her mother would normally look after, as she looked after all the details of the family's trouble, cleaning it up. But just now she seemed bewildered, beyond solving things, beyond finding scarves. She had folded her hands in her lap. Marion did the same. Her mother held out her hand to Marion, and gripped her daughter's hand briefly; then they dropped their hands back into their laps. They sat, just sat, like a family waiting for a boat, a train, anything to take them away from here so they could go and keep going and never look back.

Marion stared into the knowledge of something new. If she hadn't gone into the breakfast room and found her mother on the floor, she would not have known he'd tried to choke her. Mom would never have told her. Mom would have risen from the floor eventually, and tidied the room. She would have said there'd been an accident with the ink bottle, that someone had dropped it by mistake. She would have found a scarf. None of them would ever have known what the Old Man had done. Marion stared at the curtains by her chair. Back and forth they idled in some unlikely summer breeze. Her eyes brimmed. What else didn't she know? How many other times had her father attacked her mother, with no one the wiser?

Sidney spent the afternoon in a state, running between the house and the shop. The front door would soar open; they'd hear him stride down the hall into the kitchen, then back up the hall into the main bedroom, then out into the hall and back through the door again to the outside. He traced this route over and over during the afternoon, several times in an hour. He was a man with panic to forestall, with energy to burn. To Marion and Ethel in the breakfast room, he sounded like he was building to a repeat of the morning. Already, Marion saw Mom sprawled on the floor again, finished off this time.

I'm not letting him do it. I'm not letting him do it. I'm not stopping now; I'm not letting him do it. She heard her father leave the house one more time, then rose from her chair, patted her mother on the hand, and went to the kitchen where she dragged a chair into the hall, up beside the front door. She went to the woodbox beside the hall stove and selected the biggest junk of wood she could lift. She knew she had to bring it down on his head with enough precision and force to take him down, to kill him, with the first blow. She knew she had one shot at it and one shot only, the next time he flung open the door and came flying through. She had to make it good. If she didn't, she'd be killed, and then in his next breath her mother would be killed too.

She seized the wood, dragged it up in her arms, and climbed on the chair to wait.

~

Winter came once more, and then spring and another summer too. Marion no longer cared about the trouble she might get into, if she'd ever cared. But the way the Old Man had of taking things out on Mom made her careful, staying out of his way. Her mother's bruises faded. Nothing was ever said about George Hicks's visit and what it had wrought – not by the Old Man, not by Mom, and not by Tom or Marion. Marion and her father seldom spoke after that. If they passed each other in the house, it would be because he ran into her by accident. He'd sidle past her, shuffling step by step with his back to her, sighing all the while as if she were some kind of precipice he must take care to inch by, as if one false step might plunge him headlong into contagion. It was a production, avoiding Marion and shaming her, and he made everyone watch.

Two years passed, Sidney sidling and sighing, and Marion worried for her mother as she'd never worried before. Boys around the Bay signed up for the war after George Hicks had been through; Col Forward and Cyril Penney went from right here at home, straight to their deaths. Marion had seen the portrait Cyril had done for his parents at the studio in St. John's. He'd been brandishing a swagger stick like the officers carried. If Marion had had one the day her father choked her mother, and choked her too, maybe they'd be free of him now. It was small and lithe, a mere baton, but it had a lethal little metal ball at the end. She wouldn't have tired of holding it over her head, waiting for her father to come in, as she'd tired of holding the firewood. It had all been an ill-conceived plan anyway; she realized that now. Her father's step was always purposeful, never more so than the day George Hicks visited, and he would have been long past the door by the time she'd have managed to jump out from behind it and bring the wood down on his head; she'd have to have thrown it at him and run away. It was too much to consider waiting for him at the open side of the door. He'd have seen her, standing there over him like winged vengeance, and he'd have had time to react. She couldn't imagine she'd have been faster than him. She'd never bested him in her life, never even considered that she could.

But none of that mattered. Her father never gave her the chance to win or lose, only to surrender. The fact was, after all his agitated back-and-forthing that day, once she stood on the chair with the wood in her arms and waited for him beside the door, he hadn't come back for hours. By that time she'd long given up. Exhausted, her arms aching with the weight of the wood, she'd climbed back down and replaced it in the box and the chair in the kitchen, and gone to sit with her mother again. Tears had streamed down her face; she couldn't even hold them back from Mom.

Could she get away to nursing school in St. John's? She was so young. Maybe they'd take her because of the war shortages. Maybe she should show them her hospital corners, the way she had with first aid, tell them how she'd taken care of Jack, of Mom, all those cuts and bruises. . . . No, she couldn't tell anyone that.

~

As spring stretched into July now, Mom planned a birthday party for her; her fifteenth. They'd be unlikely to be together for another. Marion had made her cake already. She'd see Gwen Jones today – their fathers might be into it cats and dogs but Marion and Gwen were still great friends – and Net Penney. Margaret too. All her friends would be there. Especially Phyl. Phyl and Marion spent a lot of time together, studying and planning their lives. They had the same Scottie hats out of the Eaton's catalogue. Phyl was sweet on Marion's brother Tom, and Tom himself was back now for Marion's birthday, taking a day or two from his summer working for Dr. Olds. When the Bonnie Nell's distinctive whistle had shrilled in through Big Tickle the night before, well before Marion and Phyl could sight her from the government wharf, they'd jumped up and down. Tom wasn't aboard, though, and neither was his X-ray gear; that was the year the *Bonnie Nell*'s schedule was disrupted by diphtheria in the north and he was having to hitchhike around Green Bay, packing and unpacking his gear with every ride he found. Tom had come in on a passenger boat just this morning.

This was the second birthday party Marion had had in her life. Her first had been held at Fan An's Ensign shop at the top of the government wharf. There'd been no ice cream parlour in the old Ensign, but Ethel had made her birthday girl a freezer of ice cream just as she did on Education Day and Parents' Day, turning up at the school with cones and the freezer that Tom and Harry had been discharged early to go home and crank. Marion had been eight that day, and she wore a new dress, pale pink, with a black velvet sash around an empire waist. The sash matched the black velvet Peter Pan collar. She was on top of the world, and now here she was again, that many years old again almost, celebrating another birthday. This was to be grown-up, an evening affair in the parlour at Campbell's Point. Still, they'd have ice cream. All these years later, Tom was outside cranking a freezer now. He'd do films for the hospital Wednesday evening and Thursday, and all day Friday and Saturday. But now it was Tuesday, Marion's birthday, and Tom was cranking. Uncle Dolphe still had the island's only cow, so Mom had got in extra canned milk. Harry would miss his dasher on a day like this. But it had been his choice to leave them, and if he was already sorry it only went to show how Mom had been right. Harry had continued going to the Labrador, leaving school once he'd done his grade ten. Ethel had been upset. He was only fourteen, with his whole life ahead of him – and none of it, she wished, on the grey waters of the Labrador. "I can't stop you," she told him, "but it will come back against you one day."

Tears had rolled down her face as she'd packed his trunk with cans of rabbit and seal, chocolate bars, chewing gum, jars of the mustard pickles he loved. Supplies as well: oil drops for earache, flannel bandages and Mercurochrome, cotton tow and Vaseline for his mouth and his hands, too, when the salted ropes burned them. Harry worried about that trunk. Who took a trunk to the Labrador? Where could you put it? Mom hadn't even packed a trunk for the Old Man in his skippering days. But he was glad for the cotton and the Vaseline. Tom had come home from his one trip to the Labrador with his hands torn to ribbons. In the end, he'd figured out a way to use his feet to work the ropes that lowered the heavy fish tubs into the holds.

The Wisemans weren't big on celebrating birthdays. The most excitement they risked was a game of Canasta or Flinch. They'd beg Mom to play, after homework. It was bliss to be with her, seeing her relax, even though they couldn't scream and bang on the table for Flinch if Sidney was near. And who really knew whether he was near or not, where he'd pop out from next? No one really knew when anyone's birthday was, anyway; no one, that is, except Mom, who knew right down to the minute when each of them had been born. Sidney never wanted birthday parties. No commotions, thank you, especially not any from his children. Hitler's birthday was the same as the Old Man's, Tom informed them. What do you expect? Adolf and Sidney shared a birthday, April 20. If the Old Man had a birthday at all, they agreed. If he wasn't hatched.

In fact, Sidney had an innocuous birthday in May. Ethel told them that, but Marion was doubtful. April 20 sounded likely to her. Just last week they'd heard on the wireless that the Germans were stepping up their U-boat attacks now that the *Bismarck* had been sunk. Just a month ago they'd invaded the whole of Russia.

Skipper Sid followed the war on the wireless, stretched out summer and winter on the daybed in the kitchen. Only when the battery faded would he swing his feet over to the floor and sit up. Then he'd have to tip his head in and glue his ear to it. They all liked to listen to the BBC news at six, but more often than not the battery was fading. There wasn't any point in getting more in; over the winter, stored batteries didn't keep.

The war was the one thing that could get Skipper Sid up and off the daybed. Harry had been to the Labrador many times now on the *James Strong,* sometimes for two runs in a season. The crews were workhorses, and even after the season they kept working. They returned and unloaded the catch, then left again for commercial coasting for Strong's until December, when the seas roughened and the ice came in. Now that the war was on, they patrolled the coast for the war office. The Home Guard had approached Skipper Sid as a naval veteran of the first war. He went on patrol too, taking Jack. Jack and her father, together in the close quarters of the Old Man's passenger boat. Marion could almost understand it. It was like Jack, to put aside the past as if it had never happened and hope for a future – something, anything, in a future with his father.

Skipper Sid was a spotter for German planes. The war office sent in drawings of Luftwaffe bombers like the Heinkel and the Junkers, but also of the British Lancaster – that was the one Tom was in – the Flying Fortress, the Liberator, and the Mitchell, and the whole family studied them. They followed the war on the radio; it carried news and war reports and announcements about traitors. They loved to laugh at Lord Ha-Ha, the German propagandist from Galway who came on every evening to tell everyone how badly the war was really going for the Allies. Marion wondered if it wasn't really true. Mom had called up the stairs to her one January night a few years before that King George was gone. It was sad, especially with a war coming. Then there's been that mess with the new king and the American woman, and they waited for a bellwether. Then one night they heard Winston Churchill on the radio. The battery was fading as it always was, but the voice made them shiver. There was strength in that voice, like Mom's, and wisdom and succour too. Surely they'd all survive; surely they'd flourish in the end, emerging victorious, vindicated.

By now they all knew the code the government used on the public airwaves for advising lighthouse keepers of U-boat attacks. Sometimes, crowded around the radio in the evenings, they longed for something more than *A for apple, N for nuts – all normal,* but when excitement came they didn't hear about it until later, long after the fact, with no advisories at the time at all except what Randolph Crowell picked up from the coastal stations on his wireless at the post office. The post office wireless was always tuned to the good frequencies where the marine warnings and emergencies were broadcast. Otherwise, there was very little drama, very little anything at home as there'd been in the first war, where there'd been espionage and close calls and boardings and captures.

Captures! Marion breathed to Phyl while they lay in the grass and tanned, taking their shift as spotters. Back in the Great War, one early August morning in the last days of fighting, a German sub attacked the SS *Erik* off the south coast of Newfoundland, took her crew aboard and sunk her.

Sunk her!

"Everything happens on the south coast," Phyl complained. "The tidal wave, everything."

"Well, we had the sealers lost off the SS *Newfoundland*, the Keans. The east coast had that," Marion said, as if it was an achievement. *We have the Old Man*, she might have said, but even to Phyl she didn't say much about that. The next morning, back in the Great War, the crew of the *Erik* was transferred to a Newfoundland banker called the *Wallie G*. Everything seemed to have turned out all right. Now, in this war, some of the best excitement involved the *James Strong* itself. Once, she picked up a load of depth charges for the U.S. Army from Argentia, built in 1940 as one of the largest American naval bases outside the States. Her pass through Trepassey Bay saw the crew stacking the explosives in the schooner's hold. By nightfall, they'd finished. Harry was just making his last climb up from the hold for his mug-up when a U-boat surfaced beside them, played its searchlights over them, and then let them go.

But the *James Strong*'s worst moment involved Uncle Harold.

Harold Wiseman was never the same that summer of '42, the crew said afterward, once he got the wire about Janet. He'd forgotten to fly the flag that the war office had mandated, and even when the British warplane circled them and circled them, to see who the hell they might be, friend or foe, Harold didn't seem to know where the thing was. It was the flag he'd have to lower to half mast when they came through

Big Tickle and into port, so if it was lost, it might just as well stay lost. One of the men found it below decks and hoisted it up on a gaff over his head, running around the deck and waving it at the gunner in the plane. The *Strong* had been fishing at Solomon's Island all summer; that's where Randolph Crowell had eventually raised her with the news of Janet. For Harold, July crawled by, and most of August too. All he could think of was his beautiful wife, gone forever, and all his children left. It was awful, being suspended like this – that's how he felt, as if nothing could be put to right, put to rest, until he got home. He imagined Janet looking out for him, waiting to say goodbye until he got home. He just wanted to go there, wherever it might be now that Janet was gone, and yet here he was in the middle of nowhere, responsible for his men, their families, their commitments, their fortunes and their futures. Whether disaster hit the sea or the shore, a skipper went on; he owed it to his crew, if enough remained. Their own families depended on the catch. When you took on a crew you took on the weight of the world, as well as the weight of the dead – and the weight of the dead was heavy indeed. By the end of August the *James Strong* had more than two thousand quintals of fish in her hold, and to Harold it all felt a trifle next to the burden of his grief. He had to bring her through the Strait of Belle Island between the top of Newfoundland and the bottom of Labrador, then down the French Shore to Strong's wharf and home. For all his fever to go he seemed inert, and he anchored one last night at Lard's Arm on the Labrador Coast.

That night, the German U-boats were busy in the Gulf of St. Lawrence.

The next morning the *James Strong* set sail, crossing nearly immediately into a debris stream of wood, flotsam, rations, chunks of furniture. The British warplane was already overhead, circling. *U-517* and *U-165* had started the tag-team campaign that would cause most of the shipping losses in the Gulf during the war, trying to pinch off convoys bringing building materials to Allied bases going up in Goose

Bay, as well as convoys travelling from Nova Scotia to Greenland on their way to the European front. On August 27, the pair attacked two small convoys and sank a U.S. Army transport. The *Chatham*, carrying nearly six hundred men, was the first troop ship lost in the war, but the *Strong* didn't see bodies; the HMCS *Trail* and U.S. Coast Guard vessels made a quick rescue that plucked all but thirteen men out of the icy, oily waters and took them to shore at St. Anthony. The next day the U-boats hit more ships, keeping up the attack whose debris the *James Strong* sailed through because rescue vessels did not radio any warning to the rest of the convoy.

To Harold Wiseman's men aboard the *Strong*, it looked like they'd missed a party. They were too young and stupid to take it seriously, one said. After a season off Solomon's Island they were up for a bit of fun. Only the skipper was uneasy. Without Janet, he would not be easy about anything again.

~

It was a hot night, and crickets sang outside. She was carrying a pitcher of lemonade into the parlour for her friends when he stopped her. He beckoned in that way he had, with a forefinger. A gnarly forefinger. "You. Marion. Come here."

It was the first time he had spoken to her in nearly two years.

She followed him into the breakfast room, where he sat himself down again in his nest of magazines and newspapers. There was her mother's *McCall's*, under his feet. The coastal boats brought it in month after month, and at the end of the winter five or six all at once, tied in a bundle with all the other winter issues of newspapers and magazines they got, bundle upon bundle. But Mom never had time to read her *McCall's*.

"What you got there then?" Her father smiled broadly. He had such an affable face, disarming. It was hard for anyone who didn't know to understand what lay behind it.

She stood, queasy. She wanted to shift her feet apart a little to hold her place and keep herself from falling, but instead she stood motionless, like a rock. She'd budge not an inch in front of him in case he thought he was having some effect on her.

"Lemonade," she said dumbly.

"I can see. What you got down there?" He angled his chin in the direction of the parlour.

"A party."

"A party! Well, now."

He knew that. She hated him. Mom told him everything, especially anything like this that might upset him if it weren't all laid out for him beforehand, on a platter, for his approval.

"It's my birthday." She raised her chin to match his.

"Is it now!"

He knew that too. Mom would have reminded him: *Marion's birthday today, Sid. She's fifteen, imagine! Wouldn't it be nice now if she had a really lovely day!*

"Fifteen. I'm fifteen."

"Are you now?" The face again, genial. Marion's lemonade pitcher dragged at her hand like a dead weight, a rusty anchor cut loose and sunk and she gone down with it already.

"Fifteen, yes."

"And who you got in there?" Again, the chin tipped toward the parlour. He was starting to gear up now, in that way he had. She held her breath.

"My friends."

"Who?"

"Phyl, Netta, Margaret –"

"You got Gwen Jones in there?"

"Gwen, yes. Gwen's here." He knew that. He knew everyone who was in the parlour. She'd seen the top of his head when he'd crept up the front steps to peer in the window.

"Sid Jones's girl Gwen. You got Sid Jones's girl in there?"

"Yes." Her voice was coming from somewhere, faint.

"Do you now."

She stared at him.

"I asked you, do you now?" Suddenly he was roaring, the face turned monstrous, and she jumped, sloshing lemonade on her dress. Just as she'd had the new pink dress for her eighth birthday, she had another new one now for her fifteenth. It was cotton with a dirndl and a middy collar. Mom had seen it in the Ayre's flyer and brought in for her, and already she knew she wouldn't wear it again.

"Yes."

"Well now, you get her right outta there, missy. I don't want Sid Jones's girl in my house." He turned away from her in his chair, and his heel ground into Mom's *McCall's,* tearing the cover.

~

She doesn't remember leaving the room. Behind her, he shakes out his newspaper on his lap, satisfied; she hears the satisfaction. The hallway she does remember, walking up the corridor to the parlour. There is wainscot on either side; she walks a tunnel of wainscot and above it the wallpaper she helped her mother pick out six years ago when they came here. Every room in the house has wallpaper, even the kitchen. She has helped her mother choose every bit of it. It is cheerful, demure, tasteful; it is all a lie. The paper here in this hallway has small pink morning glories on vines, some leaves on the vines, a few violet blooms scattered through the pink. What are flowers doing in this house? It seems a long way suddenly, down this corridor, and for some reason it is not a place she knows. Somehow holding the lemonade against her calms her down. Ice chips she'd climbed up the ice house for and chipped at herself with the pick – these swim away to nothing in her pitcher as she walks, it is so hot a night and so cold at the same time. She stands in the parlour doorway and hears herself speaking. "I'm sorry, folks," she says, "but the party's over." She doesn't know why she chooses that way out. Something Mom has taught her, perhaps – that there is dignity in choosing all or nothing, there is

honour in forfeit if it spares someone's feelings, if it spares even one
person embarrassment or shame. Marion doesn't reason it out. She
only knows that Gwen is her friend and that Gwen is not to be embar-
rassed, not if Marion can help it, and so they all will have to go. "I'm
sorry, folks, but the party's over." There; she has said it. One of the
Strongs' boys has draped his jacket over a chair, it's that hot, and after
a long silence he picks it up and puts it on. Another pause, an endless
pause in which only her heart beats, marking the time, and then the
others stand, brush off their knees, put down their glasses and put
down their plates. Margaret has had her hand out to Phyl, passing
her cake. Netta has been in the middle of a story. Gwen has been
laughing. Marion has been in the middle of her fifteenth birthday,
and now it is gone, passed like a dead thing. Will she ever have
another? She shakes her head, trying to rattle the thoughts out. If she
stays here longer surely she will go mad. Her friends are like a life-
line leaving; she should attach herself and let them carry her away,
out the door, across the porch, down the steps. Her brother Tom
stares at her from across the room. Tomorrow he will take X-rays,
and the next and the next, and then he will be gone. Phyl will cry.
Marion will cry too. She looks away. There is something in her
throat. "Gwen," she says as her friend passes her in the doorway.
She seizes Gwen's hand and squeezes. "Thank you for coming. Do
come again."

VIII

REST

"Penny," said Tom in Marion's ear. Marion and Jack had flown from St. John's to Gander. From Gander, they'd gone to Springdale in the Norseman ski plane that Pop Hefferton had ordered for them through the minister of health. In Springdale, they picked up Tom. Stuffed in behind Marion with Jack at his side, behind the pilot, he had to bend right down to her ear to be heard over the drone of the plane. His voice sounded like a stranger's. "Penny for your thoughts."

"Slippers." Marion was white. There was something wrong with her voice too. She'd been staring out the window of the plane into the white. Her voice was white. White shrouded her brothers and herself, wound through them, all around them. At altitude the mists of February were white like ice fog.

"Slippers?"

"Yes." Even in her fur tops her feet were cold; the plane was freezing; and she'd been thinking about slippers. She turned toward Tom in the back seat, shifting so that she could see him. It was all right that he saw the mess her face was in. His wasn't much better. They loved each other; they'd grown up with the Old Man together. They'd seen each other cry a lot. She could see that he felt it too, the difference there was to their tears this time. This time, they might never stop. She couldn't see Jack's face at all. Beside Tom, Jack sat staring out the other window. "I was thinking about slippers," she said to Tom. "The way we all used to run out to him when he was first home from the Labrador, to get our slippers. You used to practically throw yourself over the gunwale of the *James Strong,* before they'd even lowered the gangplank."

"I was running to him. He was my father."

"He wasn't, though."

"I didn't know it then."

"You were still so tiny. It's a wonder you didn't fall in and drown."

"Well, we all nearly drowned, didn't we?"

"We were all so tiny then. That was the only way we'd ever have wanted to see him. He hadn't got geared up yet."

"We were innocent then."

"Until we had the innocence beaten out of us."

"Mom, most of all. None more innocent than Mom, starting out. And look what's become –"

It was ridiculous, having a conversation like this at the top of your lungs, hollering it out. They stared ahead at the ice crystals on the windshield. "They were sealskin," Marion added finally, shouting.

"Beaded."

"From the Labrador Indians."

Silence again, remembering. "How the hell was it," Tom yelled, "that the likes of him got the sizes right? They were all the right size. And yet when it came to us, he never got a blessed thing right in his life."

"Mom told him the sizes before he went." This from Jack, who had turned his head. He wasn't shouting at all, but somehow they heard him.

"Ah." They stared at Jack together, and spoke as one.

The Mother, the Mother. Jack thought about writing it in the frost on the window of the ski plane. He lifted his hand, then dropped it again on his lap – there, it was over. Everything was over. They were down on the ice with a thump and a swoosh. He stared one last time at the window. He'd wanted to see the writing, that was all. His hand was nearly indistinguishable from his mother's. When he was a small boy he'd trained himself to write just as she did. Since St. John's he had said nothing much, just stared, and now he said nothing more. His skin was translucent, glassy, as if no life was getting through to pink it up; his eyes were dusky. He'd suck in a breath occasionally, shudder as if he were cold. Now he climbed out and walked ahead of Tom and Marion on the ice across the harbour, toward the house where the Mother would never live for him again.

Marion and Tom couldn't keep up; they walked behind. There were drifts on the ice that they had to kick away, but Jack ploughed through them as if he couldn't see.

"Jack's not doing too well," Marion said.

"Jack!" said Tom.

They walked in silence. Climbing the icy slope to the house, they went in through the back door. In his own way, their father was there to meet them. *Hello Marion,* he mewled as she passed him in the kitchen doorway. It was the first time he'd said her name in nearly fifteen years, and she resisted the urge to push him out of the way. He did the same, then, to Tom and Jack, as he had to Harry when Harry had arrived earlier, from Gander. He was trying to sound sick, put-upon. But for Randolph Crowell, who sat all day in the breakfast room as if he knew there should be a man there, as if he knew children needed some kind of man about the house, they might have spat at him. As far as they were concerned, their mother was dead because their father had killed her.

It was Harry's wife, Jean, who'd called Marion in St. John's. Randolph Crowell had wired Harry and Jean in Gander the day before: Ethel had collapsed. They'd get a plane to take her out; they'd do it now, a storm was blowing in. Then another wire, another call from Jean: there'd been trouble at the house, Randolph said, while Ethel lay sick; a row with Sidney, and Grace had nearly hit him with a poker.

The Old Man had been drunk, Harry said, disgusted. The Old Man was drunk now more often than not. Mom never said so ever, not when they'd been growing up and not later either: in her letters she never mentioned trouble of any kind. But the boys knew. The boys said Skipper Sid always drank, had done from the beginning. It wasn't another evil he grew into, they said; he'd always done it. To hear them tell it he'd emerged a drunk from Aunt Lizzie's womb. It wasn't true, but it was an explanation.

Marion had been leaning over the dryer in her kitchen in Linden Court when Jean called. She'd been folding one load of diapers while another load tumbled. She leaned on the dryer and felt a hand at her back, eventually – not Ray's, surely. It was Audrey's. Since her marriage had broken up, Audrey and her little girl Pam had been living in the building too. Marion and Audrey had trained together at the Grace, and Mom and Pop Hefferton, Audrey's parents, had had Marion over to their house on Cornwall Crescent as often as she could come. They knew Marion's own family was far away, up the coast in an outport.

Now there was someone standing by Marion, and it was Audrey. They draped themselves down over the dryer and cried side by side, while it sent up its heat. It was February; it might have felt good, but Marion felt nothing. Audrey would ask her father to get a plane with skis out to Little Bay Islands, one that could land in any weather and bring Marion's mother in to hospital in Gander, all the way to St. John's if necessary.

There's no plane, Audrey, that can land in any weather.

There'll be one. Pop will find one.

Pop Hefferton was the education minister in Joey Smallwood's first cabinet. Pop Hefferton could talk to the health minister. He could make things happen.

And then the last wire, the last call. Mom was gone. *Gone.*

At the Gander airport, where he worked, Harry had been up to the control tower and on the wireless with Randolph Crowell. The ice was fine, Mr. Crowell said. They'd be sure to be able to land for the funeral, he said. The ice had been fine for landing the day before as well, Mr. Crowell said. They'd had men out to check it. He just hadn't been able to convince the pilot of that. What a shame. *Had he landed when I told him to, and taken your mother out – I couldn't believe it when I saw him circle and leave.* Mr. Crowell was a man of few words, an excellent thing in a wireless operator.

Now, walking the ice that the pilot had circled and turned his back on, leaving their mother to die, Tom and Marion could have stamped on it, heavy as lead, stamping over and over for as long as it took to break through and drown. And Jack, ahead of them, might have looked around to see them go and then simply lain down himself, on this ice that had been with them all their lives, cold and flat and thick and dead; without even trying Jack could have lain down and died.

~

Ethel spent her last night at Grace's, down just before you got to the mill. Even with Ron and his wife, Nell, living at the house at Campbell's Point with her, she hadn't been able to stick it out with Sidney one more night. She arrived at Grace's distraught; Sidney had threatened her with a gun. That night, Ethel and Grace watched out Grace's window. It was already snowing, and through the snow the figure of a man seemed to loom toward the house, carrying something on his back. Was it Sidney, with his rifle? The figure passed; the dread of the moment ran down.

She slept well that night at my house, Marion

She slept the sleep of the dead, Grace

It snowed through the night, that deep February snow that in the east brings only weariness. To get to the shop the next day Ethel had to pick her way through drifts up to her knees. Ethel Wiseman & Co.

opened early, and she was one of the first out and about. Little Bay Islands wasn't a place where anyone shovelled, where anyone cleared the road. No one had gone ahead of her, tracing her a path in the snow and stamping it down. Ron was already in the shop when she arrived; he'd come down the few steps from the house, following the rope. Ethel had had no rope, no help. She was breathless now, all in, clammy and sweaty and with a pain in her back that seared around to the front beneath her arm. She staggered behind the counter and collapsed in the chair there, slipping as she went down, catching the silver bread knife from the Royal Stores on her sleeve. It clattered from the counter and spun on the floor. On a morning like this, with snow in the air, there was so little light for it to catch.

"Ron, my son," Ethel said, "I'm going to be with the saints today."

~

I picked her up in my arms, and a frail thing she was. I carried her to the house and put her to bed. If I'd come upon him I would have kicked him with my boot. Nell, Nell, watch Mom – I called down to Nell, and then I ran down around the harbour to Grace. Couldn't run, really – had to tramp most of the way. There was one set of tracks, only, Mom's. She'd had some go of it, getting up from Grace's. She'd come through hell. Well, all her life she'd come through hell, sure. I'd just done the same myself. We'd had Betty over to Halifax for another check. Three or four she was, then, and she still couldn't hold her head up right. One side of it all sunk in there from the forceps. Nell had been eclamptic her last month. Springdale, you know. Maybe we should have gone to St. John's. It was always the same – all of life in the outports, every blessed thing a man could want, and never enough when you needed it. Lie on the floor on her blanket, that's what Betty would do. In her red velvet dress – the one with the white collar. So pretty. She cried so much, all her seven years. Cried and cried every moment of every one of those seven years. She

broke my heart. A beauty of a girl, she was, my girl Betty. Blond curls.
Oh, the sweet of her. So we'd been bringing Betty and everything we
had in the world over from Springdale on the snowmobile to Little
Bay Islands, Nell and me. We were going to stay with Mom. I was out
of the air force by then, and Mom was going to train me to take over
the business. When I heard the crack I threw Nell off and threw Betty
right into Nell's arms, and then I jumped myself. Threw myself out
flat and rolled so that I'd spread my weight. And then we watched
our things go down through the ice into the black with the snow-
mobile, and Betty cried. Marion canvassed all her friends in Halifax
and St. John's for baby clothes, for any clothes at all because Nell and
me'd lost everything too.

I couldn't believe it – I lost everything coming home to Mom, and
then Mom died and I lost everything again.

Nell, I said. Nell. Tell me, someone. How much can you lose?

~

Ethel sponged herself down and changed her nightdress while she
waited. She got more nighties together, hoping for the plane. Somehow,
she got herself out of bed, got a basin and a cloth; somehow, she
managed all that. She was short of breath, her chest ached and
fluttered, and a sheen of perspiration misted her face however much
she sponged it off. *I do not ask, O Lord.* The time crawled, the time
flew. *I do not ask.* It was to Wilbert, her nephew, that her thoughts
turned. Her sister-in-law Mary had brought the boy up after Plinny
had drowned on the Labrador. Ethel hardly knew Mary; she was
older, and Salvation Army. Ethel remembered Plinny only vaguely;
Sidney's brother, Aunt Lizzie's son. Good she remembered better, the
dance of his hair on his forehead when he turned toward her in the half
light thrown by the oil lamp. *Good, now, he has such a face. There he*
is, the evening half finished and not so long ago one of Lizzie's huge
dinners down all of us, there he is turning a potato over and over in

its jacket in the ashes in the stove. But her thoughts didn't stay long with Good, nor with anyone else in Sidney's family, except Plinny, Sid's brother who'd drowned on the Labrador, his pipe in his mouth. Plinny had left a little boy, three months old, who'd never known his father. The boy had grown up, fatherless, and joined the RCMP. He liked to hunt and there he'd been one day, shooting turrs out of season with Dr. Olds, an officer of the law breaking the law and all the world finding out. Well, so what? It must have been a lot of what to him, that was certain. He'd taken his children for a drive a last time, and then he'd parked the car and set the brake and walked into the woods with his service revolver.

Wanting to see your children a last time. *Do not do not ask. I am going the way of all the earth.* Ethel could understand everything about it now.

Later, when she lay waiting for the plane and dying, and him going around moaning and reeking, Grace threatened him with a fireplace poker. And didn't she go and put it down. Are you daft? I said.

She lay down on the bed again. She asked for Sidney. "If your father came in right now I'd tell him I love him," she told Grace.

Are you daft? I said. Don't put it down. Do it!

But Sidney wouldn't come in. He sat in the breakfast room sulking, accusing Ethel of shamming.

Why in the world did she love him like that, Marion?

And then, waiting for the plane to come back another day and try the ice again, Ethel had a second heart attack and died.

Do not do not ask

Tom and Marion and Jack came in on the plane she should have gone out on. When I came in I could have jumped out of the sky with the hurt of it. I knew all the pilots out of Gander, for God's sake. I'd been working customs for ages already, I knew all the boys. Why wouldn't he set down the plane? I raised Randolph on the wireless and he said the ice was thick as earth. Why the hell wouldn't he land?

I do not ask, O Lord, that Thou shouldst shed
Full radiance here;
Give but a ray of peace, that I may tread
Without a fear

"Aunt Dora Oxford was there, Marion, from across the road."

"I don't remember."

"Surely you remember."

"I don't remember, Tom. It was years – what, fifteen years? – since I'd been driven out of my home."

Marion, oh Marion, I was so afraid to give her anything. She was in so much pain but I was even afraid to give her an Aspirin

I quit my grade ten. Well, after my grade ten. Right after, I went to the Labrador. And that was that for school. She took me aside. I remember her eyes. She had the kindest eyes. They were full of something –

Grace.

Oh Marion, that they were my darling, yes, full of grace. Harry clears his throat. *She took me aside. She was upset. Packing my trunk, crying. I can't stop you, she told me, but it will come back against you one day. And she was right. She was always right. The customs job for boss went to Garland Wiseman. We were in the same competition together, and how Mom helped me with my application! But Garland had his grade eleven, and I only had my grade ten. 'Cause I up and quit, he won that round. I got the next job up at Gander, all right, but it wasn't the boss job. If I'd got the boss job instead of Garland, maybe I could have sent the right pilot out, the right man for the job, someone who'd land on the ice, just get on with it and land. And maybe she'd be alive now*

Do not ask don't ask.

"I slept in one of the spare bedrooms over the parlour. I got out my own lipstick and put a little colour on her face. Other than that, Tom, I don't remember. I don't know who was in my room, why I didn't sleep there myself. Grace hadn't given Mom an Aspirin even; God, I wished she'd tried that. It might have saved her life. Randolph

Crowell sat in the breakfast room the whole day. Did anyone fetch him a bite to eat? Did anyone eat at all?"

"Randolph would have been fine. He was like that. He was a come-from-away, but special."

"Remember when you'd come home from the *Bonnie Nell*? Just because you'd been taking X-rays for Dr. Olds people thought you could cure their spells, set their bones, deliver their babies?"

"Well, not quite deliver their babies. I never got asked to deliver any babies."

He was drunk, Marion. The son of a bitch. I took up the poker, I told him I'd kill him with the poker

Drunk drunk drunk, the son of a bitch

"I did. Home on vacation once, what a vacation! The woman was from Sulian's. She wasn't progressing. There wasn't anything I could do for her. Just nothing. Lord, when there's nothing to be done, right? They kept sending for me all the same. I walked over twice, back and forth, back and forth. Those few days I hardly saw Mom at all. The woman refused to go to Twillingate. And when she finally did, when she finally got on the boat, of course it was too late."

"What happened?"

"The baby died."

I didn't know what to dress her in, Marion. That one was dark, but for the collar. You choose dark for a funeral, right?

Died died died. Marion's eyes fill with tears. *Oh for the touch of a vanished hand*

"I never worked the *Bonnie Nell*, Tom, but everyone knew I was off at the Grace in St. John's and that was worse. When I was seventeen and home visiting from training, my first year, I had to take Geneva Crowell to Twillingate on a passenger boat. Lorne had thrown a rock and it had hit her in the eye. Lorne was devastated. His own sister. He begged me to go along with her; I was a nurse, I guess that was why. Almost a nurse. And the day Mom died, as Mr. Crowell sat in the breakfast room, his hands just folded in his lap, I kept wanting to ask him how Geneva was. She'd lost the eye. Lorne never got over it. I kept wanting to ask how Lorne was too. Had they reconciled? It was ridiculous. Twelve years had gone by. I was living in the past. I should have been asking him if he'd take a little tea and something to eat. He must have been starved. I should have been taking care of him. But who could blame me? That day, the present was no place to be."

Nell, I said. Nell. Tell me, someone. How much can you lose?

~

She was laid out in the parlour in a pine-board casket, the wood planed at Strong's mill. Someone had covered it with white brocade. Maybe that had been Aunt Dora Oxford and her friends, the women who sat in the parlour now. So many years had passed since Little Bay Islands had been her home, since the white house at Campbell's Point had been her home; Marion didn't know Aunt Dora for sure any more. It was chilly in the room. No one had made a fire. It was winter, the coffin would travel to the church and the graveyard on a komatik, and so the men were set to close it now. They rose in the parlour, the six of Ethel's children in order, as if they knew the place they held in some script. Grace, Ron, Jack, swaying on his feet; Marion, Harry, and finally Tom.

Grace Ron Jack Marion Harry Tom. Mom. Oh, Mom Mom Mom
Jack, my child, it's why we believe in things not seen

One by one they went to their mother's coffin and leaned in to kiss her. Marion had put her own lipstick on her mother when she'd arrived.

Her lips were blue; she looked so dead

She needed a little colour. Navy blue and white in a white casket, God. Not a bit of bright anywhere. Me, I had my red dress on; I'd worn it home under my green coat, with my green hat. Mom looked awful in the dress that Grace had picked out. It was proper enough; dark navy and more navy polka dots on a white collar. Perhaps Grace hadn't realized it was a dress Mom hadn't worn in years. Mom had had such style. All those years of selecting things from Bowrings and Ayres and the Royal Stores. You developed an eye

I must have been in the pantry. I must have been helping with tea,
getting down some cups, many hands many hands maybe Mr. Crowell
got at least a cup of tea after all. I don't know. I can't remember. I
saw them then, I guess, the fluted candy dishes Mom always loved,
up there on the shelves of the pantry behind the glass. If nobody else
wants these, I said, I'll take them. Nobody else did. Did they think
about candy dishes? At a time like this? I don't know. I don't care. I
took them upstairs and tucked them into my suitcase. I took a few of
Mom's dresses from her closet, too, and I packed them. Dresses and
candy dishes and, oh for the touch oh for the touch, I parcelled the
dresses up when I got home and sent them from St. John's to Nellie
Rendell. She was living in Corner Brook by then. She was the only one
who ever knew Mom's trouble, the only one Mom ever told. Perhaps
even we didn't know Mom's trouble like Nellie did. They were beauti-
ful dresses of Mom's; Nellie would have loved them. Did she ever wear
them? Did she write to say? I don't know. I can't remember.

Once Marion's mother had met her in St. John's when she'd been
in training, and they'd gone to the second floor of the Royal Stores
with Jack Winsor. Marion's mother had put her hand to a splendid
kelly green dress. *It's yours, my child. Would you like it?*

Kindly go out and get a job and buy your own dresses, her father
had written.

~

On the slick rock ledges of Back Beach, Nellie's daughter Margaret had
held Marion out of the sea and saved her life. Years later, Margaret
had gone to Twillingate on an errand for Nellie. A man had come up
to her and asked for directions, then grabbed her hand, pulled at her
and tore the sleeve, and that was an end to the life Margaret had
known. She went to St. John's and found Tom at Memorial, where he
was in pre-med and social work. He found a home for her to wait it
out, and a placement for the child. Marion and Phyl were in St. John's
too, training at the Grace, and she'd tried to tell them. She'd waited for

them at the nurses' residence, sitting on Phyl's bed in the dorm, her
hands in her lap. It had been hot that day. Marion and Phyl had burst
in to tear off their shorts and get into their uniforms. They hadn't seen
Margaret in ages, and never anywhere but home. How thrilled they'd
been to find her there. What a rush they'd been in! A late check-in at
the nursing desk at shift start could get a girl sacked. And all they had
to do first! They'd hardly left one twelve-hour shift before they were
due on the next. Twelve hours on the schedule, but the real shifts ran
hours longer. At the end of each they had to finish all their charts,
scrub stains from the linens before they went to the laundry, clean
the bedpans. They had time to sleep or eat between shifts, but not
both. They had time to do their own laundry, but only if they gave up
sleeping and eating. Who had time to read the wretched school magazine, the *Bib & Apron*? Who'd want to? Who'd ever want to be
reminded of a bib and apron again? And the rest of the uniform too.
Their feet were forever dyed black from the stockings.

   I'm in trouble, guys, Margaret said. It was so hot. There they were,
climbing into their blue dresses and then their starched white aprons
and bibs, securing their heavy collars and cuffs with brass studs,
pinning on their hats. The studs had had to come off for the laundry,
and now they had to go back on. How Marion hated her gear. She'd
sunburned her neck; her collar tormented her. *Kindly go out and get
a job and buy your own dresses – S.H. Wiseman.* That was the note
her father had written her when he'd opened an invoice that had come
to her mother from the Royal Stores and found three of Marion's blue
uniform dresses on it, the three that she would launder and mend and
make last for the whole of her training. Her father had never written
her a note in her life, and now this. *Kindly go out and get a job.* Wasn't
this a job, labouring that many hours a day in a starched shroud
in the heat of the summer? *I'm in trouble, guys.* There she was,
Margaret, dear Marg, just staring at her hands in her lap where she
sat on Phyl's bed. Last time they'd seen each other was that day they'd
picnicked together with Margaret's brother George, and George,
horsing around as usual, had pretended to try to pull up Marion's

skirt. How was Old George anyway? Marion liked George, but it was dear Marg whom she loved. Marg, who'd held out her hand at Back Beach and saved Marion's life. Marion, whose hand was wet and slick and whose arm was nearly pulled from its shoulder and who didn't die, and Margaret, who didn't let go. *Marg, Marg, girl, we're late. Can you give us a call later? We'll catch up then.* Margaret watched them run off to their shift. She'd go find Marion's brother Tom at Memorial. It wasn't the same at all, having to explain to a man, even Tom. But he might help her.

~

Tom alone held back from the coffin, stroked his mother's hand. He was the reserved one. The last time he'd kissed his mother he'd been a child coming home from school for lunch, and she'd just coaxed him out from under Taylor's shed and saved him from Gordo Gillard.

Once he had visited in winter, from RAF training out west. He'd made it a complete surprise. Marion had been sitting at her winter roost under the breakfast room window, leaning back into the book-case with the glass doors, staring out at the white on white – and there he was, Tom emerging from the mist over the ice like a figure in a dream. A very good dream. Impossible, really, that something not hoped for could turn out so well, when all the things that they did hope for went so badly. There he was, service cap in hand, crossing the ice on an unannounced leave. He hadn't told a soul. Mom had been up from the shop and heard Marion gasp. She came over to the window and clutched her chest. Don't surprise Mom, never surprise her, Marion used to say. Don't you think having the Old Man popping up Devil-in-the-Box day after day is enough surprise for anyone? Mom's heart couldn't take surprises. The kids didn't like the halting way their mother breathed, the way she looked half the time. Mom had had her problems – gallbladder, hysterectomy, kidney – and they worried about her heart. The hysterectomy had been Dr. Cowperthwaite's solution to birth control. He was in St. John's, he was renowned, he must know. Marion liked the sound of him. He'd told Mom to give her kids raw cabbage, right off the chopping board any time she and Ede were making dinner. But Dr. Cowperthwaite could do nothing about Mom's asthma or her heart, and he had sent her to Halifax for tests.

When Tom had come home on his visit, they'd held a party in his honour at the Orange Hall. He was bashful. So he was going to the front to fly missions in a Lancaster, so what? Couldn't he just wear civvies to the party all the same?

Tom, my son, for our friends and neighbours it's a lot of what. They'll expect to see a uniform, Mom had said.

Tom had surprised his mother that day, coming home out of the blue. Out of the white, Marion said, not out of the blue. Out of the white of the ice and its mists, as if they lived in some deep magic where things emerged and were drawn back again. He'd surprised his mother that day, but it was she who'd surprised him now. He knew she'd die someday. He knew they all would. He just never believed it.

Oh for the touch of a vanished hand. He reached for his mother's again, patted it, thought he could never let it go. And then he let it go, and stepped back.

~

Of all her friends, it was Margaret Rendell whom Marion had told first about the CHEs. Margaret had put her hand out to hold Marion's in it. "You're so smart," she said. "How can you be so smart?"

Marion was always the best of students, and when things got too bad for her to stay at home, Mom asked her if she thought she might go to Springdale to supply-teach. Springdale's teacher was ill, and the word had gone out around Green Bay. Did anyone know a young lady who could stand in? Did Aunt Et know anyone? Mother and daughter hugged on the government wharf. All around them, porters loaded the *Clyde*. She was only going across Hall's Bay, but it might have been the wide Atlantic itself. Held in her mother's arms, she'd felt something turn in her chest as if part of life itself had shut down, the part held together this far only by levers and snaps and valves that her mother had had the key to and operated daily. She was just sixteen. It would be a long while before she'd feel able to strike out on her own. She did strike out from home, it was true, because she had to, she was forced – but she didn't feel able, and years later, on a train from Badger to St. John's when she'd been up to visit Mom, she still didn't feel able. She must have shown something: fear; the kind of fear you should never show to a dog or to anyone else. A Salvation Army officer in uniform left his seat down the aisle for the one next to her. "Might I ride along here?" he asked; she nodded. He'd sat and been a barrier between her and the soldiers going down to the St. John's for shipping out. That was all he'd done, and that was everything. The soldiers were rowdy, excitable, afraid, and she was terrified of them.

She excelled in her year at the Springdale school. The board stopped looking for anyone else. They wanted her to stay. She was barely sixteen, so what? Look at how she'd held the classroom together, all five grades, a mere slip of a thing. She had primary, one, two, three, and four; forty-eight students in all. Elsie Hickman had grades five, six, seven, and eight, and Principal Skinner had the nines to twelves. Marion had Haddrell Spencer in her lot, a great hulking child in with all her little ones because he didn't want to be in school and couldn't get beyond grade four. Marion didn't know what to do with Haddrell and told Principal Skinner so, but Principal Skinner thought she could manage just about anything. She was accomplished. The board thought too; she had something and they wanted it.

She didn't want them. It was 1942 by then; Frederick Banting had crashed in his light plane over the Straight Shore; a nurse friend of Mom's from Ladle Cove had attended at the site. The war was on, had been on for years and should have been over by now, and they needed nurses in St. John's. Everyone else had gone to the front. She was seventeen when she got in, though Admitting said you had to be eighteen. There were only six in her class, though Admitting said the school needed three times that many to run. And no more than three. Most years, the Grace turned candidates away, but now the war caused shortages everywhere. Phyl was a year ahead, and said enrollment had been no better the previous year. They were exhausted all the time, too pressed, too busy, too supervised and clock-watched; time was too short, that was all. *Kindly go out and get a job.* One day Margaret Rendell turned up and Marion didn't have time for her. It had been a complete surprise, to find Margaret there at all. And another surprise to find that, afterwards, the memory of Margaret never left.

~

She went up early in the morning, a frosty one, before the plane came in to take her back into Gander and then on to St. John's. How windy the trees were, all around! That's how it seemed to her, as the expression had it: *wind sighed through the trees.* The snow was beaten down now, and she could not believe that in Newfoundland, in any outport and even this one, her own, it had ever before been that cold. She didn't mind it. It was the sort of cold you could get used to. You could laugh at how it hurts, couldn't you? Hadn't they? Like that time Ron stuck his tongue on the axe when he was chopping wood, and they all laughed and laughed, even Ron around the axe. Sure they all knew how serious it was. How could you live in a place like that and not know how serious it was? But still you had to laugh. Had Mom laughed? Mom had had to tend to Ron and his axe, warming the water to pour over his mouth while she calmed him down. What had Mom thought? Had she just gone into the white inside? Had Marion ever really known her mother at all?

Marion had another life now. But did she have to go back to it?

Entreat me not to leave thee, or to return from following after thee, she said aloud as the wind sighed around her, for she knew the words perfectly. *Whither thou goest, I will go,* Naomi had said to Ruth and

Marion said to Ethel, *and where thou lodgest, I will lodge, thy people shall be my people, and thy God my God. Where thou diest, will I die, and there will I be buried.*

~

She is home just a day when Aunt Mill comes and plants herself with her knitting in the living room of Ray and Marion's apartment at Linden Court. Ray and Marion have moved there, back to St. John's from Halifax, where they'd gone for Ray's schooling. They went to Halifax in '48 as immigrants to a foreign country, carrying their X-rays, but now they're back and the girls are toddling. Linden Court is fun for them. Alex and Nancy Hickman's kids are there and Hubert and Betty Malloy's too, and there is a wading pool on the grass, and their borrowed Aunt Audrey is there with little Pam, and their mother has plenty of friends. Soon they will all live in a grand house on Laughlin Crescent, for Ray is sought after and well paid and prosperous, and for all that he remains cold, the man who wished his own mother could be a lady like Marion's but all the same couldn't manage to get to her funeral. "Dear Miss Wiseman," someone on the railway train had written in her book the year she met him, "Let x = *a nice young man; Let* y = *a pretty miss; Let* z = *a cross old mother-in-law: Then wouldn't* x + y − z *be bliss?" It has only lately struck her that in Ray she has married a cold man who is charming, that she is repeating her mother's calamity with her father. Once she said something to him at a party, something he didn't like, it seemed, though it was only about how well his friend Lester had looked, and he turned on his heel and left her standing there alone in the middle of the dance floor, everyone staring. Aunt Mill likes Ray and is disappointed that he is out when she calls. Tell me, tell me, Aunt Mill says, what hymns did you sing at the service? Cheryl will be two next week, Cheryl with the sloe eyes, and she has pulled a blanket over her head to peep out at Aunt Mill from the middle of the living-room carpet of Linden Court. Aunt Mill is a strange creature, stiff and stretched with braids of hair wound around her ears like muffs. Watching Cheryl, Marion's heart breaks and breaks and goes on breaking at the thought that her mother will not see her daughter one last time*

Wynken and Blynken are two little eyes, Marion has already begun to tell Cheryl that,

> *And Nod is a little head,*
> *And the wooden shoe that sailed the skies*
> *Is a wee one's trundle-bed;*
> *So shut your eyes while mother sings*
> *Of wonderful sights that be*
> *And you shall see the beautiful things*
> *As you rock in the misty sea*

Marion hots up Aunt Mill's tea. She pours the tea so that she can keep looking down, so that she does not have to look up quite yet. She can't remember what hymns they sang, whether there were hymns sung at all

"Onward Christian Soldiers"? Aunt Mill is looking at the date square on her saucer. Really, she'd have rathered lemon

Mmm. Marion is non-committal. "Shall We Gather at the River"? We sang that, Marion tells Aunt Mill, though it isn't true. That's what Mom herself played for old Aunt Lizzie all those years ago, on the organ with the galleries and the mirrors, once everyone had arrived and the service started in the parlour of the Tickle house. And then afterwards they hadn't gathered at the river at all, but at the Tickle wharf, where Aunt Lizzie's pine plank coffin had been set across two seats in the motorboat. The wood for Aunt Lizzie's coffin had also been planed at Strong's mill, for Strong's has been in the business of life and death at Little Bay Islands forever. Marion, in her white gloves and her blue suit, had had to sit right behind the thing in the motorboat. Good heavens, what if they caught a wave and the boat tipped? Their little convoy motored over to the government wharf. From there Aunt Lizzie's coffin was carried up the road past the Orange Hall to the cemetery that someone had decided should be put halfway between the northern and southern harbours, to fit everyone in. Marion looks at Cheryl under the blanket on the floor. Cheryl is three years younger than Marion was then, in those white gloves in that motorboat. What is Cheryl storing away under her blanket now? What will she remember in years to come? Why can Marion remember her wretched grandmother's funeral from twenty-five years before, and not her beloved mother's from last week? What hymns? What hymns? The hymn Mom would have liked, Marion knows, though she does not say so to Aunt Mill, is that one that Harry loves too, the one about a garden. "I come to the garden alone, while the dew is still on the roses." Well, it was strange, wasn't it?

> *I do not ask that flowers should always spring*
> *Beneath my feet;*
> *I know too well the poison and the sting*
> *Of things too sweet*

On Little Bay Islands they never had roses, never a thing like roses. Mom chose all that flowered wallpaper for the house at Campbell's Point. She'd always wanted a flower garden, longed for one. But life was tough there, the ground was poor, the time no good for prettiness. Mom grew roses at Ladle Cove; she saw roses in the florists' windows in St. John's, in books, in catalogues. And Harry, well, Harry doesn't care about gardens and roses at all. Harry cares about the breakers at Tilt Cove and moose and the brace of the autumn air in from the east when the season opens. What Harry loves is what Mom loved, that's all; and more than anything he loves that part where "He tells me I am His own; And the joy we share as we tarry there, none other has ever known." They had all belonged to Mom in that way, exclusively. When there was so much to barricade yourself away from you all became very small, you packed yourself into each other's hearts and lived there, watching and waiting, barely breathing

Whose heart will Marion pack herself into now?

Cheryl gurgles from under her blanket. Aunt Mill is knitting something very complicated with cables on a long circular needle whose tips throw light around the room. Cheryl would like to catch that light. Marion can remember no hymns. Had there been a minister? A lay reader? Who? She does not know. All she remembers is sitting between Jack and Ron, her arms around them in the pew as if they were huddling against a storm blowing in

   Jack is a mess

   They are all a mess

   There was someone in front of them, in the pew ahead. She thinks it was Tom and Harry and Grace, and they have a storm coming down on them too. She does not know any longer who pulled the komatik with the casket to the cemetery, just past Strong's field by Bert Strong's house, Bert Strong who mourned Ethel all his life, and now he can really get started. The cemetery is just at the bottom of the climb to the Burnt Woods, where they waited once with Ede, Mom's mountain goats, until the sun came up to see their way to go and pick berries while the rest of Little Bay Islands slept. No one walked with anyone, Marion remembers that. They made a single track, tramping down the snow, and the sled went first. No two could walk abreast, no three; certainly not six, the six mourners whom Mom has left. All the same she felt someone take her hand – Marion, it's Margaret. Didn't she hear that? And yet there was no one there at all. In the snow and the wind Marion was confused, everyone was confused, everyone was lost. She does not remember where the Old Man was. Maybe in the back. She does not recall if the Old Man was there at all. She doesn't think Jim Strong was at the graveside; no, she remembers that Jim Strong came struggling through the snow to meet them as they came back, a tall man struggling and floundering through that same snow that had killed Mom. How come the snow got to stay, how come Mom didn't get to stay but the snow did? Jim Strong knocking snow from his hat and saying come have a cuppa tea, Marge says come in come in, come have a cuppa tea. And they did; at that moment they would have done anything that anyone said.

   Marion barely remembers the tea at Strongs'. She is back at the cemetery and Aunt Mill is back at the cemetery too, knitting, knitting, flashing her needle tips resolutely around the room. Who could have dug a grave in February? Aunt Mill asks

Newfoundlanders could have, Newfoundlanders did, Marion says,
not kindly, as if Aunt Mill had never been one in her house on
LeMarchant Road by the butter factory. Newfoundlanders. They're
not afraid of hard work and they never wait for anything

∿

"We were all there. Surely you remember, Marion."

"I don't remember, Jean."   ·

"Surely you remember the order of service."

"What order of service? Who did it?"

And so Jean tells her, Harry's Jean with the memory like a vault.
Jean and Harry went in right away, by chopper. One of Harry's
buddies from the airport took them, setting the chopper down
between Salt Rock and Campbell's Point. They walked in on the ice.
Snow had still been blowing from the storm that killed her –

The Old Man killed her, Jean.

Yes, my darling, I know, Marion.

– hurling wraiths across the ice. It had been a bumpy ride in. Still,
they'd had a better landing than the take-off they had going out a few
days later. The chopper didn't get enough lift, and they thought they
were going to crash into the Burnt Woods. Harry hadn't seemed to
notice; Harry hadn't seemed to care. *I could have jumped out of the*
sky with the hurt of it. When they arrived, Jean put on tea. She
roughed out the order of service in the breakfast room on Mom's
mahogany table, copied it out, Harry popping his head in, keeping an
eye without. Jean knew what Mom had liked, what hymns, what readings. Sidney was roaming. Already Harry had had enough of him.
Sidney had grown so much worse. They could abide him earlier, at
least, Jean said, that first year after Marion went to St. John's when
Jean and Harry married and lived at Campbell's Point while Jean
taught, before they got away to Gander. But at the end they couldn't
stomach him at all. "The way they all jumped on him afterwards,

Marion, landsakes" – Jean puts her hands to her head, shakes it, as if after all this time she can loosen the memory and dump it – "Harry and Tom and Ron." Marion and Jack had gone back by then; Grace hid. The three boys confronted the Old Man. *Well, the Old Man said. I never knew she'd die. I thought she'd live another fifteen years.* Like he'd been clocking her, marking the schedule, figuring out his own plans by hers.

I thought she'd live another fifteen years – that's what he said, Marion, can you imagine?

I thought she'd live forever – that's what I thought, Jean, can you imagine?

They drove him out of the house after that, Jean says.

Marion knows that part. How her brothers rebuked the Old Man, getting every hurt off them he'd ever put on, trying to shake off every scar he'd ever marked into them with his brute fists. How they rebuked him except for Jack, who had left already and never got his say and wouldn't have taken the opportunity if he'd had it. How Tom and Harry and Ron drove the Old Man packing that very day – *too late, boys, too late too late* – and how he never set foot in the house again.

It was the Reverend Nathan Abbott, Jean says. He took the service. "Surely you remember, Marion?"

I don't remember. But how could she have forgotten that?

"The hymns were 'Abide With Me' – we sang that in the parlour, and 'Shall We Gather at the River' –"

No.

"Your mother loved that one."

She played it for old Aunt Lizzie, all those years ago. How could Marion have forgotten they sang it for Mom too?

"And at the church, 'Jerusalem My Happy Home,' and then 431, 'I Do Not Ask, O Lord.' That's the one with that lovely last verse. *Joy is like a restless day*" – here Jean began to sing in her velvet voice – "*but peace divine like quiet night; Lead me, O Lord, till perfect day shall shine through peace to light.* Your mother loved it. Harry didn't have to tell me that, sticking his head through the breakfast room door while he kept an eye out for your father. I knew she loved that one. She used to play it on the organ when we lived there."

Yes, she did. I remember that

"It had that nice first verse, too: *I do not ask, O Lord, that Thou shouldst shed full radiance here* – and then at the graveside 466, 'When the Day of Toil is Done.' And the readings at the church, the Twenty-Third Psalm, of course, and then Psalm 121. *I will lift up mine eyes unto the hills –*"

Jean is on a roll now, and nothing can stop her. Marion wishes she wouldn't recite it. *I will lift up mine eyes unto the hills, from whence cometh my help. My help cometh from the Lord, which made heaven and earth. He will not suffer thy foot to be moved: he that keepeth thee will not slumber. Behold, he that keepeth Israel shall neither slumber nor sleep. The Lord is thy keeper: the Lord is thy shade upon thy right hand. The sun shall not smite thee by day, nor the moon by night. The Lord shall preserve thee from all evil: he shall preserve thy soul. The Lord shall preserve thy going out and thy coming in from this time forth, and even for evermore.*

Marion is speechless. Marion cannot think about her mother, and the Lord of Psalm 121. Bruises. Welts. Tears. Chokeholds. A child near death. Another, and another. A kidney, a fall. All gone down now, all gone down to death. Where had He been through it all, the Lord of Psalm 121?

"Who was there?" she manages to ask.

"Well, most everybody. Most of Little Bay Islands. Everyone who could come. Everyone loved your mother, Marion. You know that."

"Was he there?"

"Your father? He disappeared."

∿

It came up on the *Clyde* from St. John's, crated in a wooden box made to size from one-by-three-inch spruce lumber with an insulating liner of corrugated cardboard. Past Farewell Island and the Wadhams and the Funks it came, past Deadman's Bay at the east corner of the Straight Shore, past the muddy hole of Musgrave Harbour, past Maud, staring out her window in Ladle Cove, past Ethel's old schools at Carmanville and Frederickton, past Seldom and Change Islands and Chapel Island and Comfort Cove. It bypassed Twillingate and the Notre Dame Bay Memorial Hospital altogether, for nothing could be helped there now. On it went, winding around Exploits Islands, past Fortune Harbour and Fleury Bight and out over the top of Long Island, and finally through the Big Tickle of Little Bay Islands to the government wharf. Jim Strong took receipt, talking to the purser on the wharf and signing the papers on behalf of Thomas Wiseman, who'd ordered it from St. John's. Jim Strong saw to the transporting of the stone to the cemetery, saw to its planting in the ground. Years later, after Jim was gone and Marge too, Marion visited to find the grave overgrown. A young boy named Ernie Grimes helped her find grass shears over at Phyl's. Such an unlikely item to find in Little Bay Islands, but Phyl had them still and young Ernie fetched them, and together they cleaned up the grave. For once Marion wasn't tired, and she kept up with the boy. Marion seldom slept well, but last night when she'd arrived she'd slept in Mom's old bed with the tubular steel frame Mom had enamelled dark brown. The panels that barred its crescent headboard and footboard were stamped out with decorative sprays of small holes. You could count them, lying there, and feel yourself drift *on a river of crystal light into a sea of dew.* . . .

Marion had had a wonderful peaceful sleep in Mom's bed, and now she kept up an animated conversation with Ernie Grimes.

She was a come-from-away; someone new, different, exciting. He was dying for a chat. He wanted to get through high school and leave Little Bay Islands to join the RCMP, he told her.

Wasn't it strange, Marion thought, how he wanted to leave when all she'd ever wanted was to stay? So seldom did things make sense. Wasn't it strange that she'd been driven out of her home, and here was young Ernie, who couldn't wait to get away?

Don't throw me in the briar patch, whatever you do don't throw me in the briar patch. Do you know that story? Marion asked Ernie Grimes.

Ernie didn't. T'was your dear old mom, now, he said, clipping back the last of the grass and the weeds.

There was not a rosebush on the grave, not a forget-me-not. *I do not ask that flowers should always spring beneath my feet.* It was hard to find anyone to keep a grave up; flowers were a difficult choice. Phyl Taylor's parents' graves had gravel spread on them. That kept the weeds away, at least.

Tom and Phyl couldn't place the boy Ernie. These days, Little Bay Islands was getting to be such a different place. *All the changes since our day, Marion, you can't imagine!* Perhaps one of the kids from Mack's Island – weren't they Grimeses there now, in the old house where the Forwards had had the swing? Phyl frowned, called over next door to Aunt Dora Oxford. Wasn't Ernie Grimes long dead? Yes he was now, sure, Aunt Dora said. He'd been the fella what chewed tobacco just when no one did any more, that special kind he had brought in special too. There'd been no end to his gut, and spitting tobacco like that, well. He'd had a grandson, and wasn't that lad dead too, drowned or worse? Wasn't he?

Marion didn't think so. Ernie Grimes had been very much alive. Raring to go. When he'd helped her sweep away the last of the grass around the stone, he'd sat back on his heels and read the inscription.

Ethel W. Wiseman

1892–1957

At Rest

"Look at that," he said. "*At rest.* Will you look at that."

ACKNOWLEDGEMENTS

Several books helped me sketch in Newfoundland's past: the Reverend Charles Lench's *The Story of Methodism in Bonavista* (1919); Gary L. Saunders's *Doctor Olds of Twillingate* (1994); David Macfarlane's *The Danger Tree* (1991); Col. H.W.L. Nicholson's *The Fighting Newfoundlander* (1964); and the marvellous and indispensable *Encyclopedia of Newfoundland and Labrador*, initially the undertaking of Joey Smallwood.

Thanks to Alan McWhirter of Connecticut and Gil McWhirter of Edmonton, for adding what they knew of their own Newfoundlanders at war, and to Capt. Paul Furlong, OC B Company, 1 Royal Newfoundland Regiment in St. John's, for telling me more about mine. Thanks to Doug Baker at Humber Memorials in St. John's, and to Carl Hustins.

I'm grateful to Joel Yanofsky and Jeffrey Round, extraordinary readers and cheerleaders. Thanks to Cal Barksdale and Marilyn Biderman, to Lisan Jutras for her sharp eye, and especially to Dinah Forbes for her firm hand and hard work, and for letting me do all the complaining. I'm indebted to Bjorn Haagensen, my lucky star, for absolutely everything, not just the expert, tireless research. I could not have done this book without him.

Understanding one's world, Santayana said, is the classic form of consolation. Fleeing it is the romantic form. As with any story about a family, some of the family are inclined to escape it, others to stand and deliver. I thank all the Wisemans, the classicists and romantics alike, especially my cousin Craig Penney, who for so many years beat the bushes to recover the family story, and who shared it generously.

My mother, Marion Wiseman, has been my north star, her part all forbearance. Who wants to remember? Who wants to forget? She never flinched at remembering, she worried a lot and cared more, and she loved her mother, Ethel Wellon Wiseman, the way I love her.